S0-BSL-118

LANGUAGE AS SOCIAL ACTION:
SOCIAL PSYCHOLOGY
AND LANGUAGE USE

LANGUAGE AS SOCIAL ACTION: SOCIAL PSYCHOLOGY AND LANGUAGE USE

Thomas Holtgraves
Ball State University

2002
Lawrence Erlbaum Associates, Publishers
Mahwah, New Jersey   London

President/CEO:	Lawrence Erlbaum
Executive Vice-President, Marketing:	Joseph Petrowski
Senior Vice-President, Book Production:	Art Lizza
Director, Editorial:	Lane Akers
Director, Sales and Marketing:	Robert Sidor
Director, Customer Relations:	Nancy Seitz
Editor:	Bill Webber
Textbook Marketing Manager:	Marisol Kozlovski
Editorial Assistant:	Erica Kica
Cover Design:	Kathryn Houghtaling Lacey
Textbook Production Manager:	Paul Smolenski
Full-Service & Composition:	Black Dot Group/ An AGT Company
Text and Cover Printer:	Sheridan Books, Inc.

This book was typeset in 10/12 pt. Times Roman, Bold, and Italic.
The heads were typeset in Americana, Americana Bold, and Americana Bold Italic.

Copyright © 2002 by Lawrence Erlbaum Associates, Inc.
All rights reserved. No part of the book may be reproduced in any form, by photostat, microform, retrieval system, or any other means, without the prior written permission of the publisher.

Lawrence Erlbaum Associates, Inc., Publishers
10 Industrial Avenue
Mahwah, New Jersey 07430

Library of Congress Cataloging-in-Publication Data

Holtgraves, Thomas.
  Language as social action : social psychology and language use / Thomas Holtgraves.
    p.   cm.
  Includes bibliographical references and index.
  ISBN 0-8058-3140-1 (alk. paper)
    1. Sociolinguistics. 2. Speech acts (Linguistics) 3. Interpersonal communication.
4. Conversation analysis. I. Title.
P40 .H663 2001
306.44—dc21   2001033703

Books published by Lawrence Erlbaum Associates are printed on acid-free paper, and their bindings are chosen for strength and durability.

Printed in the United States of America
10 9 8 7 6 5 4 3

For Marnell, Noah, and Micah

Contents

Preface

This book grew out of my interest in, and research on, various aspects of language use. Language, of course, is an extremely broad topic and one that is of interest to scholars in a variety of disciplines. As a social psychologist, my concern has been with language as social action, how social variables play a role in our use of language, and how language use plays a role in our social life. The topics I discuss in this book are all related in some way to these two general issues.

Research on the social bases of language use is widely scattered across a variety of disciplines, including philosophy, anthropology, sociolinguistics, cognitive psychology, pragmatics, social psychology, communication, and others. My goal in writing this book was to bring together in one place research from these different areas so as to provide a fairly comprehensive, interdisciplinary summary and integrative review of the literature dealing with language as a social action. This is not an exhaustive book on language use; the topics I cover here are ones that I have found most illuminating and relevant for understanding the role played by language in social life. It is thus a selective review, but one that I think captures many of the most fundamental aspects of language as social action.

Although I draw from many different research traditions in this book, the material and my approach is probably most relevant for the areas of social psychology, cognitive psychology, and communication. Until recently, language research has been outside mainstream social psychology. There are important exceptions, of course, most notably the work of Roger Brown, Robert Krauss, and Howard Giles, scholars whose efforts have influenced my own work and whose research I cover extensively in this volume. Cognitive psychologists, on the other hand, have tended to ignore the social aspects of language use. Again there are important exceptions, most notably Herb Clark, whose research has had an obvious impact on my work and the writing of this book.

My research on language has been supported by grants from the National Science Foundation, the National Institute of Mental Health, and the Ball State University Office of Academic Research and Sponsored Programs. The writing of this book was supported in part by a sabbatical award from Ball State University. I would like to thank the following people who read either the entire book or selected chapters: Robert Krauss, Boaz Keysar, Marnell Holtgraves, Bosuk Yoon, Howard Giles, Michael Schober, and the students in Robert Krauss's Spring 2000 *Human Communication* course.

I have found language to be a fascinating topic and one with unlimited potential to increase our understanding of social life. My hope is that this volume will be able to convey that view to others.

LANGUAGE AS SOCIAL ACTION: SOCIAL PSYCHOLOGY AND LANGUAGE USE

Introduction

The Social Bases of Language and Linguistic Underpinnings of Social Behavior

It is hard to think of a topic that has been of interest to more academic disciplines than language. Linguists, of course, but also philosophers, sociologists, psychologists, communication scholars, computer scientists, and many others have pursued its study. Why? What is it about language that makes it so important for so many disciplines? For many scholars, it represents the medium through which we encounter reality; our language both reflects and creates that reality. For others, it represents a uniquely human ability—an ability that reflects the essence of what it means to be human. And for others, language is a system that allows people to communicate or transfer propositions among themselves.

Language is truly an multidisciplinary topic; unfortunately it is not often an interdisciplinary topic. However, it should be, and in this book I attempt to provide an interdisciplinary review of language use as a human social action. The key words here are *social* and *action*. What this entails, first of all, is a consideration of language *use*, rather than treating language as an abstract, symbolic system. In other words, my concern will be with what people are doing when they use language, with the actions they are performing as they speak. People use language to accomplish various things—they request and compliment and criticize, and so on. But it is not only an action, it is also a social action, an action involving other people. This fact both shapes the nature of the activity—people must

1

coordinate with others in order to understand and to be understood (Clark, 1996a)—and its consequences—linguistic actions affect how interactants think and feel about each other.

There are many disciplines that have been concerned with language as social action. For example, philosophers, computer scientists, and microsociologists have treated language in this way, and psychologists have provided empirical tests of some of their ideas. The role of context, or the structural properties of talk, have been described in detail by conversation analysts, most of whom would be considered anthropologists or microsociologists. The interpersonal implications of language use have been the focus of research conducted by anthropologists, sociolinguists, and communication scholars, whereas research on language and thought has been undertaken primarily by psychologists and anthropologists. Perspective taking and coordination have been studied most extensively by psychologists, although conversation analysts have made some important contributions here as well.

In this book I will draw from these different orientations and disciplines. But the overarching approach taken here is primarily social psychological. It is a social psychological perspective in the sense that language will be viewed as a behavior that is both influenced by other people, as well as a means for influencing the behavior of others. How we talk—what we try to do with language—is extremely sensitive to the social context. What we say and how we say it is influenced by our perceptions of our interlocutors, what they can be presumed to know, our relationship with them, and so on. But at the same time, when we use language we alter the behaviors, thoughts, and feelings of others. It is this reciprocal relationship between language and the social context that makes language use a truly social psychological phenomenon.

LINGUISTIC UNDERPINNINGS OF SOCIAL PROCESSES

Because of the reciprocal relationship between language and the social context, language use is an extremely important component of many social psychological phenomena. In many respects, person perception and memory, impression management, attribution, relationship development and satisfaction, and even research methods are inherently linguistic phenomena. Consider an example. Data collection in social psychological research usually involves language in some way. Research participants are given verbal instructions; they are asked to report their impressions, solve a problem, make a judgment, and so on. Researchers have generally been careful with their use of language in these situations, making sure their instructions are clear, the wording of their questions unambiguous, and so on. Only recently has research been conducted that demonstrates how certain conversation principles influence how participants interpret (and hence respond to) research questions (e.g., Schwarz, 1996). Obviously language is an important component of social psychological data collection; *how* it influences this process is less clear and only now beginning to be researched.

It is somewhat surprising, then, that in the main, social psychologists have not contributed extensively to the study of language. Now, it is not the importance of language for social psychology that has been disputed; there has been a chapter on language in every edition of the *Handbook of Social Psychology*. Granted, with the exception of the recent chapter by Robert Krauss, these chapters have not been written by social psychologists. But the fact that they have been included is testimony to the obvious centrality of language in the social psychological enterprise.

Of course, acknowledging the centrality of language in social life is not the same as understanding how and in what way it is central to social processes. This point was well made by Krauss and Fussell (1996), who note that the current relationship between social psychology and language is similar to the pre-1970s relationship between social psychology and cognition. The rise of social cognition research in the 1970s, with its emphasis on the detailed examination of the cognitive underpinnings of social thought, represented a new attempt to explore the role of cognition in social psychological processes. So even though social psychology had always been cognitive—its central concepts such as attitudes, values, and so on are cognitive constructs—social cognition research was a new attempt to explicate how those processes work. Similarly, although social psychologists acknowledge the importance of language in social life, there has been a dearth of empirical research designed to explicate *how* language works and the manner in which it is central to social life.

But this is not to say that the importance of language for social psychological phenomenon has been completely ignored. It hasn't. There are researchers in various disciplines who pursue topics related to language and social psychology. For example, scholars have begun to examine the role of language in prejudice and stereotypes (e.g., Maas, Salvi, Arcuri, & Semin, 1989), social reasoning (e.g., Hilton, 1995), and person perception (e.g., Berry, Pennebaker, Mueller, & Hiller, 1997). And in fact there is a journal—*Journal of Language and Social Psychology,*—and an association—*International Association of Language and Social Psychology*—that serve as testimony to the scholarly interest in things both linguistic and social psychological.

Moreover, for some theorists language use is the *essence* of many social psychological phenomena. For example, some of the language-based approaches to the self (e.g., Gergen, 1989; Harre, 1986; Sampson, 1983) take language to be the site for the construction of the self; the self is not a bounded, unitary, entity but rather something that is continuously created through our use of language on different occasions. In a sense the self is a story (e.g., McAdams, 1993), one that is continuously being written and rewritten.

Similarly, the ethogenic approach to social psychology (e.g., Harre & Secord, 1972) also places great emphasis on language. In this case the focus is on the linguistic accounting procedures that people use to make their actions war-rantable and understandable to themselves and to others. It is assumed that behav-ior, and the accounts that people provide of their behavior, reflect an underlying rule structure, a rule structure representing social competence in much the same way that grammatical rules underlie our linguistic competence.

Both of these examples are part of an emerging stance toward social psycholo-gy that has been termed discursive social psychology (e.g., Potter, 1996, 1998; Potter & Wetherall, 1987; Edwards & Potter, 1992). In general, this approach is critical of mainstream social psychological research. It is asserted, for example, that many presumably stable social psychological constructs such as attitudes are inherently variable; they only appear to be stable, unitary, entities because social psychologists force these phenomena into a priori conceptual categories. Atti-tudes are often contradictory and inconsistent over time and settings, and only by examining how attitudes are linguistically constructed can this be seen. Discur-sive social psychologists thus recommend language as a topic of study in its own right, not as reflecting some intrapsychic structure.

Many of the aims and assumptions of discursive social psychology are consis-tent with those taken in this book. I assume that language and social psychology are related in many ways, and that research should attempt to explicate this link. But discursive social psychology largely adopts an antiexperimental stance; studying language use is viewed as an *alternative* to traditional psychological experimentation. Although I strive to be methodologically inclusive in this book, I also assume that experimentation remains a viable and valuable means for exploring language use. As a result, discursive social psychology is not treated extensively in this book.

SOCIAL BASES OF LANGUAGE

Just as social psychologists in the main have tended to ignore the role of lan-guage in social psychological processes, many research traditions concerned with language have tended to ignore the social bases of language use. For exam-ple, most branches of linguistics, with the obvious exception of sociolinguistics, treat language as an asocial phenomena. Similarly, most psycholinguists adopt what Clark (1996a) refers to as an individualist perspective; the production and comprehension of language is assumed to be the result of an isolated individual producing or comprehending language in a vacuum. And of course it *is* a single individual who constructs an utterance and a single individual who decides what that utterance means. But the form that an utterance takes and the manner in which it is interpreted cannot really be understood apart from the social context in which it is produced and understood. For example, a speaker will often be concerned with protecting or managing an identity, both hers and that of her interlocutors. This concern may be reflected in the manner in which she phrases her utterances (language production), and, simultaneously, her interlocutors awareness of these concerns may influence the manner in which her utterances are interpreted (language comprehension). The very fundamentals of language use are intertwined with social concerns; an understanding of how language is both produced and comprehended will require a consideration of its social dimensions.

OVERVIEW OF MAJOR THEMES

Language Use as Action

Language can and has been viewed as an abstract system, a system that can be analyzed apart from its use. This has been the tradition in linguistics for the past 40 years (e.g., Chomsky, 1965). In this approach, researchers attempt to understand how an ideal speaker/hearer produces and comprehends utterances. But in this case there really is no speaker. It does not matter how or why an utterance might be used; such issues are deemed unimportant, or at the very least not relevant for understanding language competence. Many philosophers have also treated language as an abstract system—a system that is evaluated based on its correspondence with the external world and the extent to which that correspondence can be verified. Again, the how and why of language use is ignored.

But language can also be viewed as a tool, a tool that is used for accomplishing particular ends. To *use* language is to perform an action, and it is a meaningful action, with consequences for the speaker, the hearer, and the conversation of which it is a part. This is a very different view of language. To understand meaning there must be a speaker. And context is critical. What a speaker means with an utterance (what he intends to accomplish) can only be derived with some reference to a context.

It is this action dimension of language that forms the heart of chapter 1— "Speech Acts and Intentions: The Things We Do with Words." In this chapter, I summarize the fundamentals of speech act theory (e.g., Searle, 1969) and review some of the relevant empirical research bearing on issues raised by this approach. There are a number of specific issues treated in this chapter. When language use is viewed as an intentional action, then the link between language and action becomes critical. Do people recognize (at some level) the actions that a speaker performs with an utterance? What is the nature of this recognition? What psychological states are required for a speaker to successfully perform an action with language? Is the recognition process the same regardless of how the linguistic action is performed? What knowledge is required to produce and understand linguistic actions? And, just what actions can be performed with language anyway? Speech act theory is a theory of action, and as a theory of action it is in large part a social psychological theory.

Language Use as Interpersonal Action

Not only is language use an action, it is simultaneously an interpersonal action. By interpersonal action I mean that what we do with language—the actions that we perform (e.g., a request)—have implications for the thoughts and feelings of the involved parties, as well as the relationship that exists between them. Our words are typically addressed to other people, and people are not abstract entities devoid of feelings, goals, thoughts, and values. People's language use—how they perform actions with language—must be sensitive to these concerns. We cannot always say exactly what we mean because we generally do not want to threaten or impose on or criticize our interlocutors. Of course we have the same feelings and goals and thoughts and values; we do not want to be criticized and threatened and imposed on, either. These interpersonal concerns are related. By attending to others' feelings we increase the likelihood that they will attend to ours. Language appears to be remarkably responsive to these concerns. Many, if not all, languages allow speakers to perform threatening actions (e.g., requests, criticisms) in ways that attend to these feelings.

I consider the interpersonal determinants of language production in detail in chapter 2—"The Interpersonal Underpinnings of Talk: Face Management and Politeness." In this chapter, I focus primarily on politeness theory (Brown & Levinson, 1987), a comprehensive framework for understanding how interpersonal concerns motivate many aspects of language use. Politeness theory, although not without problems, has the advantage of postulating links between interpersonal variables and numerous aspects of language use; it is truly a social psychological approach to language use.

A number of issues are considered in this chapter. For example, why do people often not say what they mean? And why is it possible to say the same thing—perform the same linguistic action—in so many different ways? Also, why are we more circuitous with some people than with others? Are there underlying principles (e.g., face management) that account for this variability, and are such principles valid across cultures? Does this linguistic variability play a role in person perception and recognition of a speaker's intention?

Language use is interpersonal in another way; it is a rich source of identity-relevant information. Many aspects of our language use (accent, speech rate, politeness level, etc.) provide pieces of information that can be used by others in forming impressions of us. And many of these variables can be strategically altered as a means of managing the impressions we convey to others. Hence, language use plays an important role in both person perception—how we perceive others, and them us—and impression management—how we strategically vary our talk to achieve particular effects.

I discuss these ideas in chapter 3: "The Interpersonal Consequences of Talk: Impression Management and Person Perception." A number of related issues are discussed in this chapter. For example, what linguistic (and extralinguistic) variables play a role in person perception? *How* do these variables play a role in person perception? Are people generally aware of these effects, and if so, do they strategically manipulate these variables as a means of managing their impressions? What is the role of the social context in these processes? And to what extent do pragmatic principles guiding conversations play a role in person perception and impression management?

Language Use as Contextualized Action

Conversation utterances are not isolated things; they always occur in the context of other conversation turns. This context is important for interpreting the meaning a speaker intends to convey with an utterance, as well as the interpersonal consequences of her remark. In this way, meanings (both intended and unintended) reside not so much in an utterance as in the placement of that utterance in a sequence of conversation turns. The structure of verbal interactions is obviously crucial, and in chapter 4—"Conversational Structure"—I consider some of the various issues related to structure. Most importantly, in what ways are conversations structured? How is this structure achieved? That is, what mechanisms allow people to coordinate their actions so as to produce a coherent conversation? How, for example, are topics introduced, maintained, and changed? How does conversational structure contribute to the production and comprehension of meaning? And what are some of the interpersonal consequences of conversational structure?

Language Use as Coordinated Action

As an interpersonal action involving other people, language use is a collective action. It is collective in many senses, but of crucial importance is the need for interlocutors to coordinate their relative perspectives, to have some sense of how their conversational partners will interpret their utterances. Perspective taking is important for many levels of language use, from the sense and reference of an utterance, to the specific speech act that is performed, to the interpersonal consequences of an utterance. To successfully perform an action with language requires some degree of perspective taking.

But how good are people at taking another's perspective? Are there systematic errors in this process? What conversational mechanisms are used by conversational participants to signal their recognition of each other's perspective? To what extent does perspective taking allow for the establishment of truly mutual knowledge? I consider these and other issues in chapter 5—"Conversational Perspective Taking."

Language Use as Thoughtful Action

Finally, language use is thoughtful action, thoughtful in the sense that much human cognition, especially human social cognition, is mediated by language use. Now, research on the relationship between language and thought has something of a checkered history. An early, relatively extreme view that language fully determines thought (the so-called Whorfian hypothesis) has proved largely untenable. But clearly language and thought are related in various ways, and in chapter 6—"Language and Social Thought"—I deal with several issues that underlie this potential relationship.

The most crucial issue is determining which aspects of language are related to which features of thought. In that vein, much of this chapter focuses on the effect of language use (rather than language as an abstract system) on social thought. Language provides a vehicle for perceiving and thinking about others, and so the form that our thoughts and perceptions take may be influenced by language. For example, the dimensions along which we perceive others might be determined by the existence of specific lexical items that are available in our language; it is difficult to perceive others on dimensions for which one has no words. Moreover, the informational value of some words can extend beyond the dimension or category they denote. For example, certain verbs can carry information regarding the causal locus of the act that is referenced. And the very act of putting things into words might affect the representation of that information. That is, the *use* of language—for example, telling a story to another person—can affect what we (and our interlocutors) think and remember about others.

CONCLUSION

Language is one of those things that we often take for granted. It's almost like breathing—necessary for life but not something we pay much attention to unless problems develop. But unlike breathing, language has profound implications for our *social* existence. It plays a role in virtually every aspect of our dealings with others. For example, requests—from the mundane "Can you pass the salt?" to the profound "Will you marry me?"—simultaneously define and alter our relationships with others in both small and large ways. Understanding what we are doing when we use language can aid our understanding of what it means to be a social being. One of the goals of this book is to make a contribution in this direction.

1

Speech Acts and Intentions: The Things We Do With Words

People do things with their words. They order and promise and criticize and apologize and so on. In other words, to use language is to perform an action. As obvious as this is, an action view of language has had a relatively short history, and many of the implications of viewing language use as action have yet to be pursued in any detail. Moreover, viewing language as action, especially as a social action, makes clear many of the social psychological underpinnings of language use.

There is a strain of thought in philosophy, developed primarily at Oxford University beginning in the 1930s, that is concerned with the analysis of the ordinary use of language. Two related lines of research within this tradition are of particular importance, and I will use them as the starting points for this chapter. The first, termed speech act theory, was developed by John Austin and later elaborated on by John Searle. Speech act theory explicitly conceptualizes linguistic meaning as use; what we mean with an utterance is the use to which the utterance is put. In the first half of the chapter I describe this approach and the issues that it raises for understanding language use. The second strand of thought revolves around the concept of conversational implicature, an approach to nonliteral meaning that was developed by Paul Grice. Grice's views have been extremely influential and a central concern within the field of pragmatics. In the second half of this chapter I examine his ideas, placing particular emphasis on the recognition of speaker intention in general and illocutionary force in particular. Much of this discussion will be centered on the comprehension of indirect speech acts and the various processing models that have been proposed and tested.

JOHN AUSTIN AND THE DEVELOPMENT OF SPEECH ACT THEORY

In the early part of the last century there existed a major theoretical approach to language—termed logical positivism—that claimed all utterances were to be evaluated exclusively on the basis of their verifiability. In this view, if the truth of an utterance could not be determined, the utterance was viewed as meaningless. The intent of logical positivism, of course, was to eliminate the imprecision inherent in human languages. But the outcome of the approach was extreme—many everyday conversational utterances were viewed as simply meaningless. A truth-conditional approach to language (without the requirement of verifiability) exists today in the various logical approaches to language, particularly those attempting to develop a formal semantics (e.g., Kaplan, 1979).

It is against the backdrop of logical positivism that the development of speech act theory should be viewed. Both Ludwig Wittgenstein (1953) and John Austin (1962)[1] independently, and almost simultaneously, proposed action-oriented approaches to language that clearly articulated the weaknesses inherent in the truth-conditional view. I give priority to Austin's work here because, as the developer of speech act theory, his work continues to have a specific relevance for language theorizing.

Austin's (1962) speech act theory arose from his observation that it simply is not possible to determine the truth value of many utterances. For example, the truth of the utterance "I promise to do it tonight" cannot be determined. The utterance has no relationship with the external world, and so truth conditions cannot be established. As we will see in moment, this utterance can be evaluated on many different dimensions—it may or may not be sincere, for example—but attempts to ascertain its veracity are useless; it is neither true nor false.

This led Austin to propose a (preliminary) distinction between performative utterances and constative utterances. Constatives are utterances for which a truth value conceivably could be determined. Thus, one could ascertain the truth of the utterance "It's raining out" by looking out the window. Performatives (e.g., "I apologize"), on the other hand, are used in order to perform some act (their occurrence

---

[1]Although not published until 1962, Austin's theory was developed much earlier—in the 1930s—at approximately the same time that Wittgenstein was developing the ideas contained in *Philosophical Investigations* (1953).

changes the world in some way), and hence they are not amenable to a truth-conditional analysis. Although one cannot determine the truth value of performatives, there are various ways in which they can go wrong, or to use Austin"s term, be infelicitous. For example, if I utter the performative "I declare war on Canada," I will fail to substantially alter the world. My remark will have no effect (it misfires according to Austin) because I have no authority to declare war. My utterance, although neither true nor false, is clearly infelicitous.

Austin proposed three sets of conditions required for the felicitous performance of performatives. First, there must be a conventional procedure performed by an appropriate person in an appropriate context that has a conventional effect. For example, a minister can perform a marriage by uttering, in the appropriate context, "I now pronounce you man and wife." Second, the procedure must be executed correctly and completely. Third, the person performing the act must have the requisite thoughts, feelings, or intentions (e.g., to perform a felicitous promise the speaker must intend to perform the promised act).

Performatives, then, are a class of utterances that are conventionally used as a means of performing certain actions. They can be either successful or not but are neither true or false. Constatives, on the other hand, report or describe the world and hence should be amenable to a truth-conditional analysis. But it is Austin's fundamental insight that these acts, too, are subject to felicity conditions. To assert something felicitously requires, among other things, that the speaker sincerely believe that what is being asserted is true. To perform an assertion is to take a particular stance regarding the nature of the world. If I say to someone, "It's raining out," I commit myself to that proposition; I have taken a specific stand and performed a specific action. So even assertions have a performative feature. On the basis of these and other problems, Austin abandoned the performative-constative distinction in favor of a theory of illocutionary forces or speech acts.

On this view, *all* speech acts have a dimension of meaning (or propositional content) *and* a particular force. In other words, one is *doing* something with one's words. But what exactly is one doing? In Austin's speech act theory, any utterance involves the simultaneous performance of a number of different acts. First, one is performing a locutionary act. That is, one is making certain sounds (a phonetic act) that comprise identifiable words that are arranged on the basis of a particular grammar (a phatic act), having a certain sense and reference (a rhetic act). When John says to Mark, "I will do it tonight," the sound produced by John will be recognized by Mark as words with a particular meaning and a particular reference (e.g., "I" refers to John, the speaker). In a sense, the locutionary act involves the dimensions of language (phonetics, syntax, and semantics) with which linguists have traditionally been concerned.

In addition to the locutionary act, the speaker is also performing a particular "act in saying," or what Austin termed an illocutionary act. The illocutionary act is the conventional force associated with the uttering of the words in a particular context. Thus, John's utterance—"I promise to do it tonight"—will have the force of a promise (if performed felicitously).

Finally, a speaker is simultaneously performing what Austin termed a perlocutionary act. The perlocutionary act refers to the effects the utterance has on the hearer. For example, the effects of John's verbal promise may include Mark's recognition that John is making a promise, his relief that he has done so, his hope that he will keep it, and so on. Perlocutionary acts are hearer based. Although obviously prompted by the speaker's utterance, the effects may extend well beyond anything intended by the speaker. Thus, perlocutionary acts are indeterminate and not necessarily intentional.

It should be clear from this brief review that Austin's speech act theory, together with the latter Wittgenstein (1953), marked the beginning of a new way to view language. The emphasis on language as action rather than as an abstract system for describing reality marked a fundamental shift. It raised new issues and posed new questions, and although Austin dealt with some of these issues, they have been developed further by other theorists. It is to those issues and theorists that we now turn.

JOHN SEARLE: SPEECH ACT TAXONOMY AND FELICITY CONDITIONS

Beginning with his dissertation, Searle (1969) systematized and extended speech act theory in several directions. For the present discussion, his most important contributions include his specification of illocutionary force via the felicity conditions, his taxonomy of speech acts, and the notion of indirect speech acts. Each of these issues are considered in turn.

Maintaining a view of language use as action, Searle (1969) argued that the conditions for the felicitous performance (in Austin's sense) of a speech act can be viewed as constituting the performance of that speech act. That is, the felicity conditions for a particular speech act must be met for that act to be performed successfully, and the meeting of these conditions constitutes the performance of that speech act. Moreover, speech acts differ in terms of the specifics of the conditions underlying their performance, and hence these conditions (in conjunction with some others to be discussed below) serve as a framework for comparing different speech acts.

The original felicity conditions proposed by Searle (1969) have been modified only slightly over the years, and other important components of illocutionary force have been proposed. These original four conditions, however, remain central to understanding the nature of what it means to perform a particular speech act. Note that there are other conditions that are not unique to speech act performance that must be met also (e.g., both speaker and hearer must speak the same language). A summary of these conditions, with illustrations for the act of requesting, is presented in Table 1.1.

TABLE 1.1
Summary of Felicity Conditions for Requests

Condition	Example for Request
Propositional Content	Predicates future act by the hearer
Preparatory	Act has not yet been performed
	Speaker believes hearer is able to perform act
Sincerity	Speaker sincerely wants hearer to perform act
Essential	Utterance counts as an attempt to get the hearer to perform act

1. *Propositional Content:* A fundamental feature of speech act theory is the conceptualization of an utterance as having both a propositional meaning and an illocutionary force (Austin's locutionary and illocutionary acts). Logically, speech acts are often represented as having the form $F(p)$, where F is the illocutionary force and p the propositional content. Although it is possible for two utterances to have the same force yet different propositional meaning, or the same meaning but different forces, force and propositional content are not completely independent. The propositional content condition states that certain illocutionary forces specify what is acceptable in terms of propositional content. For example, promises and requests require the specification of future courses of action, and hence "I promise to study hard last night" and "Please, study hard last night" make little sense.

2. *Preparatory Condition:* For any particular speech act, there are one or more conditions, usually concerning the beliefs and desires of the interlocutors, that are presupposed in the (felicitous) performance of the act. To felicitously perform a request, a speaker must believe that the hearer has the ability to perform the requested act and that the hearer would not perform the act unless requested to do so. The felicitous performance of an assertion requires the speaker to believe the truth of the proposition and that the hearer is not aware of the proposition. An apology requires the belief that the act for which one is apologizing is bad. And so on. In some instances the preparatory conditions specify the nature of the social relations existing between interlocutors. For example, to order someone to do something requires the speaker to have power over the hearer.

3. *Sincerity Condition:* In performing a particular speech act, the speaker expresses a certain psychological attitude regarding the propositional content of the utterance. For example, in performing a promise a speaker expresses an intention to do the act that is being promised. A person can make a promise with no intention of keeping it, of course, but such an utterance would not be felicitous. The sincerity condition, then, is a requisite psychological state the speaker must have in order to perform a particular speech act; it is the specification of

a particular relationship between the speaker's mental state and the propositional content of his words.

4. *Essential Condition:* The uttering of a particular expression in a specific context "counts as" the performance of a specifiable act; the essential condition specifies the particular illocutionary point of an utterance. In most contexts, the uttering of "Please close the door" counts as a request for the hearer to shut the door.

Now, the essential condition states that an utterance in context will have a conventionally recognized illocutionary point, and according to Searle (1979), there are five basic, primitive illocutionary points. These five points are exhaustive, and mutually exclusive, and they are derived from a consideration of the possible relations between one's words and the world (as it is or could be). This represents an important attempt to classify, in a systematic manner, actions that speakers can perform with their utterances. Although other taxonomies have been proposed (e.g., Bach & Harnish, 1979), Searle's is probably the most well known. His taxonomy is in the following list and summarized in Table 1.2.

1. *Directives:* A directive counts as an attempt to get the hearer to perform some future action. Prototypes include requesting, ordering, and questioning. With these speech acts, a speaker is attempting to alter the world in some way with words. Hence, directives represent a world-to-words fit; the speaker is attempting to bring the world in line with words.

2. *Assertives:* An assertive counts as an attempt to represent an actual state of affairs, to commit the speaker to something being the case. Prototypes include asserting, concluding, informing, predicting, and reporting. With assertives a speaker is attempting to depict the nature of the world. Hence, rather than attempting to get the world to match one's words (the world-to-words fit of directives), one is attempting to get one's words to match the world; assertives represent a words-to-world fit.

3. *Commissives:* A commissive counts as an attempt to commit the speaker to a future course of action. Prototypes include warning, promising, threatening,

TABLE 1.2
Taxonomy of Illocutionary Points

Illocutionary Point	Direction of Fit	Examples
Directive	World-to-words (hearer)	Request, order
Assertive	Words-to-world	Conclude, predict
Commissive	World-to-words (speaker)	Promise, warn
Declarative	World-to-words and	Declare war
	Words-to-world	Perform marriage
Expressive	Null	Thank, apologize

and guaranteeing. As with directives, the speaker of a commissive is attempting to alter the world in some way; commissives thus reflect a world-to-words fit. Unlike directives, however, it is the speaker's (rather than the hearer's) subsequent actions that will alter the world.

4. *Declaratives:* A declarative counts as an attempt to bring about a change in some institutional state of affairs. Prototypes include declaring war, performing a marriage, and calling a base runner "out." For a declarative, the relationship between the world and a speaker's words is bidirectional; declaratives have a double direction of fit (both words-to-world and world-to-words). The point of a declarative (e.g., declaring war) is to alter the state of the world (world-to-words) by stating that the propositional content matches the state of the world (words-to-world).

5. *Expressives:* Expressives count as attempts to express a psychological state. Prototypes include thanking, complaining, greeting, and apologizing. For expressives, there is no fit between words and the world. Instead, the point of an expressive is simply to express the speaker's inner psychological state or to express a particular attitude that is represented by the propositional content of the utterance.

Although there are only five illocutionary points, there are far more than five different speech acts that one can perform. The illocutionary point, then, is only one component determining illocutionary force. Distinctions between speech acts with the same illocutionary point can be made in fairly principled ways. One such way is in terms of the felicity conditions. For example, a request and a command have the same illocutionary point; they are both directives, or attempts to get the hearer to do something. But they differ in terms of their felicity conditions; a command requires (as one of its preparatory conditions) the speaker to be in a position of authority over the hearer, a condition not required of a request.

Other components associated with differences in illocutionary force include degree of strength and mode of achievement (Searle & Vanderveken, 1985). Degree of strength involves the sincerity condition of the speech act and refers to the strength of the speaker's belief or desire. For example, to claim and to guess are both assertives, but the degree of strength is stronger for the former than for the latter. Mode of achievement refers to differences in the specific means used for achieving a particular illocutionary point. For example, requests and commands are both directives, but they have different modes of achievement; with a request the speaker leaves open the option of refusing, but with a command the speaker must invoke a position of authority over the speaker. And compare both of these with the act of begging, a speech act that is also a directive, but for which the mode of achievement is to get another to do something by being humble.

Searle's taxonomy and specification of illocutionary force are attempts to systematize the observations of Austin and hence are important contributions to the development of speech act theory. Searle provided a framework for specifying more precisely the actions that can be accomplished with language, as well as the relationship between those actions, one's words, and the mental states of the interlocutors. Searle's approach is not without problems, and his critics are many (as discussed later). But there is no doubt that Searle has contributed greatly to the development of an action-oriented view of language use.

SPEECH ACTS AND INTENTIONS

Speech act theory provides an account of language use as intentional action. That is, speakers, in performing an illocutionary act, are *trying* to do things with their words. This emphasis on intentional action stands in stark contrast to the deconstructionist view that an author's intention is ephemeral and indeterminate (e.g., Gibbs, 1998, 1999). In speech act theory, intentions are crucial.

An early and important paper outlining an intentional view of communication was published by the philosopher Grice in 1957 (see also Grice, 1989). In this paper, he made an important distinction between signs and signals. Signs convey information, but a recognition of that information does not require a recognition of the speaker's intention to have that information recognized. For example, if I start to fall asleep in the evening, my family may infer that I am tired. My falling asleep means that I am tired, but I am not intending them to recognize this by virtue of my falling asleep. Signals, on the other hand, convey nonnatural meaning (or meaning-nn) and are communicative acts that achieve their ends by virtue of the hearer recognizing the speaker's intention to achieve those ends. In other words, the hearer's recognition of the speaker's intention fulfills the intention. If I say to my family that I'm really tired, I mean for them to recognize that I intend for them to believe that I am tired. Their recognition of my intention fulfills that intention. Communicative intentions are intentions of a peculiar and complex sort; they are reflexive intentions. They are satisfied by virtue of the recognition of their existence.

Now, exactly what intention does a speaker intend to have recognized with an utterance? In general it is illocutionary force. This is an important point because our utterances can have numerous effects above and beyond what we intend. These perlocutionary effects (i.e., the effects the utterance has on the recipient) do not require recognition of the speaker's communicative intention. I might, for example, try to convince you of a particular point by making a series of assertions about that point. But, whether or not I actually succeed in convincing you (convince is a perlocutionary act; one cannot say, "I hereby convince you of x") does not depend on your recognition of my attempt to convince you.

The perlocutionary–illocutionary distinction is an important one (although not without some problems). It is clearly important to distinguish between what a speaker intends to communicate with an utterance and what effects that utterance has on the hearer. Obviously a speaker's intention and its effect on the hearer are not completely independent; some perlocutionary effects are tied to the illocutionary act, and the illocutionary act can be viewed as a means of achieving a particular goal (a perlocutionary effect). For example, we generally perform a request (an illocutionary act) with the goal of getting the addressee to perform the requested act (a perlocutionary effect). But we may have additional goals. We may, for example, attempt to make the request politely so as to avoid offending the recipient, and the recipient's recognition of this conveyed politeness can also be regarded as a perlocutionary effect (see chap. 2 for detail on politeness). Both of these perlocutionary effects are intended by the speaker—she wants the addressee to perform the requested act and to recognize that she is making this request in a polite manner.

At the same time, some perlocutionary effects may be unintended because an utterance can yield a wide variety of inferences and emotional reactions. The recipient of a request may feel put upon, used, angry, frustrated, and so on. And these effects might be quite idiosyncratic. This is why deconstructionists argue that the interpretation of a text is largely independent of the author's intention in producing that text. But as Gibbs (1998) points out, the fact that multiple interpretations are possible (i.e., a remark can have multiple perlocutionary effects) does not diminish the fact that at an earlier stage of processing the speaker's intention, and the hearer's attempt to recognize that intention, plays a crucial and fundamental role in interpretation.

One problem with the perlocutionary–illocutionary distinction is that certain illocutionary verbs do not seem to be characterizable in terms of a reflexive intention. One obvious example in this regard is "brag." If I want to successfully brag, I *do not* want my audience to recognize my intention to brag. This is similar to what Jones (1964) referred to as the ingratiator's dilemma. We sometimes intend to perform acts such as bragging, being ingratiating, and so on. But our success at performing these acts depends on others not recognizing our intention to perform them.

RECOGNIZING ILLOCUTIONARY FORCE: HOW DO PEOPLE KNOW WHAT OTHERS ARE DOING WITH WORDS?

If language use is action, how do we recognize what action is being performed with an utterance? Do we even need to recognize it? And what does it mean that a specific action is recognized as having been performed? One might think these questions trivial and obvious; we generally seem to know, quickly and without reflection, what people are doing with their words. But these questions are far from trivial; this issue is a tremendously difficult and thorny one for language researchers across a wide variety of disciplines.

For Austin (1962), the recognition of illocutionary force was largely conventional and based on the performative verb, along with sentence mood and type. A performative verb (when used in the first-person singular in the predicate of the main clause of the sentence) names the action that it performs. In uttering "I promise to do it," the performative verb *promise* names the act (promising) that is performed. Performative verbs, then, represent a universe of possible illocutionary acts, and it is important to understand them and their properties as a means of understanding what it is that people do with words. In this regard, it is interesting to note that the set of performative verbs varies among cultures. This is because many performative verbs (especially declaratives such as christening, declaring war, etc.) are constituted by the existence of certain cultural institutions, and because those institutions vary among cultures, words (and the actions they perform) that make sense in one culture may not make sense in another culture (see chap. 6 for further discussion).

If people do recognize illocutionary force when comprehending an utterance (an issue that is far from settled—see the following), what is the nature of that recognition? One possibility is that recognition of illocutionary force is componential. That is, because illocutionary force is determined by a small set of conditions (the felicity conditions along with a few others), then comprehension might include recognition of those conditions. In this view, the comprehension of a request would involve a recognition of the speaker's *desire* that an act be performed (the sincerity condition), her belief in the hearer's *ability* to perform the act (a preparatory condition), and so on.

This componential view of speech act meaning has received some limited empirical support. Using sentence verification (Experiment 1) and reading time (Experiment 2) procedures, Amrhein (1992) found convincing evidence that variations in the polarity of two components—speaker ability and speaker desire—underlie the comprehension of four quasi-performative commissive verbs (promise, hope, guess, agree). For example, the comprehension of "promise" entails recognition of the speaker's desire and ability, "hope" entails recognition of the speaker's desire but not his ability, "agree" entails the reverse, and "guess" entails neither. In addition, in these studies the degree of speaker committedness (similar to strength of illocutionary force) was largely accounted for by the combination of these intentions. Components of intentions—such as ability and desire—are fundamental features of social action, and it makes sense that interlocutors would orient to them (e.g., Heider, 1958).

Still, the exact nature of the comprehension of illocutionary force and whether illocutionary force is even recognized is not clear. Surprisingly, there has been little psycholinguistic research on this issue. This is a particularly important problem because many times illocutionary force is not specifically named with a performative verb, as was the case with the sentences used in Amrhein's (1992) experiments. Instead, most of the time the performative is implicit. For example, "I'll be there without fail" or "I'll clean it tomorrow, I guarantee it" would, in most contexts, function as promises, yet neither contain the performative verb "promise." Does comprehension of these utterances involve activation of the implicit performative verb "promise," and if so, how does this occur? Regarding the former question, there is some evidence that implicit performative verbs are activated during comprehension and do form part of the comprehender's representation of the remark (Holtgraves & Ashley, 2001). Regarding the second question, Austin, Searle, and others have suggested that intonation, the context, and background knowledge all contribute in various ways to the recognition of illocutionary force. But this tells us very little about *how* this is accomplished.

In speech act theory, utterances have both a propositional meaning and an illocutionary force, and comprehension involves a recognition of both force and propositional meaning. But there are alternatives to this approach for which illocutionary force recognition would not be required. One view, termed the *performative hypothesis* (Gazdar, 1979; Levinson, 1983), suggests that all sentences have a performative clause as the highest clause in deep structure. Now, this clause can be deleted, which produces implicit performatives. Thus, "I say to you that it is raining out" becomes transformed into "It's raining out." In this view, illocutionary force is simply the performative clause, and this clause is true simply by being uttered (hence, its truth or falsity is not an issue). Thus, there is no need for a speech act dimension of illocutionary force. In a different vein, Katz (1977) has attempted to explain speech act force in terms of grammatical competence (illocutionary force is assumed to be embodied in the grammatical structure of a sentence) and pragmatic performance (contextual factors interact with embodied illocutionary force to create speaker meaning).

There are a number of syntactic and semantic features of sentences that provide some support for these views. For example, sentences may contain adverbs that appear to be modifying the implicit performative clause as in "Frankly, I don't give a damn" (derived from "I say to you frankly that I don't give a damn"). Even if the performative hypothesis could explain these features, it fails to capture in any way the fundamental nature of language use as action. Consider the following:

1. I apologize for what I did.
2. I apologized for what I did.

The performative view would treat these two utterances as the same (differing only in tense). But does not the first statement constitute the performance of a specific action in a way that the second statement does not? To apologize with one's utterance is a very different thing than saying that one has apologized.

A very different alternative to speech act theory comes from the large and growing body of research in artificial intelligence and intentional communication (e.g., Cohen & Levesque, 1990). In much of this research illocutionary force is not viewed as an elementary unit of analysis; interactants need not recognize the illocutionary point of each utterance. Rather, people are viewed as rational agents possessing goals and plans designed to achieve those goals. Mutual awareness of this fact prompts interactants to attempt to recognize each other's plans and goals, as well as possible obstacles to those goals. Consider the following exchange at a fast-food restaurant.

Bill:	Small coke and fries, please.
Counterperson:	Would you like ketchup with that?
Bill:	Yes, please.

Bill's first utterance is a request. Does the counterperson's comprehension of his remark include a recognition that it has the illocutionary force of a request? And if so, does the representation of the request consist of a recognition of Bill's *desire* to acquire the items, his *belief* in the counterperson's ability to provide the items, and so on? Or, alternatively, might the counterperson simply view Bill as a rational agent with the goal of acquiring some food items, and that he plans to achieve this goal by purchasing these items from the counterperson? For the procedure to function smoothly, the counterperson may not need to recognize the illocutionary force of Bill's remark. And, in fact, in this example the counterperson does not respond to the illocutionary force of the request, but instead anticipates subsidiary goals that Bill might possess. Whether or not people, at least in some instances, recognize more general plans of actions designed to achieve particular goals, rather than recognizing discrete illocutionary forces, remains to be seen.

Finally, the prototypical exchange considered by speech act theorists is a single speaker directing an utterance to a single hearer. But talk exchanges are not limited to dyads; many times multiple participants are involved. Does this change the nature of speech act performance? According to Herb Clark and his colleagues it does (Clark & Carlson, 1982; Clark & Schaefer, 1987). When there are multiple parties involved in a conversation, a speaker's utterances might be directed toward a single, specific addressee. But when this occurs, the speaker's utterances must be designed with other participants in mind. For example, the speaker must use language that will allow participants (not just the designated addressee) to identify referents and illocutionary force; she must do this so that all participants (not just the addressee) can keep track of what is being talked about, thereby allowing them to contribute to the conversation at a later point in time.

According to Clark and Carlson (1982), this problem is solved via the performance of informatives. Informatives are logically prior speech acts directed at all participants, and it is via the performance of an informative that the addressee-directed illocutionary act is performed. For example, when the professor tells Hillary in front of the class to read some newly assigned articles for an upcoming exam, he is informing the entire class (including Hillary) of his suggestion (he is performing an informative). It is through his informing the class of the suggestion that the suggestion to Hillary is performed. Note that when a speaker addresses a single hearer, the analysis is the same as the standard speech act analysis. The important point is that speakers must be sensitive to the presence of participants other than an intended addressee, and they must design their utterances with those other participants in mind.

INDIRECT SPEECH ACTS

Recognition of a speaker's intention is particularly problematic because, as a moment's reflection reveals, people very frequently mean more than what they say. In speech act terminology, the intended illocutionary point is often different from the literal illocutionary point. This can be seen quite clearly with requests. For example, the remark "It's warm in here" has the literal illocutionary point of an assertive, a statement about the way the world is. But in many (though not all) contexts the intended illocutionary point is that of a directive, an attempt to get the hearer to do something (e.g., open a window).

Many speech acts, such as requests, are almost always performed indirectly (Ervin-Tripp, 1976). We rarely say to someone "Shut the door," preferring instead to make our requests indirectly with "Can you shut the door?" "Would you mind shutting the door?" and so on. This presents something of a problem for theories of language comprehension. Specifically, if illocutionary force is often conveyed indirectly, how do hearers determine the intended illocutionary force of a speaker's remark? Note that the related question of why people speak indirectly in the first place is covered in detail in chapter 2.

Language researchers have developed two main approaches to the issue of the comprehension of indirectness. The first focuses on the inferential processing assumed to occur when a hearer recognizes the intended illocutionary point. The second approach suggests that inferential processing is not necessary and that the intended illocutionary force is recognized directly. Both approaches will be covered in some detail here because they raise important issues regarding language comprehension.

Inferential Approaches

All inferential approaches assume that an indirect remark has both a literal illocutionary force as well as a conveyed (or indirect) illocutionary force and that hearers must engage in an inference process in order to recognize the conveyed illocutionary point.

One of the earliest inferential approaches for understanding the comprehension of indirect requests was proposed by Gordon and Lakoff (1975). In their view, hearers are assumed to recognize the literal meaning of an utterance such as "Can you pass the salt?" and to reject that meaning whenever it is blocked by the context. Thus, in most situations in which this utterance would be used (e.g., eating dinner), the literal meaning cannot be what the speaker truly means. So, how does one determine what the speaker really intended? Gordon and Lakoff postulated the existence of what they termed conversational postulates, or inference rules, stating, for example, that "Can you x?" translates into "I request you to do x."

One of the most interesting aspects of this approach is the linkage of mechanisms for performing indirect requests with the felicity conditions underlying requests. In general, people can perform indirect requests by questioning hearer-based preparatory conditions such as ability, willingness, and so forth and by asserting speaker-based preparatory conditions. This relatively simple model accounts for a wide variety of indirect requests as can be seen in Table 1.3.

This analysis can be extended to speech acts other than requests (although it does not work quite as well). More important, there is evidence that this approach can explain the production of indirect requests in many different languages (Brown & Levinson, 1987). That different languages would develop identical means for performing requests indirectly provides support for the characterization of requests in terms of the underlying felicity conditions (i.e., these conditions are referenced in the indirect performance of these acts), as well as the idea that requests are face threatening and hence performed indirectly so as to lessen that threat (see chap. 2).

Searle (1979) also proposed an inferential approach to comprehending indirect speech acts. In essence, Searle argued that indirect speech acts involve the performance of two distinct speech acts, each with a different illocutionary point. There is a literal illocutionary point, as well as an ulterior, intended illocutionary point that is conveyed via the performance of the literal illocutionary act. Continuing with the classic salt example, the person at the dinner table who says, "Can you pass the salt?" is simultaneously performing two distinct speech acts. The first act is a query about the hearer's ability to pass the salt; this is a question, or request for information. Simultaneously, she is also performing the speech act of requesting the hearer to actually pass the salt (i.e., to perform an action).

But how is this accomplished? How does the hearer recognize that there is an ulterior speech act being performed? And how does he recognize what that ulterior act is? Searle (1975; pp. 46–47) lays out a detailed reasoning process by

TABLE 1.3
Preparatory Conditions Underlying the Linguistic
Forms of Indirect Requests

Request Form	Preparatory Condition
Can you shut the door?	Question hearer's ability
I want you to shut the door.	Assert speaker's desire
Would you shut the door?	Question hearer's willingness
Did you shut the door?	Question whether or not act has been performed

which the hearer is assumed to recover the primary illocutionary point. This process involves 10 distinct steps (with Searle suggesting that more are actually necessary), but in essence involves two fundamental stages. The first stage is a recognition that the literal illocutionary force is not the intended meaning, and that there is some other illocutionary act that is the intended act. This stage is based on the theory of conversational implicature proposed by the philosopher Grice (1975), a theory that will be discussed in some detail later. The second stage—occurring after the realization that an ulterior meaning is intended—is a procedure for determining the intended illocutionary act. In many cases, references to various preparatory conditions will guide the hearer to the speaker's intended, indirect meaning. Thus, "Can you open the door?" and "Would you pass the salt?" reference the hearer's ability and willingness to perform certain actions, thereby guiding the hearer to directive interpretations. This approach works fairly well for examples like this (at least it is plausible; whether it is supported by psycholinguistic research will be discussed later). But there are numerous ways in which people can perform indirect speech acts, and many of them are not based (at least directly) on the felicity conditions underlying the intended act. How, for example, does one infer that "I'm thirsty" really means "Please get me something to drink"? In these cases, it is not at all clear how a hearer determines the intended speech act. Despite this limitation, Searle's approach has been influential, due, in part, to its reliance on Grice's proposals regarding conversational implicatures. It is to those proposals that we now turn.

Grice's Theory of Conversational Implicature

Grice's theory of conversational implicature was first presented as the William James lecture at Harvard University in 1967, and then later partially published (Grice, 1975, 1989). The theory is brief and rough and not completely worked out. Yet, its essential insights are profound; the theory has had a tremendous impact on a number of different areas of research.

In this theory, Grice is essentially concerned with how it is possible for people to mean more than what they say; in other words, to convey nonliteral meaning. He proposes that this is possible because interlocutors abide by what he termed the cooperative principle (CP). The CP is simple and straightforward and states simply that one should: "Make your conversational contribution such as is required, at the stage at which it occurs, by the accepted purpose or direction of the talk exchange in which you are engaged" (p. 45).

This very general requirement states that people should communicate in a rational and efficient manner; say what you mean, just the facts, don't wander around, and so on. This general requirement is further specified in terms of the following four conversational maxims:

1. *Quantity*—Make your contribution as informative as required (i.e., do not be either overinformative or underinformative).
2. *Quality*—Try to make your contribution true, one for which you have evidence.
3. *Manner*—Be clear. That is, avoid ambiguity and obscurity.
4. *Relation*—Make your contribution relevant for the exchange.

To abide by the CP when conversing, then, one's utterances should be clear (manner), truthful (quality), relevant for the topic (relation), and the right size (quantity). Of course conversationalists rarely abide by these maxims. They are often irrelevant, they sometimes say too much or too little, and so on. But it is usually the case that people will mutually assume adherence to the CP and maxims, and this assumption serves as a frame for interpreting a speaker's utterances. That is, a speaker's utterances will be interpreted *as if* they were clear, relevant, truthful, and informative. For example, saying, "Can you pass the salt?" at the dinner table is a violation of the relation maxim (i.e., in this context, inquiring into another's ability to pass the salt would not be a relevant contribution). But, because the hearer assumes the speaker is being relevant, he will search for an ulterior meaning (and make a conversational implicature); he will interpret the utterance in such a way so as to maintain adherence to the conversational maxims. It is in this way that violations of the CP serve as a trigger to search for an ulterior meaning (i.e., the first stage in Searle's model).

The "Pass the salt" example is an instance of an implicature that arises to preserve adherence to a specific conversational maxim. Additionally, speakers will sometimes intentionally flout or violate a maxim, in which case it is simply not possible for the hearer to assume the speaker is adhering to the maxims. For example, abrupt topic changes ("I hope it stops raining soon") in response to personal questions ("How did you do on that Chemistry exam?") function as relevance violations and convey much more than their strictly literal meaning (possible gloss: I didn't do well on the exam). In this case, it is obvious the speaker is not complying with the relation maxim. But the hearer will usually still assume overall cooperativeness on the part of the speaker and, as a result, generate a conversational implicature that makes sense of the violation. Much figurative language can be explained in this way. Consider, for example, tautologies such as "Boys will be boys" or "War is war." These are clear violations of the quantity maxim; they are essentially uninformative. Yet these utterances will in most contexts convey clear nonliteral meanings.

Grice's theory can be regarded as an important adjunct to speech act theory. It provides a mechanism by which speakers convey, and hearers recognize, illocutionary force. And it does so in a way that is both simple and broadly applicable. Conversational implicatures are important because (in most views) they are not derivable from semantics alone; one cannot generate the intended meaning of a person's utterance (illocutionary force) by considering the words and their organization in isolation. Rather, the context, including the interlocutors' mutually assumed knowledge, are crucial for determining a speaker's meaning. It is in this way that Grice's framework is clearly a social psychological model of communication; interactants must mutually assume cooperativeness if communication is to succeed (see chap. 5).

Importantly, Grice's theory applies to *all* action, not just linguistic communication. That is, the CP and corresponding maxims are assumed to underlie rational interaction of any sort, verbal and nonverbal. Imagine, for example, two people cooking dinner together. In order to do this successfully they need to cooperate, and their cooperation involves making their contributions to the joint endeavor relevant (e.g., if asked to stir the sauce one should do it immediately, not later), truthful, and so on. Like speech act theory, Grice's theory is about action as much as it is about language.

Over the years, scholars have noted several weaknesses with Grice's theory. First, Grice was not particularly clear regarding the specific implicature a hearer will be most likely to make. The general answer is that the implicature will be one that makes the utterance a cooperative response, one that would "fit" in the conversation. No doubt this is true, but in many instances there are numerous possibilities in this regard; the theory narrows down those possibilities but does not specify exactly how an utterance will be interpreted. This, of course, is impossible to specify in advance. Still, additional interpretive constraints, especially those derived from the social bases of communication, could be developed. One possibility, for example, is that the addressees' recognition that the speaker is engaging in face management (Goffman, 1967) may serve to make certain interpretations more likely (Holtgraves, 1998). This proposal is considered in detail in chapter 2.

Second, as Krauss and Fussell (1996) point out, it is not entirely clear what will constitute a maxim violation; it has been notoriously difficult to specify maxim violations in any formal way. For example, what constitutes an appropriately informative reply? And what exactly is a relevant response? Moreover, what counts as a maxim violation may vary as a function of characteristics of the speaker. Politicians, for example, can be quite skilled at violating the relevance maxim, so much so that the violation may not even be noticed. And if it is noticed it may simply be written off as an attempt to avoid answering a question (i.e., an implicature will not be generated, although perceptions of the speaker may be affected). In short, Grice's conversational maxims may not be invariant over social contexts.

Along similar lines, some concern has been raised about whether the conversational maxims are cross-culturally valid, a point never raised by Grice, although he seems to have pitched his theory, implicitly at least, as being cross-culturally valid. Some researchers, however, have noted that the maxims may not be valid in certain cultures. In a well-known paper, Keenan (1976) argued that people in Malagasy routinely withhold information from one another (information is a culturally prized commodity), an action that is in clear violation of the quantity maxim. As a result, violations of this maxim do not usually result in conversational implicatures (as presumably would be the case in most other cultures). There is a more general criticism here. It has been suggested that Grice's view, with its emphasis on individual autonomy (i.e., the individual is the source of his utterances) has relevance only in Western cultures (Fitch & Sanders, 1994). It is possible that any maxims people follow in communicating cooperatively will vary over cultures, reflecting, perhaps, differences in what is regarded as rational interaction.

Third, Grice's stipulation that there are four (and only four) maxims has been criticized. Some have argued that additional maxims are required (e.g., Leech, 1983), others that four is too many. Regarding the latter, Sperber and Wilson (1986) have argued that there really is only one conversational maxim—be relevant—and that the other maxims are simply instances of this more general requirement. In many respects this seems correct; by failing to provide an informative response (quantity maxim) one is also failing to provide a relevant response.

These are all-important questions that need to be pursued. It is clearly important to determine the specific content of conversational maxims, how they might vary over settings and cultures, the reasoning processes that link maxim violations with particular interpretations, and so on. But the answers to these questions will not alter the basic Gricean insight that *if* a person believes a maxim has been violated (whatever the personal and contextual features bringing about that belief), then some interpretive work will be undertaken. Nor will they alter Grice's fundamental point that conversational maxims (whatever they may look like) serve as a basis for rational interaction, and hence as a framework for interpretation, thereby allowing people tremendous flexibility in the manner in which they communicate their intentions.

Idiomatic Approaches

An alternative view of indirect speech acts argues that the types of inferential processes discussed so far are not required for the recognition of nonliteral or indirect meanings. Rather, the intended indirect meanings are assumed to be idiomatic, or noncompositional. In this view, "Can you pass the salt?" is regarded as an idiomatic expression for (indirectly) requesting another to pass the salt. In this case, the hearer need not recognize and then reject the literal meaning (a question about the hearer's ability to pass the salt) in favor of a directive reading (an attempt to get the hearer to pass the salt). Instead, the hearer is assumed to directly recognize the (indirect) meaning of the remark.

There is a certain intuitive appeal to an idiomatic approach, especially for utterances like "Can you pass the salt?" Simple reflection suggests that on hearing this utterance, we do not go through the (relatively) time-consuming process of recognizing the literal meaning, rejecting the literal meaning due to its inappropriateness in context, and then constructing an alternative interpretation.

When someone says, "Can you pass the salt?" it seems as if we know right away that the speaker is asking for the salt.

In addition to its intuitive appeal, there are certain linguistic characteristics of indirect requests that support an idiom interpretation. Consider, for example, whether or not *please* can be (acceptably) inserted into a sentence. For direct requests (but not for other illocutionary acts) *please* can be inserted in order to make the request more polite. Note, however, that this is acceptable only preverbally ("Please, shut the door"), or at the end of the utterance ("Shut the door, please"), and not anywhere else (e.g., "Shut please the door" is not acceptable). Interestingly, many indirect requests also allow the insertion of *please.* Thus, it is acceptable (and common) to say, "Could you please shut the door?" or "Would you please shut the door?" and so on. The constraints on where *please* can be inserted are identical to those for direct requests (e.g., one can't say, "Could you shut please the door?"). This suggests that the underlying semantic structure of indirect requests of this sort are identical to the underlying structure of their direct counterparts.

Finally, inferential approaches are based on the assumption that one can reliably differentiate between literal/direct and nonliteral/indirect meanings. Whether this is possible has been questioned extensively by Gibbs (1984, 1994b; see Dascal, 1987 for an opposing view). Literal meaning is most often taken to be compositional (i.e., a result of the sentence's lexical items and syntax) and context free (i.e., the meaning of the sentence regardless of who says it when and where). But Gibbs argues that there are sentences that simply do not have a literal meaning. What, for example, is the literal meaning of "How 'bout a beer?" Other utterances (e.g., "Can you pass the salt?") might have a literal meaning, but it is one that is very rarely, if ever, used. Gibbs also notes that in certain instances so-called literal meaning is not context free and can only be understood with reference to a specific context. What, for example, is the literal meaning of "I've eaten" in response to an offer of a snack? Does it mean that one has, in the past, eaten a meal? No, obviously it refers to having recently eaten; but then that could not be part of its so-called literal meaning. In the end, Gibbs bases much of his argument on the lack of psycholinguistic evidence supporting the presumed role that literal meaning plays in the comprehension of utterances. This issue is discussed in more detail in the next section.

COMPREHENDING INDIRECT SPEECH ACTS: PSYCHOLINGUISTIC EVIDENCE

The question of how people comprehend indirect meanings is an extremely important one. Indirect meanings abound, and not just in conversations. Poetry, novels, and artistic expressions in general trade on the subtleties of nonliteral language (e.g., see Gibbs's [1994a] *Poetics of Meaning).* Understanding how we comprehend indirect meanings gives us insight not only into language, but also into how we think, reason, and interact with one another. Consequently, there has been a fair amount of psycholinguistic research examining how people comprehend indirect, nonliteral meanings. Most of this research has focused on whether or not inferential processing is involved in the comprehension of two broad utterance types—requests and figures of speech. The emphasis on these remarks is understandable; requests are almost always performed indirectly, and figures of speech are, by definition, indirect.

In general, inferential approaches assume that addressees (a) always first recognize the literal meaning of an utterance prior to comprehending the indirect meaning, (b) search for an indirect interpretation only after deciding that the literal reading is defective (i.e., it violates a conversational maxim), and (c) generate additional inferences in order to comprehend the utterance (Gibbs, 1994b; Glucksberg, 1991). For requests, there are several lines of research providing some support for inferential processing. First, the manner in which people respond to indirect requests suggests that the literal meaning of these utterances is activated. For example, in a series of clever experiments Clark (1979) analyzed replies to telephone requests made of various merchants. The requests were always indirect requests for information such as when the store closed (e.g., "Can you tell me what time you close?") or the price of a particular item. As one would expect, people always recognized the indirect meanings of these utterances. But one of the most interesting findings was that the replies frequently addressed both the literal and the indirect meaning of the request. Thus, in response to "Can you tell me what time you close?" people frequently responded with something like "Sure, 8 p.m." The "sure" is clearly in response to the literal meaning of the request, suggesting that the literal meaning of the utterance had been activated.

Along somewhat similar lines, much of the research on politeness (see chap. 2) provides indirect evidence that literal meaning is activated. The politeness of a request is based on the remark's literal rather than indirect meaning. For example, "Could you shut the door?" is more polite than "I want you to shut the door," even though both are indirect requests to shut the door. There is fairly extensive research demonstrating that the perceived politeness of requests is influenced by variations in literal wording (Clark & Schunk, 1980; Holtgraves & Yang, 1990, 1992). There must be some awareness of the literal meaning if politeness judgments vary in this way.

And there is also some evidence that people encode the specific wording of an utterance when that wording varies in politeness (Holtgraves, 1997a). In these studies, people spontaneously remembered the politeness wording of utterances at better than chance levels. Even when they did not remember the exact wording, they did seem to retain some gist of the politeness of the utterance. For example, if people had heard "I'd like you to read the list," they were more likely to recall an equally polite form (e.g., "Could you read the list?") rather than an impolite form (e.g., "Read the list"). These results also suggest some activation of literal meaning.

All of these findings are consistent with the provision in inferential models that literal meaning (at least for requests) receives some degree of activation. The problem is that this is not direct evidence; there is no evidence regarding the actual cognitive operations involved in the comprehension of requests. For example, it is possible that the politeness of a request is recognized simultaneously with (rather than prior to) the recognition of the conveyed, or indirect, meaning. Furthermore, it is conceivable that some wordings have conventionalized politeness values that determine perceived politeness without any activation of the literal meaning of the remark. For example, "Can you x?" forms might be conventionally more polite than "I want you to x" forms. It is possible that this difference in wording could affect politeness without any activation of the literal meaning of the utterance.

Fortunately, there is more direct evidence bearing on this issue. There is an extensive line of psycholinguistic research investigating the comprehension of what is usually referred to as figurative language (e.g., similes, metaphors, oxymorons, sarcasm, etc.; for summaries see Gibbs, 1994b; Cacciari & Glucksberg, 1994). This research is relevant for the present discussion because all figurative language is, by definition, indirect speech. In using a figure of speech a speaker is meaning more than that which is conveyed with a literal reading of the utterance. Figures of speech include metaphors (e.g., My job is a jail), idioms (e.g., Button your lips), ironic sarcasm (e.g., "A fine friend you are" when one has been anything but a friend), and many others. Note, however, that in contrast to indirect requests, the illocutionary force is generally the same for the literal and conveyed meanings. With "He spilled the beans," for example, both the literal and idiomatic readings are assertions.

In general, empirical research on figurative language has not supported the standard inferential processing model of indirectness. First, consider the claim that a nonliteral meaning is the result of an inference process. An inference process is time consuming, and so people should take longer to comprehend figures of speech than their direct equivalents. But numerous studies have demonstrated that an inference process is not required for these forms. People simply do not take more time to understand the meaning of figurative expressions (e.g., "He spilled the beans") than they do literal equivalent expressions (Gibbs, 1980; Ortony, Schallert, Reynolds, & Antos, 1978).

Second, in the standard inferential processing models, activation of the literal meaning of a remark is obligatory and must occur prior to the (optional) recognition of the nonliteral, or figurative, meaning. However, research indicates that for many figures of speech, the literal and figurative meanings are assessed simultaneously and in some cases even in a reversed order. Keysar (1998) provides the following example that illustrates this well. In Kosinski"s (1971) novel *Being There,* the president of the United States at one point asks Mr. Gardiner his opinion of the economy, and the latter responds with:

In a garden . . . growth has its season. There are spring and summer, but there are also fall and winter. And then spring and summer again. As long as the roots are not severed, all is well and all will be well. (p. 45)

Now, in most instances such comments would be taken metaphorically. And readers probably do take them metaphorically at first, but then quickly realize that it is the literal that is intended.[2] This suggests that activation of figurative meaning, rather than being optional, is sometimes obligatory and accessed in a relatively automatic fashion. Consistent with this reasoning, several studies have demonstrated that the nonliteral meaning of a figure of speech is activated even when the literal meaning is acceptable in context (Gildea & Glucksberg, 1983; Glucksberg, Gildea, & Bookin, 1982; Keysar, 1989).

In terms of requests, Gibbs (1983) has demonstrated that certain indirect requests are idiomatic and comprehended without activation of their literal meaning. In two priming studies, he found that indirect requests facilitated subsequent sentence verification judgments of targets that were indirect readings of the requests, but the same indirect requests did not result in any facilitation for targets that were literal paraphrases of the request. This indicates that people did not compute a literal reading of the utterance before determining the indirect reading (the heart of inferential models). Rather, the indirect meaning was computed first and represented independent of any literal reading.

Finally, the inferential view claims that once a literal meaning has been rejected, it will no longer play a role in determining the meaning of an utterance. But this too appears not to be the case. Rather, the literal meaning of the words in a metaphor can continue to influence the manner in which the metaphor is interpreted (Cacciari & Glucksberg, 1991; Titone & Connine, 1994).

So, there is mixed evidence here: politeness research (indirectly) supports an inferential view, but much psycholinguistic research provides support for an idiomatic model. An important fact to recognize here is that there are many different ways to convey an indirect meaning, with corresponding differences in how those meanings are processed. And there are two broad distinctions that appear to be important in this regard: generalized versus particularized implicatures and conventionality.

Particularized versus Generalized Implicatures

Grice (1975) made several important, though often overlooked, distinctions regarding how implicatures are made. Of particular relevance is his distinction between generalized and particularized implicatures. The basic difference between the two is that generalized implicatures are context independent; they

---

[2]Mr. Gardiner is a gardener with absolutely no knowledge of economics.

can arise without reference to the context. Particularized implicatures, on the other hand, are context dependent; recognizing them requires a consideration of the utterance in terms of a context, most notably the prior discourse context.

Much of the figurative language examined in prior research appears to produce generalized implicatures. For example, most metaphors and idioms seem to be interpretable independent of any discourse context. Regardless of the context, people will usually interpret "He spilled the beans" as meaning "He revealed a secret." Support for this comes from the fact that the nonliteral meaning of many metaphors is not optional; even when the context supports a literal reading, the nonliteral meaning is still activated (Gildea & Glucksberg, 1983; Glucksberg, Gildea, and Bookin, 1982; Keysar, 1989).

There is another sense in which generalized implicatures are context independent; their nonliteral meaning is derived primarily from the words in the utterance. Metaphors (e.g., My job is a jail) can be viewed as a mapping process whereby a prototypical name (e.g., jail) is used to represent an unnamed superordinate category without a name (i.e., things that are confining). The nonliteral meaning in this case is derived primarily from the concepts referenced by the words in the utterance.

Particularized implicatures have received relatively little empirical attention. The clearest case of a particularized implicature would be violations of Grice's (1975) relation maxim. Consider the following exchange (from Holtgraves, 1998):

> **Bob:**   What did you think of my presentation?
> **Andy:**   It's hard to give a good presentation.

People generally interpret Andy's reply as conveying a negative opinion about Bob's presentation (Holtgraves, 1998; see chap. 2 for additional detail regarding this process). But how do they arrive at this interpretation? Experiments conducted by Holtgraves (1999) demonstrated that the comprehension of these replies involves an inference process quite like the one described by Grice (1975): Recognition of the conveyed meaning is time consuming and involves initial activation of the literal meaning. Unlike generalized implicatures, the conveyed indirect meaning (I don't like your presentation) is optional; the indirect meaning is not activated if the context supports a literal reading.

Particularized implicatures represent a type of inference that occurs only with reference to a particular discourse context. For relevance violations it is the relation between the reply and a prior utterance—the fact that the reply is not literally relevant—that results in the generation of a specific indirect meaning. Particularized implicatures, then, are not the result of any specific feature of an utterance (there are an infinite number of utterances one could use to violate the relevance maxim), but rather a feature of the placement of an utterance in a conversational sequence. So, the particularized–generalized distinction is not a property of utterances per se, but rather a property of the manner in which an utterance is used. Idioms, metaphors, and other figures of speech might also yield particularized implicatures in certain contexts. Imagine, for example, Tom asking Bob if he should apply for a job with Bob's firm, and Bob replies "My job is a jail." Tom will no doubt recognize the metaphorical meaning of Bob's remark, that Bob believes his job is confining (a generalized implicature). But it also seems likely that Tom will construct some type of particularized implicature, something along the lines of a belief that Bob is advising him that he would not enjoy working for his firm. The particularized implicature occurs because the metaphor serves as a reply to a prior question.

Conventionality

In general, a conventional means for performing a speech act means that the literal meaning of the utterance is pro forma, not to be taken seriously. Most discussions of conventionality have focused on requests. Although there is some disagreement regarding this issue, conventional indirect requests generally have the following features: (1) they can be performed by asserting or questioning the felicity conditions that underlie requests (see p. 22 above), (2) the utterance contains the request-based propositional content (e.g., "shut the door" in "Could you shut the door?"), and (3) the preverbal insertion of "please" is allowed (e.g., "Could you please shut the door?"). Research demonstrates that people do not respond to the literal meaning of conventional indirect requests (Clark, 1979). More importantly, their indirect meanings are recognized in a direct fashion, without need for a time-consuming inference process (Gibbs, 1983; Holtgraves, 1994).

All other indirect requests not meeting these criteria can be regarded as nonconventional indirect requests, and there are a lot of them. Unfortunately, little is known about the forms they can take. One possible form has been termed a negative state remark (Holtgraves, 1994). This request is based on the following principle: A speaker can perform a request by asserting or (questioning) the existence of a negative state (or a state that the hearer can infer is negative) if there is some action that the hearer can perform in order to alter the negative state. This principle yields indirect requests such as "It's warm in here" or "I'm thirsty" to request another to open a window or get one a drink, respectively. Note that these forms do not contain the directive propositional content, cannot take *please,* and are not related (at least directly) to the underlying felicity conditions. In contrast to conventional indirect requests, the comprehension of nonconventional forms (at least negative state remarks) will, on occasion, involve an inference process (Holtgraves, 1994).

Finally, it may be possible to extend the logic of conventionality to certain responses to requests. Because requests project to a next turn, the felicity conditions underlying a request should remain relevant for that turn (Clark, 1985). As a result, these same conditions can be denied as a means of refusing to comply with the request. Thus, when Amber asks Beth for a loan, Beth's ability to loan the money can be questioned by Amber in order to indirectly perform the request ("Can you loan me $20?") and denied by Beth in order to (indirectly) refuse to comply with the request ("I don't get paid until to Friday"). Research suggests that indirect refusals performed in this way, like conventional indirect requests, are recognized directly and without need for an inference process (Holtgraves, 1999).

CONCLUSION

In this chapter I have focused on language use as human action, as opposed to treating language as an abstract system existing apart from its use. When viewed in this way language is heavily contextualized and dependent on real-world knowledge. Language users must know what actions can be performed with language and how to perform them. And, of course, they must be able to recognize the actions another has performed with her utterances.

Speech act theory provides one framework for viewing language use as action. There are obviously many unresolved issues and problems with speech act theory, several additional ones of which I note following (for a more detailed critique see Levinson, 1983). But the essential idea of speech act theory—that in using language one is performing various actions—is no doubt correct. And one of the virtues of this approach—although it has not always been emphasized—is the placement of language within the context of social activities. This can be seen most clearly, of course, with declaratives. To "declare war," call a base runner "out," christen a ship, and so on presuppose the existence of social institutions without which these linguistic actions would not make sense. To understand these verbal actions, then, requires an understanding of these institutions and the role of these utterances within them. Declaratives represent the essence of rule-governed verbal behavior, these practices (or ceremonies) are generally governed by a tightly structured set of rules, including stipulations regarding who can say what and where and when and with what effect. It is just these sorts of procedures that Austin (1962) noted and relied upon in his development of speech act theory.

It is very important to not lose sight of the fact that other illocutionary acts—assertives, directives, expressives, and commissives—are also part of various social activities. Of course, the rules are not as formal and concrete as they are for declaratives, but they exist and they do play an important role in these verbal actions. To understand, say, a directive, requires an understanding of not just language as an abstract system, but also an understanding of peoples' relations with one another—an understanding that people can and do perform actions for one another, that people have desires for others to perform such actions, that these desires can be communicated, that people have various rights and obligations, and so on. In this regard, it is important to note the importance given by Searle (1969,

1979) to social psychological variables such as status in governing speech act use.

The importance of the social nature of language use seems to have had its greatest impact on views of language production; felicity conditions specify when and under what conditions various speech acts can be performed. Interestingly, there has been no parallel development in terms of interpretation; the role of social variables in the interpretation of speech acts has generally been ignored (but see Levinson, 1979). If the production of speech acts is guided by the social activities of which they are a part, then those same variables should play a role in speech act interpretation.

Consider, for example, the role of status. As noted by Searle (1979), Brown and Levinson (1987), and many others, the relative status of a speaker is very important in determining to whom a request can be made as well as how that request is made (see chap. 2). Higher-status people have the right to direct the actions of others, and lower-status people have the obligation to comply with those directives—these are, in a sense, defining features of what it means to be high or low status. Now, the status relationship between people can also play a role in interpretation. If higher-status people have the right to issue directives, then utterances with multiple meanings might be more likely to be given a directive interpretation when the speaker is high rather than low in status. This seems to be the case. People are much faster at comprehending ambiguous remarks (specifically, nonconventional indirect requests such as "It's warm in here" as a request to open a window) when a speaker is described as being high (rather than low) in status (Holtgraves, 1994). The role of other interpersonal variables in comprehension is described in chapter 2.

The relationship between language and social variables is not one way; it is not only social psychological factors that are implicated in language use; language use is also heavily implicated in many social psychological phenomena. One of the things speech act theory provides is the conceptual machinery for understanding, at a very basic level, what people are doing with their talk. In this way it can provide a means for examining the linguistic underpinnings of social psychological processes such as how people negotiate power in a relationship (e.g., who issues the most directives, who complies with the most directives), how they request help (e.g., directly or indirectly), how they attempt to persuade and self-disclose, and so on (see chaps. 2 and 3).

Overall, then, the socially situated nature of language use is one of the enduring legacies of speech act theory. Despite this obvious strength in emphasizing the social underpinnings of language, there are certain ways in which, paradoxically, the theory is not social enough. For example, when we make a request, we impose on the other, and depending on the particulars of the setting, we may elicit resentment, feelings of imposition, and so on. Such interpersonal effects are clearly a social dimension of language use that must be systematically related to speech acts (e.g., a request will generally elicit different reactions than an apology). In general, most theoretical and empirical work on speech act theory has concentrated on the illocutionary act; perlocutionary effects have largely been ignored. This is unfortunate because it is the perlocutionary effects that make speech act theory a truly social psychological theory; the perlocutionary act refers to the effect one person has on another through their talk. Speakers, in formulating their remarks, must have some inkling of the particular effects in others that they would like to achieve and design their remarks accordingly.

A similar sort of criticism can be applied to Grice"s (1975) theory of conversational implicature. Clearly, people frequently violate the CP and corresponding maxims, and it seems that these violations serve as an invitation to look for an ulterior meaning. But why violate the maxims and convey an indirect meaning in the first place? Why not just say what you mean? The fact that all natural languages contain mechanisms for conveying indirect meanings suggests that there is something fundamental going on here, and that fundamental thing is largely a social thing. People convey their meanings indirectly to achieve various social purposes. In chapter 2 the ramifications of this notion are explored in detail.

All illocutionary acts are social acts in the sense that they are directed at another person. The performance of a speech act requires, then, a speaker who performs the act, as well as a hearer who recognizes it. This point was crucial for Austin, who regarded hearer uptake as necessary for the successful performance of a speech act. But in many respects, speech act theory and related research has given the hearer short shrift; the emphasis has clearly been speaker oriented. It is the speaker's attitudes, beliefs, and utterances that have been examined in detail. This one-sided concern is partly manifested in a large and largely unexplored area in speech act theory; namely, how does a hearer recognize a speaker's intention (or the illocutionary force of a speaker's remark)? Sentence mode and mood are woefully insufficient, as there is no clear relationship between these variables and illocutionary points. It may be that there are various illocutionary force indicators (Levinson, 1983) that aid in this process, but what they look like and how they work remains to be seen. Other than with explicit performatives, the manner in which illocutionary force is recognized and represented is unclear.

There is another problem here—one that also reflects a failure to appreciate how social psychological processes are played out in verbal interactions. The problem is this: The unit of analysis in speech act theory is a speaker's single utterance. This utterance is usually complete and well-formed—unlike real talk, which is often fragmented, elliptical, and so on. Moreover, it is usually assumed that a single speech act is performed with a single utterance. Of course they often are, but it is also frequently the case that a single speech act is performed over a stretch of dialogue as it is jointly negotiated by the interlocutors. Consider the following example of a request made, or attempted to be made, over a series of turns (much more detail on these sorts of processes is provided in chap. 4).

Al: Hi, ya busy?
Bob: Sorta, what's up?
Al: I'm having problems with my computer.
Bob: I could look at it this evening.
Al: Great, thanks.

Granted, there are multiple speech acts being performed here (a request, an offer, thanks), but note that the request is performed over (the first) three turns rather than within a single turn. This illustrates the way in which requests can be negotiated over a series of moves, giving the interlocutors options at various points (e.g., Bob at turn 2 could have said, "Yes I'm busy"—thereby diminishing the likelihood that Al would have made his problem known in turn 3, and thereby effectively preventing the request from being made). The point is that many times intentions are made manifest over a series of moves. Thus, understanding what people are doing with their words will require a consideration of how they accomplish their ends, in collaboration with another, over a series of moves, points to be discussed at length in subsequent chapters.

2

The Interpersonal
Underpinnings of Talk:
Face Management
and Politeness

Speech act theory provides a view of language as social action; language use has a force as well as an abstract content. However, the actions people perform with speech acts also have interpersonal implications. And people, being people, cannot simply perform speech acts without any concern for those interpersonal implications. To request, apologize, and criticize involves not only the performance of a directive, commissive, and assertive, respectively, but also the performance of actions with clear implications for the identities of the interactants. How people talk must be responsive to those concerns. This is why our verbal interactions with others are not always quick, clear, and maximally efficient. Instead, we hedge and hesitate, speak indirectly, gently negotiate topic changes, and so on. All of these occur in large part as a result of interpersonal considerations.

In this chapter, I consider some of the interpersonal underpinnings of language use, focusing particularly on single utterances (interpersonal underpinnings of sequences of talk are considered in chap. 4). Two general issues are pursued. First, as described in chapter 1, Grice's (1975) theory of conversational implicature has been an influential framework for examining conversational interaction. He proposed the existence of a set of maxims that serve as a framework for the production and comprehension of indirect meanings. But why do speakers violate these maxims in the first place? Why don't people speak in the clearest and most efficient manner possible (i.e., in accord with the maxims)? Second, when maxim violations do occur, how is it that hearers are able to arrive at the precise meaning intended by the speaker? The general thesis I develop in this chapter is that these questions are related and can be answered only with reference to interpersonal considerations. For most of this chapter, I focus on the first question and hence deal with issues regarding language production, or why speakers phrase their remarks the way that they do. In a final section of the chapter, I consider the second question and deal with the role of interpersonal processes in language comprehension.

POLITENESS AND LANGUAGE PRODUCTION

Politeness theory has provided a major framework for examining the interpersonal underpinnings of language use. Now, in this tradition the term *politeness* refers not to a lay conception of politeness or a set of protocols regarding how one is to behave in different social settings. Instead, politeness is a technical term, a theoretical construct invoked as a means of explaining the link between language use and the social context. Politeness is an extremely broad phenomenon existing at the interface of linguistic, social, and cognitive processes. It refers (roughly) to the way one puts things and the way one puts things is a result of a speaker's cognitive assessment of the social context. Because of its broad reach, politeness has been a topic of interest to scholars in a variety of disciplines, including anthropology, linguistics, philosophy, social psychology, cognitive psychology, communication, sociolinguistics, and others.

Several theories of politeness have been proposed (see, e.g., Fraser, 1990). But by far the most popular approach was developed by Penelope Brown and Stephen Levinson. Their theory was originally published as a book chapter in 1978, and then reissued whole as a book in 1987 (with an introductory chapter summarizing relevant research). This theory has been extremely influential, and for good reason: It represents a framework for linking the major dimensions of social interaction with the ways in which people talk with one other. In this regard, it is truly a social psychological theory of language use. Because of its importance, the present chapter is structured around this theory.

In their theory, Brown and Levinson attempt to specify the various ways in which people use language in the service of face management. In doing so, they borrow heavily from the writings of Ervin Goffman on the topic of face and face management, and it is to those ideas that we now turn.

Goffman, Face, and Face-Work

According to Goffman, face is "the positive social value a person effectively claims for himself by the line others assume he has taken during a particular contact" (1967, p. 5). Face, in a sense, is one's situated identity. But it is not a specific identity (e.g., being witty, sophisticated); rather it is the successful presentation of *any* identity. To fail to have one's identity ratified is to lose face in an encounter, to have one's identity ratified is to have face, to maintain an identity that has been challenged is to save face. Face, then, is something that resides not within an individual, but rather within the flow of events in an encounter.

When in the presence of others, one's face is on display and subject to various threats; consequently it must be maintained. This is accomplished by engaging in face-work, or undertaking communications designed to create, support, or challenge a particular line; it is the (largely linguistic) means by which face is managed during an encounter. Goffman (1967, 1971) provided several important distinctions regarding face-work. Of particular importance is his distinction, derived from Durkheim (1915), between avoidance rituals, or the avoidance of impinging on another (Durkheim's negative rites), and presentation rituals, or the displaying of solidarity with another (Durkheim's positive rites). Avoidance rituals proscribe what one should not do. Thus, people generally do not call attention to another's faults, introduce threatening topics, restrict another's movements, or in any way violate the other's territory (or face). In contrast, presentation rituals are approach based; they are the ritualized offerings (e.g., invitations, salutations, compliments) made to others as a means of affirming and maintaining a relationship.

Face-work, for Goffman, is not trivial or a sometime thing. It is the ritual attention [derived from Durkheim's (1915) analysis of religious ritual] that people must give to one another so that interactants can be mobilized to be "self-regulating participants in social encounters" (1967, p. 44). The assumption of mutual concern with face, and its accomplishment via face-work, provides a mechanism that accounts for the emergence of the interaction order from the chaos of self-serving individuals. The social order is thus created and sustained through the ritual of face-work. And this ritual is largely cooperative. Because face can only be given by others (one might claim a particular identity, but it must be ratified by others), it is in each person's best interest to maintain each other's face. Acting with demeanor (supporting one's own face) entails acting with deference to the other (supporting the other's face); threats to another's face thereby become threats to one's own face. Now, insults, challenges, and so on obviously occur, but they have their effect because of the mutual assumption of cooperative face-work.

Brown and Levinson's Politeness Theory

Brown and Levinson's (1987) theory is a direct extension of Goffman's analysis of face and face-work. It is, in effect, a more precise specification of face (what it is and what threatens it) and face-work (the specific mechanisms used for its accomplishment). I consider each of these extensions in turn.

First, Brown and Levinson argued that face is comprised of two basic and universal desires: negative face, or the desire for autonomy, and positive face, or the desire for connection with others. Positive and negative face correspond to Durkheim's (1915) concepts of positive (approach based) and negative (avoidance based) rites, and these two desires match up quite well with basic wants postulated by other scholars such as agency (negative face) and communion (positive face; Bakan, 1966) and power (negative face) and intimacy (positive face; McAdams, 1985).

Like Goffman (1967), Brown and Levinson argue that face is subject to continued threat during the course of social interaction. Positive face is under continued threat because contact and connection with others is crucial to our existence. Relationships must be maintained, and any hint of slippage (e.g., failing to return a greeting) threatens positive face. Negative face is threatened when one's freedom to engage in various courses of action (including the most insignificant actions) is diminished. In a sense, merely participating in a conversation threatens one's negative face (at some minimal level) because one is required to respond to the other person. Of course, one can eliminate this imposition by attempting to terminate the conversation, but to do so, without the appropriate moves, will threaten the other person's positive face—and in so doing threaten one's own positive face. Clearly, face concerns permeate our social interactions.

Many of the acts people want to perform are inherently face threatening. Requests, for example, threaten (primarily) the negative face of the hearer (they restrict autonomy), disagreements threaten the positive face of the hearer (they may lessen solidarity between interactants), apologies threaten the positive face of the speaker (by denigrating oneself vis-à-vis the hearer), and so on. Crossing the primary type of threat (positive or negative) with the primary focus of the threat (speaker or hearer) results in the fourfold typology presented in Table 2.1.

Things can get a little complicated because sometimes a verbal act can have multiple implications for face.[1] Consider, for example, a compliment. This act supports the positive face of the hearer (it emphasizes solidarity). But it can simultaneously threaten the recipient's negative face (at least in some cultures) because he must respond in some way, usually by acknowledging the compliment, but also by downgrading the compliment so as to comply with the injunction against self-praise (Pomerantz, 1978). Even requests, which seem straightforward on the surface, turn out under closer scrutiny to not be so clear. Although the recipient's negative face is clearly threatened, so too might her positive face, insofar as the request implies a criticism of the recipient for not having already performed the act (Labov & Fanschel, 1977). For example, "Why haven't you done the dishes yet?" threatens both negative face (via the request to do the dishes) and positive face (via the criticism for not already having done so). In general, although all directives threaten the hearer's negative face, they can also vary, in a principled way, in terms of additional threats posed by the act (Wilson, Aleman, & Leathan, 1998).

---

[1]It is even more complicated than this because the face of third (and fourth, etc.) parties may also be threatened. Although acknowledged by Brown and Levinson, this point was not developed, and very little research has been conducted on this issue.

TABLE 2.1
Typology of Face-Threatening Acts

Threat focus:	Type of Face Threat	
	Negative Face	Positive Face
Hearer	Requests	Disagreements
	Offers	Criticisms
	Compliments	Complaints
Speaker	Promises	Apologies
	Acceptance of offer	Emotional leakage
	Thanks	Compliment acceptance

Brown and Levinson's Politeness Strategies

The preceding analysis suggests a fundamental conflict for social interactants. On the one hand, they are motivated to cooperatively manage each other's positive and negative face. On the other hand, they need or want to perform social acts that are inherently threatening to positive and negative face. It is this ubiquitous (and presumably universal) conflict that motives politeness; it is an underlying pressure that affects in various ways the tone of our interactions with others. Unless one chooses to live in complete isolation (and hence avoid this conflict), one must engage in some degree of face-work or politeness.

So exactly how is this accomplished? What exactly is politeness? In one sense, all politeness can be viewed as deviation from maximally efficient communication; as violations (in some sense) of Grice's (1975) conversational maxims (see chap. 1). To perform an act other than in the most clear and efficient manner possible is to implicate some degree of politeness on the part of the speaker. To request another to open a window by saying "It's warm in here" is to perform the request politely because one did not use the most efficient means possible for performing this act (i.e., "Open the window").

The essence of politeness can be made clearer by contrasting human-human communication with human-computer communication. People communicate with a computer in the most direct and efficient manner possible, that is, in accord with Grice's maxims. We don't suggest to our computer that it perform some task—we command it to do so. We are able to do this because we need not be concerned with managing the face of our computers. Computers have no feelings or pride or sensitivity; they don't take offense if ordered to do something or if the user yells at it for some perceived misdeed.[2] But humans do have sensitivities and

---

[2]Interestingly, there is some evidence that users of natural language interfaces may actually anthropomorphize their computer system and mimic in their communications the politeness generally shown to humans (Brennan, 1998).

feelings and might indeed by offended if commanded to do something (negative face is threatened) or if criticized for some failing (positive face is threatened). Politeness allows people to perform many interpersonally sensitive actions in a nonthreatening or less threatening manner.

There are an infinite number of ways in which people can be polite by performing an act in a less than optimal manner, and Brown and Levinson's typology of five superstrategies is an attempt to capture some of these essential differences. Their superstrategies can be ordered on a continuum of politeness, or the extent to which face-work is encoded in the remark. I first describe the superstrategies and major differences between them. This is followed by an extended discussion of the specific mechanisms by which they are performed. The superstrategies and their specific manifestations are presented in Table 2.2.

The least polite strategy (actually the complete absence of politeness) is to perform an act bald-on-record. This represents adherence to Grice's maxims and hence is maximally efficient communication. For example, to perform a request bald-on-record a speaker would use the imperative (e.g., "Close the door"); to perform a disagreement would involve a bald assertion (e.g., "You're completely wrong about this"). The other end of the continuum—the most polite strategy—is simply to forgo performing the act at all.

Falling between maximum politeness (not performing the act) and minimum politeness (bald-on-record) are three superstrategies that are ranked in descending order of politeness: off-record politeness, negative politeness, and positive politeness. The defining feature of off-record politeness is ambiguity; there is more than one defensible interpretation of the utterance in context. In contrast to other

TABLE 2.2
Summary of Brown and Levinson's Politeness Strategies

Superstrategy	Substrategies
Bald-on-record	
Positive politeness	Claim common ground
	Convey cooperation
	Fulfill hearer's wants
Negative politeness	Conventional indirectness
	Avoid assumptions
	Avoid coercion
	Communicate desire to avoid impingement
	Incur a debt
Off-record politeness	Violate conversational maxims:
	Quality
	Quantity
	Manner
	Relation

Adopted from Brown and Levinson (1987).

politeness strategies, the recipient of an off-record remark must infer the speaker's intended meaning (the meaning is off-record). Politeness is thus accomplished by dissociating the speaker from the face threat inherent in the act; the speaker can always deny a face-threatening reading of the utterance.

Negatively polite and positively polite strategies are on-record, meaning that the speaker's intent is relatively clear and does not need to be inferred. As its name implies, negative politeness orients to the negative face of the interactants, or desire for autonomy. It is an avoidance-based politeness and is derived from Durkheim's (1915) negative rites and Goffman's (1967) avoidance rituals. Although the act performed with negative politeness is relatively clear, the manner in which it is performed symbolically lessens threats to one's autonomy. For example, the request intent of "Could you shut the door?" is usually clear, but by symbolically giving the recipient an option, it indicates some respect for the hearer's freedom to be unimpeded. Positive politeness, on the other hand, addresses the positive face wants of the interactants, or desire for connection. It generally functions by implicating, in some way, solidarity or closeness with the hearer. This can be accomplished in various ways and includes, for example, the use of joking and familiar address terms (e.g., in-group identity markers). Positive politeness is thus an approach-based politeness and is derived from Durkheim's (1915) positive rites and Goffman's (1967) presentation rituals.

In Brown and Levinson's view, positive politeness is assumed to be less polite than negative politeness. This is because negative politeness avoids the positively polite presumption of closeness, an assumption that may or may not be valid from the hearer's point of view. Importantly, this ordering is consistent with Durkheim's (1915) and Goffman's (1967) ordering of negative rites/avoidance rituals as being more deferential (and hence more polite) than positive rites/presentational rituals.

Note that both positively polite and negatively polite forms are on-record, meaning that the act performed is relatively clear. Still, these strategies represent deviations from maximum communication efficiency. Although the directive force of "Could you shut the door?" is clear, performing the act in this manner, rather than with the imperative, signals a polite attitude. The intent of positively polite strategies is even more clear; many times positively polite requests will include the imperative (and hence be very direct), but the imperative will be embedded within verbal markers of closeness, an embedding that is not necessary and hence violates the quantity maxim (do not say more than is necessary).

Off-Record Politeness

Off-record politeness is the prototype of indirect communication; theoretically, the face-threatening act that is performed must be inferred. Brown and Levinson adopted the Gricean framework for categorizing off-record strategies; hence, strategies can be grouped according to the specific maxim that is violated. Thus, violations of the quality maxim (say what is true) result in sarcastic irony (e.g., "That's brilliant," when it is not), metaphor (e.g., "My job is a jail"), rhetorical questions (e.g., "Did someone leave the light on?"), and so on. Violations of the manner maxim (be clear) result in the use of euphemisms and vagueness regarding the face-threatening act (e.g., "I wonder who forgot to do the dishes?"). Violating the quantity maxim (be as informative as required) can result in understatement (e.g., "It's OK" as a less-than-positive response to another's new haircut) and overstatement ("The line in the grocery store was a mile long" as an excuse). (See Kruez, Kassler, & Coppenrath [1998] for detail on exaggeration.) Quantity maxim violations can also yield interesting cases whereby the denial of a proposition generally believed to be false (e.g., Ronald Reagan is an alcoholic) results in an increase in the extent to which the denied proposition is believed to be true (Gruenfeld & Wyer, 1992; see chap. 3).

Violating the maxim of relation (be relevant) can occur in a variety of ways. In many contexts simply raising an issue will constitute a relevance violation and serve to trigger a directive interpretation (e.g., "I'm thirsty" as a request for something to drink). The relation maxim can also be violated when responding to questions that are potentially face threatening, and in this way face-threatening information can be conveyed in a polite way (this process is discussed in detail in the comprehension section that follows). For example, in response to the question "What do you think of my new coat?" the speaker can convey, in a polite way, a negative opinion by violating the relation maxim (e.g., "Oh, where did you get it?").

In general, Brown and Levinson's treatment of off-record politeness is sketchy at best, and they offer few new principles beyond the standard Gricean maxims. But their intent was not so much to explain how people comprehend off-record remarks as to show how off-record remarks can convey politeness. It is also not clear whether these strategies are truly off-record. For example, their treatment of irony and metaphor is not consistent with psycholinguistic research demonstrating that an inference process is often not required for comprehension (see chap. 1, pp. 61–74). Still, the general idea that indirect communication can function as a means of conveying a polite attitude is no doubt correct, and off-record politeness is a rich area for future research.

Negative Politeness

Negative politeness is on-record—recognition of the act performed is presumed to occur without an inference process—and oriented to the recipient's negative face (desire for autonomy). The most frequent strategy is to be conventionally indirect. Conventional indirect forms can be performed by questioning or asserting the felicity conditions underlying the act (see chap. 1). Thus, to request another to shut a door one can say "Will you shut the door?" "Can you shut the door?" "Are you able to shut the door?" "Did you shut the door?" "I want you to shut the door," and so on. It appears that all languages allow for the performance of conventional indirect requests. Brown and Levinson report similarities in this regard across the three languages they examined, and other researchers report parallels (though not identical parallels) across several different languages (Fraser & Nolan, 1981; Hill, Sachiko, Shoko, Kawasaki, & Ogino, 1986; Holtgraves & Yang, 1990; but see Matsumoto, 1988). This illustrates the possibly universal impact of face management on language, evidence that is consistent with Brown and Levinson's claim that face management is a universal motivating force for politeness.

A second strategy is to avoid presuming or assuming anything regarding the hearer's beliefs or desires (e.g., her ability to perform a particular action or his beliefs regarding a particular proposition). The primary means for accomplishing this is through the use of hedges. A common means in English (and probably other languages as well) is the use of "if" clauses suspending the relevant felicity conditions. This yields requests such as "Close the window, if you can," and "Turn up the heat, if you want," and so on. It is also possible to hedge Grice's maxims. This often overlaps with the conventional indirect forms described, but additional forms can be generated. For example, hedges on the quality maxim (and hence the sincerity felicity condition) yield assertions such as "I think abortion is wrong" (vs. the direct "Abortion is wrong"); hedges on the relevance maxim can be used to soften the imposition of topic changes, as with "I'm sorry to bring this up, but . . ." and "By the way, . . ."; and quantity hedges can be used to lessen the imposition of a request (e.g., "Could you make this copy more or less final?").

A third strategy involves attempts to lessen coercion. This includes not only conventional indirectness, as described, but also the conveying of pessimism regarding the appropriateness of the act to be performed. Output strategies include (in English at least) use of the subjunctive ("Would you open the window?" rather than "Will you open the window?"), tag questions (e.g., "You don't have any spare paper, do you?"), and remote possibility markers ("I don't suppose there is any chance you are going to the store today"). Additional strategies directed toward the lessening of coercion include attempts to minimize the imposition (e.g., "I just stopped by to get that manuscript"; i.e., my imposition is limited to just this one act, and "Could I borrow a cigarette?" vs. "Could I have a cigarette?"). Speakers can also lessen coercion by humbling themselves (e.g., downgrading a compliment with "I was sure I flunked that test") and giving deference (e.g., using formal address terms).

A fourth strategy is to communicate explicitly that one does not want to impinge on the other. This can be accomplished by providing an account or apology and thereby indicating reluctance (e.g., "I don't want to bother you, but could you give me a hand?"), admitting the impingement ("I know you're busy but could you take a look at this?"), or asking for forgiveness ("I hope you'll forgive me"). Another relatively common strategy (of a very different kind) is to linguistically dissociate the interactants from the to-be-performed act. Examples include avoiding the use of "I" ("It's true" rather than "I tell you it's true") and "you" pronouns ("Close the door" rather than "You close the door"), and by using passive rather than active constructions ("It is expected that students take this course," rather than "I expect you to take this course").

A final strategy is to simply go on record as incurring a debt (e.g., "I'd be eternally grateful for your help") or, conversely, by disclaiming any indebtedness on the part of the hearer (e.g., "I could easily do it for you" as an offer).

In general, the linguistic strategies for addressing negative face wants have face validity—they all seem to address negative face in some way, primarily by lessening the imposition and/or providing options (Lakoff, 1973). The strategies, however, are not organized in any principled way (e.g., the strategies exist at many different levels, from lexical items to phrases to hedges on maxims), and it is largely a descriptive scheme. But it is a very important descriptive scheme, illustrating as it does the rich repertoire of linguistic means that exist (in many different languages) for addressing negative face wants.

Positive Politeness

Positive politeness, like negative politeness, is on-record; unlike negative politeness, it is an approach-based strategy. The essence of positive politeness is the staking of a claim for some degree of familiarity with one's interlocutor. It is thus the language of intimacy, though in certain respects an exaggerated version of intimate talk, with the exaggeration serving to mark the positive politeness that is being conveyed. Positive politeness is also free ranging and need not (necessarily) address the threat associated with the specific act being performed; it can be used with acts threatening either positive or negative face.

Brown and Levinson outline three broad strategies for conveying positive politeness, with numerous output strategies for the first two. The first strategy is to claim common ground with the other person. This is accomplished by conveying the idea that the speaker and hearer are connected by virtue of having something in common (e.g., group membership, similarity of interests, values, attitudes). Group membership may be emphasized by using various in-group markers such as familiar address terms (honey, luv, mate, pal, bud) and/or slang ("Lend me a couple of bucks, OK?"). One may demonstrate similarity of interests by commenting on the other's appearance, belongings, and so on ("Oh, I see you got a new haircut"). Note the emphasis here on approach rather than on avoidance. Rather than ignoring another person's, say, runny nose (a negative politeness strategy), one would notice and attend to this state of affairs (e.g., by presenting the runny nose with a tissue).

An extremely important feature of common ground is a shared perspective. Thus, people often strive to find agreement with one another at some level. They may, for example, seek out safe or noncontroversial topics (the weather, sports) to discuss. They may engage in small talk and gossip. Even when disagreeing they may seek points of agreement by displaying token agreement (e.g., "Yes, but . . ."), if only for a second, and by hedging their opinions (e.g., "I kinda think that abortion is wrong" vs. "Abortion is wrong") (Holtgraves, 1997b).

A second major positive politeness strategy is to claim association by virtue of the fact that speaker and hearer are, in some sense, cooperators. Thus, speakers may indicate awareness and concern for the hearer's positive face wants (e.g., "I hope you don't think me rude, but your tie is hideous") and/or convey a promise that addresses the hearer's positive face ("I'll stop by next week"). Cooperation can also be conveyed with optimism, a strategy that again nicely reflects the difference between negative and positive politeness. Rather than indicating pessimism about the hearer's relationship with the specific act (a negative politeness strategy), a speaker can instead convey optimism ("I'm sure you won't mind if I help myself to a beer"). Also, one can convey cooperation with the use of inclusive terms (e.g., "Let's have a beer" vs. "Give me a beer"), by asking for reasons (often a type of optimism) (e.g., "Why don't we go get a beer?") and by explicitly noting reciprocity (e.g., "I lent you my notes last week so I'd like to see yours for this week").

A third and final positive politeness strategy is simply to fulfill the other person's wants in some way, directly and substantially, rather then symbolically (as is accomplished with the preceding strategies). Gift giving is the prototype here, but direct satisfaction of the other's desire for respect, sympathy, and so on are also examples of this strategy.

Like their descriptions of the other two superstrategies, Brown and Levinson's treatment of positive politeness is rich and impressionistic. And again, the strategies do appear to have face validity, although they are quite diverse and not organized in any principled way. Additional strengths and weaknesses of this typology will be considered next.

Interpersonal Determinants of Politeness

Given the tremendous variability in politeness strategies that exist for performing any particular act, what determines the particular strategy that a person will use? The choice depends on the relative weighting of two competing motives: the motive to communicate efficiently (in accord with Grice's maxims) and the motive to manage face. In general, the greater the perceived face threat of the to-be-performed act (or the weightiness of the threat in Brown and Levinson's terms), the greater the likelihood that a speaker will opt for a more polite strategy. This must be balanced, however, against pressures for efficient communication. In an emergency situation, the motive for clarity should outweigh concerns with face management (Goguen & Linde, 1983). It makes little sense to be polite when attempting to warn others of a fire.

What, then, determines the weightiness of the threat? It is the speaker's perception of act weightiness, a dimension based on the speaker's assessment of three variables: the culturally influenced degree of imposition of the particular act (Rx), the social distance between the speaker and the hearer [D(S,H)], and the relative power of the hearer over the speaker [P(H,S)]. These variables are assumed to be assessed simultaneously in determining act weightiness, and this can be depicted with the following formula:

$$Wx = D(S,H) + P(H,S) + Rx$$

Thus, increasing weightiness of an act is associated with increasing distance between the speaker and hearer, increasing power of the hearer relative to the speaker and increasing imposition of the to-be-performed act. The model makes intuitive sense. It predicts (and reflection generally confirms) that we are more likely to be polite (due to increased weightiness) to a higher-power person than to one who is lower in power than us. We are also more likely to be polite when asking for a large favor (e.g.,"Do you think I could possibly borrow your car?") than when asking for a small one ("Got a quarter?"), due to the greater imposition of the former relative to the latter.

Several features of this formulation deserve discussion. First, the weightiness of any act is based on the speaker's *perceptions* of these variables. Although there may be a general consensus (within a culture) regarding the assessment of these variables (e.g., most would agree that a general has greater power in an army than a private), in the end such assessments are in the eye of the beholder. This can result in individual and cultural variability in the assessment of face threat and, hence, differing levels of politeness in the same situation (a point to be elaborated on below). Cultures and subcultures, for example, may vary in terms of how much distance is typically assumed between unacquainted individuals, resulting in cultural differences in overall politeness (Scollon & Scollon, 1981).

Second, the variables of power and distance were not randomly chosen; they are the fundamental dimensions of social interaction and show up (sometimes under different names) in many empirical and theoretical examinations of dimensions underlying social interaction (e.g., Wish, Deutsch, & Kaplan, 1976). Note also that power and distance are related to negative and positive politeness respectively. Finally, a common reaction to this model is that there must be other variables impacting politeness. And there are. But power, distance, and imposition are high-level, abstract variables that subsume other potentially relevant variables. For example, power can be based on ethnic identity, situation-based authority, expertise, or gender. Hence, these variables are constantly shifting, and this illustrates their contextual sensitivity. In other words, it is only in a particular context that these variables have meaning. When the general goes home at night his power might be considerably diminished in his interaction with his spouse—thus, he may no longer issue orders. Similarly, the degree of imposition of an act can vary over settings and most importantly among cultures. What may be regarded as relatively imposing in one culture (e.g., an offer in Japan) tends to be perceived as relatively less imposing in another culture (e.g., the United States).

EVALUATION OF POLITENESS THEORY

To what extent does Brown and Levinson's model explain the manner in which people phrase their remarks in various settings? Is face management a fundamental and universal motivation for politeness? Do utterances vary in terms of politeness in the way predicted by the model? Brown and Levinson provided support for their model by documenting the existence of their politeness strategies in three very different languages. The parallels are indeed impressive, and the reader is referred to their work to get some sense of the evidence they provide. But they did not provide evidence for the ordering of politeness strategies, the impact of the social variables on politeness (other than their intuitions), or their conceptualization of face. Since their theory was first published, a large amount of research—experimental, ethnographic, and theoretical—has been conducted, and it is to that research that we now turn. This research has supported certain aspects of their model, but also demonstrated weaknesses and suggested ways in which the model needs to be revised.

Ordering of Politeness Strategies

One of the major claims made by Brown and Levinson is that their linguistic superstrategies fall on a universal continuum of politeness; bald-on-record is the least polite, followed in ascending order by positive politeness, negative politeness, and off-record politeness. For requests, there is partial support for this ordering (Bauman, 1988; Blum-Kulka, 1987; Holtgraves & Yang, 1990), with similar ratings reported for U.S. Americans and South Koreans (Holtgraves & Yang, 1990). It is also possible to make predictions regarding the perceived politeness of conventional indirect requests (a subcategory of negative politeness) based on the degree of hearer threat (or cost) implied by the form. For example, "May I ask you where Jordan Hall is?" is less costly (the speaker is asking permission to make the request) and hence more polite than "Would you tell me where Jordan Hall is?" Extremely subtle predictions are possible here. For example, "Could you open the door?" is less costly and hence more polite than "Would you open the door?" The latter implies the hearer has the ability, the former does not. Peoples' politeness ratings agree quite closely with this logic. Clark and Schunk (1980) found strong support for this ordering (though see Kemper & Thissen, 1981), as did Holtgraves and Yang (1990), with both U.S. American and South Korean participants. Conceptually similar results have been reported by

Hill, et al. (1986) with Japanese and U.S. American participants and by Fraser and Nolan (1981) with U.S. American and Spanish participants. These relatively close parallels across languages provide partial support for Brown and Levinson's contention that the linguistic manifestation of conventional indirect speech acts is universal.

Unfortunately, there has been much less research on the perceived politeness of superstrategies for speech acts other than requests. But extant research suggests that bald-on-record forms are perceived as less polite than various indirect forms. For example, when conveying a negative opinion, a bald-on-record form is perceived as less polite than an indirect form (Holtgraves, 1986) and is less likely to be used (Bavelas, Black, Chovil, & Mullet, 1990). Thus, in response to the question "Do you like my new coat?" it is perceived as less polite to say "I don't like it" than to convey indirectly that one doesn't like it (e.g., "Oh, where did you get it?"). For expressing an opinion that is at odds with one's interlocutor, it is more polite if done indirectly (e.g., "I kinda think abortion is wrong") than directly (e.g., "Abortion is wrong"; Holtgraves, 1997b).

Despite the supportive evidence, there are a number of problems with Brown and Levinson's typology. Criticisms of their typology have focused on two general issues. First, is the typology a reliable and valid scheme for classifying the politeness of utterances? There are several related points here. One frequent criticism of the classification scheme is that many times an utterance will contain multiple politeness strategies (Baxter, 1984; Craig, Tracy, & Spivak, 1986; Tracy, 1990). Thus, positive politeness (e.g., in-group identity markers) may occur in conjunction with a conventional negatively polite form, thereby making unambiguous classification of the utterance problematic. No doubt politeness strategies are mixed within a turn. Note, however, that a single utterance can perform multiple speech acts and hence create multiple face threats. For example, requests that simultaneously function as a criticism may motivate the speaker to use both negative and positive politeness in her remark (e.g., "Honey, why haven't you done the dishes yet?").

Sometimes the occurrence of multiple politeness strategies may be more apparent than real because markers of politeness can occur for reasons other than politeness. For example, variability in address forms (which may be related to politeness) can be a result of differing social relationships or be part of an attempt to (re)negotiate a relationship. Compounding the problem is the fact that certain markers of politeness, such as hedges, can function as either positively or negatively polite, depending on the context. The assignment of utterances to politeness categories is not a clear-cut task. It represents the analyst's judgment of the utterance as a whole (not a simple counting of politeness markers) in a particular context. But note this too presents a difficulty because politeness can be conveyed over a series of turns, thereby making analysis at the speech act level problematic (as Brown and Levinson note). For example, a speaker might use an impolite form when making a request and hence appear to threaten the recipient's negative face. But this impolite request may have occurred after a prerequest (e.g., "Are you busy?"), a move that performs the face-work (Levinson, 1983). This issue will be discussed in more detail in chapter 4.

The second major issue concerns Brown and Levinson's ordering of the politeness strategies. Although this ordering has received partial empirical support, at least for requests, there has been one major exception to the predicted ordering: Negatively polite forms are usually ranked higher in politeness than off-record forms. It has been suggested that off-record forms carry a cost in terms of efficiency (Blum-Kulka, 1987; Leech, 1983); their use threatens the recipient's negative face because she must expend some effort in order to infer the speaker's intended meaning (it is thus an imposition). There is a potential, additional cost with off-record forms; their use gives the impression of manipulativeness on the part of the speaker (Lakoff, 1973).

This research, then, raises the issue about whether politeness should be equated with indirectness, as many authors have argued (Brown & Levinson, 1987; Leech, 1983; Lakoff, 1973). This is an important issue because it deals with the essence of what politeness is. For requests and other directives, indirectness provides the recipient with options, thereby lessening the imposition and increasing politeness (Lakoff, 1973). But research demonstrating that off-record forms are not the most polite forms clearly contradicts this logic. Moreover, Dillard, Wilson, Tusing, and Kinney (1997) found that the perceived politeness of messages was positively correlated with message explicitness (or directness), the exact opposite of the presumed politeness-indirectness link.[3]

Clearly, indirectness can occur for reasons other than politeness, and politeness may be conveyed by means other than indirectness. So, politeness and indirectness are not identical. However, several things need to kept in mind here. First, very indirect utterances (i.e., off-record forms) may not function as truly ambiguous messages in an experimental context. For example, providing participants with a set of requests to be rated informs them that all of the utterances are requests, and this eliminates the ambiguity of off-record forms, their defining feature. Also, it is very difficult to scale indirectness (other than perceived indirectness); to do so requires an empirical examination of the cognitive processes involved in comprehension, an endeavor that has yet to be undertaken. So, attempts to determine the exact relationship between politeness and indirectness will have to await further research. In the meantime, a weaker ordering might be proposed, whereby indirect remarks are generally perceived as more polite than their direct counterparts, but variations in indirectness may or not correspond to changes in perceived politeness.

---

[3]Note, however, that the message occurred between people in a close relationship, and according to Brown and Levinson's politeness theory, it is in close relationships that more-direct/less-polite speech is expected.

A related criticism concerns the proposed ordering of negative and positive politeness. Some researchers have questioned whether negative politeness is always more polite than positive politeness. More specifically, it has been argued that these forms are qualitatively different and hence cannot be ordered on a uni-dimensional continuum (Baxter, 1984; Lim & Bowers, 1991; Scollon & Scollon, 1981; Tracy, 1990). There is some merit to this argument; it seems unlikely that the proposed ordering will be valid across all types of face-threatening acts. For directives (threats to the hearer's negative face), the proposed ordering makes sense both theoretically (negative politeness grants the hearer greater autonomy than positive politeness) and empirically (Holtgraves & Yang, 1990). On the other hand, for acts that primarily threaten the hearer's positive face, positive politeness may be more polite than negative politeness (Lim & Bowers, 1991). Consider, for example, the various ways in which disagreements and criticisms can be per-formed. One can convey a (more polite) criticism with positive politeness (e.g., "We've been friends a long time but I need to tell you that you didn't do a great job here") or off-record politeness ("The middle section of the proposal is not as good as the beginning"). But how would one perform a criticism with negative politeness? The primary threat with a criticism is to the recipient's positive face, and so it makes sense that the polite performance of this act will entail the use of positive politeness. But negative face is not threatened here (unless the criticism implies some needed action on the part of the recipient), and so it seems largely irrelevant. In research on disagreements, instances of negative politeness were virtually nonexistent (Holtgraves, 1997b).

One possibility in this regard is that politeness strategies can be ordered on the basis of a specificity principle; a strategy that orients to the specific type of face threatened will be regarded as the most polite strategy. Thus, negatively polite strategies would be more polite for acts threatening the hearer's negative face, and positively polite strategies would be more polite for acts threatening the hearer's positive face.

Finally, research on politeness strategies has focused almost exclusively on lin-guistic politeness, even though Goffman (1967) emphasized the nonverbal facets of politeness and Brown and Levinson (1987) noted it as a possibility (though they did not develop it in any way). Recently, however, there have been some attempts to examine this aspect of politeness. For example, Ambady, Koo, Lee, and Rosen-thal (1996) examined the verbal and nonverbal politeness of South Korean and U.S. American participants as they conveyed good or bad news to people varying in power. Politeness was conveyed both verbally and nonverbally, and the social context affected the two components in a similar manner. Also, Trees and Manusov (1998) examined the perceived politeness of messages varying in both verbal and nonverbal politeness. These authors identified (and manipulated) spe-cific nonverbal behaviors assumed to be related to increasing politeness (e.g., raised eyebrows, touch, less distance) and decreasing politeness (e.g., greater dis-tance, lowered eyebrows, lack of touch, loud voice). Perceived politeness was affected by both verbal and nonverbal politeness. Importantly, the two components interacted; when impolite nonverbal behaviors occurred, linguistic politeness had relatively little effect on overall perceived politeness.

Clearly, nonverbal behaviors are an important though underresearched aspect of politeness. How something is said can be just as important as what was said in terms of the overall politeness of a message. Moreover, it seems likely that verbal and nonverbal behaviors will interact in complex ways, in terms of both determining the overall politeness of a message, as demonstrated by Trees & Manusov (1998), but also in terms of determining the speaker's intent with a message (e.g., nonverbal accompaniments may disambiguate the meaning of off-record forms).

Obviously, the Brown and Levinson typology is problematic in many respects. It is overly broad and simplistic and in some instances difficult to use unambiguously with actual talk. The notion of degrees of politeness (and hence a politeness continuum) is intuitively reasonable but unlikely to be constant over speech acts. What their typology has accomplished, though, is to illuminate the rich variety of linguistic (and more recently nonlinguistic) means by which interactants manage face. The typology is an attempt to specify exactly how face motives show up in the patterning of talk. In this sense, it has been a useful scheme, albeit one that needs to be modified in various ways.

Effects of Interpersonal Variables

A considerable amount of research has examined the impact of power, distance, and imposition on politeness; this has clearly been the most popular arena for empirical tests of Brown and Levinson's model. The general strategy in this research has been to manipulate one or more of these variables and to examine their impact on politeness. The most popular method has been to ask respondents what they would say in various situations or to rate the likelihood of using different utterances in different settings. But researchers have also examined what people actually say, both in the field and in the laboratory.

In general, relatively consistent effects have been found for the power variable, with increasing levels of politeness associated with increasing levels of hearer power. This has been found with experimental studies of requests (Holtgraves & Yang, 1990, 1992; Leitchy & Applegate, 1991; Lim & Bowers, 1991) as well as with observational studies of actual requests (Blum-Kulka, Danet, & Gherson, 1985). The impact of power on address forms has long been known (Brown & Ford, 1961; Brown & Gilman, 1989), and these findings can be interpreted within a politeness framework (Wood & Kroger, 1991). The link between power and address forms may well be universal.

In addition, power has been found to have the predicted effects on the politeness of messages conveying bad news (Ambady et al., 1996), reminders and complaints (Leitchy & Applegate, 1991), accounts and apologies (Gonzales, Pederson, Manning, & Wetter, 1990), questions (Holtgraves, 1986), criticisms (Lim

& Bowers, 1991), teasing (Keltner, Young, Heerey, Oemig, & Monarch, 1998), and no doubt other speech acts as well. In an intriguing examination of politeness in Shakespeare's tragedies, Brown and Gilman (1989) reported that the predicted effects of power on politeness occurred for a range of speech acts, including requests, address forms, complaints, and others.

Fairly consistent support has been found for the imposition variable, with greater politeness occurring for acts representing a greater imposition. This effect has been found for requests (Brown & Gilman, 1989; Holtgraves & Yang, 1992; Leitchy & Applegate, 1991), expressions of gratitude (Okamoto & Robinson, 1997), accounts and apologies (Gonzales et al., 1990; McLaughlin, Cody, & O'Hair, 1983; Schlenker & Darby, 1981), recommendations (vs. reports) (Lambert, 1996), as well as other speech acts (Brown & Gilman, 1989; Leitchy & Applegate, 1991). There have been some null findings reported (e.g., Baxter, 1984), though they are clearly in the minority.

Finally, the results for relationship distance have been the most problematic and unclear. Some researchers (Holtgraves & Yang, 1992; Wood & Kroger, 1991) have reported greater politeness in more distant relationships, as the theory predicts; others have found the reverse (Baxter, 1984; Brown & Gilman, 1989), and some have reported no relationship between distance and politeness (Lambert, 1996). The underlying logic for this variable is that in unfamiliar relationships (high distance) the potential for aggression is unknown, and so interactants must use politeness to signal the lack of an aggressive intent. This concern is assumed to be less important between people in a close relationship. Now, part of the problem here might be in terms of how the distance variable is conceptualized. If it is viewed exclusively as degree of familiarity between interactants, then there is some support for the theory. But if distance is viewed as encompassing both familiarity and liking (affect), then the theory appears to be in error. When the effects of familiarity and liking are separated, increased liking is usually associated with increased politeness (Brown & Gilman, 1989; Slugoski & Turnbull, 1988), and this is the opposite of the theory's prediction.

Brown and Levinson assumed the perceived weightiness of an act to be a simple sum of perceived power, distance, and imposition; they proposed an additive model. Empirical research, however, demonstrates that this assumption is clearly unwarranted. Numerous researchers have examined the simultaneous impact of two or more of these variables on politeness and have reported the existence of interactions between them; the effects clearly are not additive. For example, researchers have reported Power by Distance interactions (Blum-Kulka et al., 1985; Holtgraves & Yang, 1990; Lim & Bowers, 1991; Wood & Kroger, 1991), Imposition by Power interactions (Holtgraves & Yang, 1992; Gonzales et al., 1990), and Imposition by Distance interactions (Holtgraves & Yang, 1992; Leitchy & Applegate, 1991). The general meaning of these interactions is simply that as estimates of any one of the three variables become quite large, the effects of the other two variables become much smaller. For example, a person making a very large request (high imposition) will probably be quite polite regardless of the recipient's relative status. Also, Wood and Kroger (1991) have argued that the three variables are not equally weighted and that power should be weighted more heavily than the other two variables.

The linking of power, distance, and imposition with politeness is one of the great strengths of Brown and Levinson's model. It demonstrates (and research has partially supported) how broad social variables work down into the minute patterning of linguistic and nonverbal behavior. The model is obviously too simple; the variables interact in various ways and are probably not weighted equally. But empirical research is contributing to the refinement of these links. Some researchers have argued that other dimensions might need to be considered (Slugoski & Turnbull, 1988), including more situation-specific rights and obligations (Fraser, 1990; Tracy, 1990). Note, however, that power, distance, and imposition are abstract, high-level variables that should subsume many other more specific variables that have an effect on politeness. And this makes sense. But it is doubtful that this framework encompasses everything regarding variability in politeness. Consider, for example, research demonstrating that people, when formulating requests, specify the most salient obstacle (e.g., unwillingness, lack of memory, inability, ignorance) that the recipient must overcome in order to comply with the request (Francik & Clark, 1985; Gibbs, 1986). This is not completely inconsistent with politeness theory, of course. Specifying obstacles is one way of performing a request indirectly, and in so doing one is conveying a polite attitude (it is more polite than if one used the imperative). But the different obstacles that might be referenced indicates an orientation to an essentially nonsocial feature of the setting (except insofar as it reflects speaker-hearer coordination).

Or consider the role of emotion in politeness. Forgas (1999a, 1999b) has recently demonstrated how a speaker's emotional state can influence the level of politeness. In several experiments he found that people in a sad mood tended to prefer greater levels of politeness than people in a happy mood. In this case, politeness is being influenced by intrapersonal rather than interpersonal processes. But why does mood affect politeness in the first place? One possibility is that a person's mood influences their perceptions of the interpersonal context (power, distance, and imposition). So, people in a sad mood may perceive themselves as being relatively low in power or perceive an act as being relatively more imposing, and it is these perceptions that affect their level of politeness. Whether mood and other intrapersonal variables can be handled within the Brown and Levinson (1987) framework remains to be seen.

The role of emotion in politeness production illustrates a potential blending of the intra- and interpersonal; emotional states influence social perception, which then influences politeness levels. Note that this illustrates the potential for consistent individual differences in politeness, a phenomenon that has been somewhat overlooked (Holtgraves, 1997c). People may differ from one another in their levels of politeness, in part, because they differ in their perceptions of interpersonal situations. Introverts, for example, may perceive relatively greater distance between themselves and others and, hence, produce higher levels of politeness. Extraverts, on the other hand, may perceive relatively less distance and, hence, favor the use of relatively less-polite but more approach-based strategies (i.e., positive politeness).

Status of the Face Concept

Is face management *the* fundamental and universal motivation behind politeness? Don't people sometimes attack each other's face via insults and challenges? Isn't there individual and cultural variability in politeness? In other words, are people in all cultures always concerned with the collective management of face? Well, no, they are not. And these facts have raised a number of issues regarding the conceptualization of face and face management as they relate to politeness.

First, people sometimes engage in aggressive face-work and perform speech acts that directly threaten (rather than support) another's face (Craig et al., 1986; Penman, 1990; Tracy, 1990; Tracy & Tracy, 1998). Obviously such occurrences need to be explained within a theory of politeness, and the Brown and Levinson model clearly gives short shrift to such occurrences. The lack of politeness (bald-on-record) is not the same as aggressively threatening another's face. One possibility would be to expand the model to include an aggressive face-work strategy, a strategy that would be less polite than bald-on-record (Craig et al., 1986). In this regard, some language researchers have proposed that certain speech acts can be ordered on a mitigation-aggravation continuum (Goguen & Linde, 1983; Labov & Fanschel, 1977; McLaughlin et al., 1983). It is important to note, however, that aggressive face-work (insults and challenges) has its impact, in large part, because it is assumed that people will be face supportive. It is thus the presumption of politeness that is assumed, not its actual occurrence. So although people may engage in aggressive face-work, they succeed in doing so because of the underlying presumption of cooperative face-work.

A related criticism is that there has been an overemphasis on the management of the hearer's face at the expense of face-work directed toward managing one's own face (Craig et al., 1986; Penman, 1990; Ting-Toomey, 1988). Although the self- vs. other-face distinction is included in the Brown and Levinson model, the politeness strategies they consider are clearly oriented toward the hearer. This is because face management is assumed to be cooperative; threats to the other's face are threats to one's own face. So, by supporting the other's face, one is supporting one's own face. But clearly there are times when there is a trade-off between protecting one's own face and managing the face of the hearer. Consider the giving of an account for violating a norm, an act that is interesting because of the simultaneous threat to both the speaker and the hearer. The occurrence of a violation threatens the offended person's positive face (e.g., an insult) and/or negative face (e.g., spilling a drink on the host's carpet), as well as the offender's positive face (a desire to look good) and/or negative face (remedial work must now be done). A concession (admitting fault) with an apology supports the hearer's positive face (and possibly negative face if restitution is included), but will simultaneously threaten the speaker's positive and negative face. Conversely, refusing to provide an account will prevent the speaker's positive and negative face from being threatened, but will increase the positive and negative threat to the offended person (Gonzales, Manning, & Haugen, 1992; Holtgraves, 1989). Although not necessarily a zero-sum situation, for certain speech acts, there does appear to be an inherent tension between giving and receiving face; the more attentive a speaker is to the hearer's face, the more the speaker's face is humbled. Thus, estimates of act weightiness may need to incorporate the perceived cost to the speaker for using a particular politeness form.

Finally, one of the most important issues surrounding politeness is its status as a cultural universal. Although few would argue with the claim that politeness exists in all cultures, the claim that positive and negative face are universal desires motivating the form that politeness takes has been questioned by many researchers. These arguments take several forms. Some have argued that the Brown and Levinson politeness continuum does not hold in all cultures. Katriel (1986), for example, argues that in Sabra culture in Israel there is a preference for a direct, straightforward style; greater directness (the lack of politeness) is seen as more attuned to the interactants' face than is politeness via indirectness.

A second general critique is that negative face is relevant only in Western cultures, or cultures where there is an emphasis on individual autonomy. For example, Rosaldo (1982), in her analysis of Llongot speech acts, argues that directives in that culture are not particularly face threatening, referencing as they do group membership and responsibility rather than individual wants and desires (see also Fitch & Sanders, 1994). Hence, directives in that culture will usually not be performed politely. Similarly, Matsumoto (1988) argues that in Japanese culture, interactants orient toward their relationships instead of emphasizing individual rights; hence, negative face wants are relatively unimportant. As a result, strategies normally viewed as addressing negative face may take very different forms in Japan. For example, deference can be indicated by increasing imposition on the hearer (by displaying dependency) rather than by attempting to lessen an imposition.

Clearly there is great cultural variability in terms of politeness. The crucial question is whether this variability is a result of differing cultural conceptions of face or whether these differences can be explained at a lower level of abstraction. Brown and Levinson (1987) assumed positive and negative face to be universal desires, but that cultures will vary in terms of what threatens face, who has power over whom, how much distance is typically assumed, and so on. In this view, politeness can serve as a framework for examining cultural differences. Thus, certain acts are more threatening in some cultures than in other cultures, and hence, greater politeness will be expected for those acts in the former than in the latter. For example, directives appear to be more threatening in Western cultures than in Ilongot culture and, hence, are more likely to be performed politely in the former than in the latter.

There have been several demonstrations of the utility of politeness theory for explaining cross-cultural differences in language use. Recall that the theory predicts greater politeness as a function of perceived distance, imposition, and power. Now, cultures and subcultures may systematically differ both in terms of the default values for these variables, as well as in terms of the weighting given to these variables. Regarding the former, Scollon and Scollon (1981) report that Athabaskans tend to assume greater distance when interacting with unacquainted individuals than do English-speaking Americans. As a result, the former display a preference for negative politeness strategies and the latter a preference for positive politeness strategies, preferences that can result in misunderstanding when members of these groups interact.

In terms of the weighting of the variables, Holtgraves and Yang (1992) and Ambady et al. (1996) have demonstrated that South Koreans weight the power and distance variables more heavily than do U.S. Americans. This means that South Koreans tend to vary the politeness of their remarks as a function of power and distance to a greater extent than do U.S. Americans. This is an important finding and one that dovetails nicely with the concept of individualism-collectivism. In collectivist cultures such as Korea, strong distinctions are drawn between in-groups and out-groups, and this results in greater overall variability in social interaction (Gudykunst, Yoon, & Nishida, 1987; Leung, 1988; Wheeler, Reis, & Bond, 1989). Hence, the findings for politeness are consistent with the overall pattern of greater behavioral responsiveness to social situations for collectivists relative to individualists. Another possibility in this regard has been suggested by Ting-Toomey (1988), who has argued that the politeness of people in collectivist cultures focuses more on other-face, while the politeness of people in individualistic cultures focuses more on self-face.

The concepts of face and face-work have great utility in terms of explaining the patterning of language behavior over contexts. Is face a universal concept? Possibly. Do people in all cultures have both positive and negative face wants? Possibly, but they will probably be weighted differently. Do acts threaten face in the same way in all cultures? Definitely not. The specific manifestations of face threat show great cultural and subcultural variability. Again, with politeness theory we are at a relatively high level of abstraction, a level that provides a framework for explaining cross-cultural similarities and differences in language use. And the importance of such a framework should not be underestimated. Examining cross-cultural variability in language use without such a framework would result in a purely descriptive enterprise, a listing of features that appear to be cross-culturally different, but which at a higher level may reflect similar underlying motivations. Now, one problem with the theory, as with any broad theoretical enterprise (e.g., Freudian psychoanalytic theory), is that it may border on the non-falsifiable. For example, failing to confirm politeness theory predictions in one culture can be explained away by arguing that face was manifested differently in that culture. Obviously, specification of the manifestations of face within a culture needs to be undertaken before the theory can be tested within that culture.

POLITENESS AND COMPREHENSION

As the preceding review suggests, politeness is a pervasive and universal feature of human language use, and research has demonstrated how it motivates the manner in which people phrase their utterances in different settings. But what about language comprehension? If politeness impacts language production, should it not also play a parallel role in language comprehension? This possibility has received only limited attention; politeness research has focused almost exclusively on language production. Still, there are some possibilities worth mentioning.

A fundamental mechanism for conveying a polite attitude is to speak in a less than optimally efficient manner, that is, to violate (in some sense) Grice's conversational maxims and speak indirectly. This, of course, raises again an issue discussed in chapter 1: How do hearers recognize the intended meaning of a speaker's utterance? As we saw in chapter 1, many indirect remarks do not require an inference process for comprehension (Gibbs, 1983). And in terms of the Brown and Levinson model, one can conclude that this would be the case for most, if not all, on-record politeness (i.e., positive and negative politeness). On the other hand, the defining feature of off-record politeness is that an inference process is required for comprehension. Now, whether or not that is actually the case awaits further empirical research; no doubt the intended meaning of some off-record forms will not (depending on the context) require any inferential processing. But some will, and that requires an explanation.

Brown and Levinson adopted wholesale the Gricean framework for the production and comprehension of politeness. Thus, interlocutors are rational agents with mutual awareness (not necessarily conscious awareness) of the impact of conversational maxims on the communication of meaning. Speakers can communicate indirect meanings, along with a polite attitude, by relying on the ability of hearers to detect a violation and infer the intended meaning.

Assuming the initial stage of an inference process does involve the hearer's recognition of a maxim violation, what guides the hearer toward the recognition of an alternative (and presumably intended) indirect meaning? Grice (1975), of course, was largely silent regarding this issue, suggesting simply that hearers will generate an inference that is consistent with the conversational exchange. But how is this to be determined? In theory, there are an unlimited number of inferences that a hearer could make.

There have been some more specific proposals in this regard. For example, Sperber and Wilson (1986) have argued that interpretation is guided by a relevance principle. Hearers are assumed to construct the most relevant interpretation of an utterance, where the most relevant interpretation is one requiring the least amount of effort (due largely to accessibility) and providing the greatest number of contextual implications. In a similar vein, Hobbs, Stickel, Appelt, and Martin (1993) have proposed a computational model based on a general principle that hearers construct an interpretation of textual ambiguity (indirectness) in the most efficient manner possible. Importantly, neither of these proposals include interpersonal considerations, even though interpersonal considerations are a major reason for indirectness.

It is here that politeness theory may be useful. First, when encountering a maxim violation of some sort, it is likely that a hearer will attempt to explain why the violation occurred. This is consistent with several lines of research. For example, people generally try to explain why unscripted or unexpected actions have occurred (Hastie, 1984). Moreover, the comprehension of a text often involves a search for meaning, and that search is guided by an attempt to understand why something is mentioned in a text (Graesser, Singer, & Trabasso, 1994). Readers also generate causal inferences as a means of achieving coherence in their representation of a text (Singer, Halldorson, Lear, & Andrusiak, 1992).

Second, given that indirectness is motivated in large part by politeness, it seems likely that hearers, on encountering a maxim violation, will consider the possibility that the speaker is engaging in face management. This recognition can then serve as the basis for generating an interpretation of what a speaker means with an utterance. Consider again the following exchange from Holtgraves (1998):

Bob: What did you think of my presentation?
Al: It's hard to give a good presentation.

Al's reply is a violation of the relation maxim; it fails (at the surface level) to provide the requested information. So Bob will need to generate an inference in order to make sense of the reply. Now, Bob could interpret Al's reply as meaning that he really liked the presentation (despite its difficulty), or that he is sympathizing with the difficulty of performing this activity, and so on. But in most instances Bob will not generate those interpretations. Instead, he will probably recognize that Al is engaging in face management. And because it is a negative opinion of Bob's presentation that would be face threatening in this situation, the most likely interpretation is that Al does not have a positive opinion of the presentation. If the opinion was positive there would be no need to violate the relation maxim; a positive opinion would not be face threatening.

There is some research that supports this reasoning. For example, respondents tend to interpret replies to personal questions that violate the relation maxim (as in the above example of Andy and Bob) as conveying negative information (e.g., a negative opinion or a negative disclosure). Moreover, when face management as a possible motive for violating the relation maxim is removed, then utterances violating the maxim become very difficult to comprehend. That is, people take longer to comprehend the reply "It's hard to give a good presentation" when it is made clear that the presentation was good (and hence politeness is not a motivation for the maxim violation) than when no information about the presentation is provided (Holtgraves, 1998).

It needs to be emphasized that relevance violations will not always be interpreted as conveying negative information. Rather, the claim is that they will be interpreted as conveying negative information if it is negative information that is face threatening. There are times, however, when positive information might be threatening. For example, imagine a conversation between two siblings, Mark and John, in which Mark always outperforms John in school, much to John's chagrin. Mark is aware of John's feelings and generally tries to manage his face. Now, when John asks Mark how he did on his chemistry test, and Mark fails to answer directly (e.g., "Let's go get a pizza"), John will probably interpret the reply as conveying positive information (i.e., he did well on his exam) rather than negative information. In this context it is positive information that may be face threatening, and so the reply will tend to be interpreted as conveying positive information.

The production and comprehension of politeness should go hand in hand. If politeness is conveyed by deviation from maximally efficient communication, then interactants must have some means for recovering a speaker's intention. If these deviations are motivated by politeness, then it seems reasonable that recognition of this motivation will play a role in the interpretation of an utterance. In a sense, this is a specific example of the more general process of coordination in language use, a topic to be covered in more detail in chapter 5.

CONCLUSION

In this chapter I have examined some of the interpersonal implications of speech act performance. Speech act theory (Searle, 1969) has focused almost exclusively on illocutionary force, or the action that a speaker can be said to have performed with an utterance. But speakers are often doing more, sometimes much more, than just performing speech acts. To say "Shut the door" to someone is to perform a directive; but by virtue of performing the directive in this way, with a bald-on-record form, the speaker is also communicating a lack of concern for the recipient's face and possibly implicating that he views himself as being higher in power than the hearer. To say "Could you shut the door?" to someone is to also perform a directive, but by virtue of performing the directive this way, with a negatively polite form, the speaker is also communicating a concern for the negative face of the recipient and by implication that he may not view himself as having power over the recipient.

So, understanding language use as social action requires a consideration of the speech act performed with an utterance, as well as the interpersonal implications of performing the speech act in this way in this particular context. Language use is sensitive business; one can't just blindly issue directives, make offers, engage in disagreements, and so on. One can, of course, but in so doing one is communicating a lack of concern for the other's face and thereby relinquishing all rights to civil treatment from the other person.

A speaker's level of politeness, then, reveals her view of the interpersonal context. In this way, politeness theory can provide a theoretical mechanism for examining some of the linguistic underpinnings of social life. Consider a few examples. Recently, there has been much interest in how cultures differ in the manner in which the self-concept is elaborated (e.g., Markus & Kitayama, 1991). Politeness theory provides a framework for examining how such differences might play out in social interactions, particularly cross-cultural interactions. By definition, people in collectivist cultures perceive closer relationships with in-group members and more distant relationships with out-group members, than do people in individualistic cultures. And this difference is manifested in their talk; in-group–out-group differences in politeness are greater for collectivists than for individualists (Holtgraves & Yang, 1992; Ambady et al., 1996). Or consider gender differences in language. To the extent that men are less polite than women (e.g., Tannen, 1990), such differences may be a result of systematic gender differences in the perception of one's relative power (or relationship distance), and it is these differences that explain differing levels of politeness.

Particularly important is the contribution that politeness theory can make to our understanding of the effectiveness of communication patterns in small group interaction. Goguen and Linde (1983), for example, examined the communications of aircraft personnel and found, consistent with politeness theory, that lower-status members tended to be relatively indirect (polite) in their communications to higher-status superiors. But the surprising finding (and a disconcerting one for frequent fliers) is that this occurred even in emergency situations, when communicative efficiency concerns should have trumped politeness concerns.

There are many other areas of social psychology that have received little attention from a linguistic perspective, and politeness theory can provide a wedge into the role that language plays in these processes. Consider impression management. Despite its popularity as a research area (e.g., Jones, 1964), we actually know very little about how people manage their impressions during the course of an actual interaction. Clearly, it is through the use of language that we attempt to convey our identities, and politeness is one aspect of language use that may play a crucial role in this process. One's level of politeness can be strategically varied in order to convey power or competence or closeness or distance and so on. This possibility is discussed in more detail in chapter 3. The list goes on. For example, how do people effectively request help? How do they most effectively influence others? Politeness theory provides a comprehensive, high-level framework for examining how linguistic variability plays a role in these and other social psychological processes.

Politeness is a phenomenon existing at the interface of linguistic, social, and cognitive processes; it is conveyed through language and is a result of a person's cognitive assessment of the social context. Politeness theory, on the other hand, is a tool or framework that can be used to examine the interaction of these different phenomena, and as such it provides a rich multilayered approach to language use. Still, politeness theory has a number of potential problems, many of which have been noted in this chapter. A major problem is that in many respects it is an overly simplistic view that overlooks important features involved in language use or forces them into an inappropriate framework. Now, one of the ways in which politeness theory is too simple is the almost exclusive reliance on speech acts as the unit of analysis. One problem with this is that politeness theory then adopts, by default, all of the weaknesses of speech act theory. And one of the major weaknesses of speech act theory and politeness theory is that illocutionary force and politeness may be conveyed over a series of moves, rather than within a single turn of talk. That is, rather than being performed on an utterance-by-utterance, turn-by-turn basis, speech acts may be performed, and face-work undertaken, over a stretch of talk. Moreover, neither speech act theory nor politeness theory has much to say about how conversations are structured or the manner in which turns of talk are related to each other. It is just those issues that I discuss at length in chapter 4.

3

The Interpersonal
Consequences of Talk:
Impression Management
and Person Perception

One of a person's most distinctive features is how she or he talks. Consider, for example, how often we recognize one another from small samples of talk at the beginning of a telephone conversation. Our accent, speech rate, vocabulary, and so on all serve to identify us in terms of age, sex, ethnicity, status, social class, anxiety level, and more. When we communicate, we cannot help but influence the impressions others form of us. In Goffman's (1959) terms, many of these effects reflect impressions "given off," nonstrategic features of our (linguistic) behavior that are used by others in forming impressions of us.

But talk is also strategic; we make numerous communicative choices. We can talk fast or slow, loud or soft; we can use a plain vocabulary or be particularly esoteric. We can vary our style of talk. As we saw in chapters 1 and 2, any speech act can be performed in a variety of ways, and for many speakers there are choices regarding dialects and even languages. The linguistic choices a person makes reflect, at some level, an attempt at impression management, or impressions "given" in Goffman's terminology. So, whether strategic or not, language use is a rich source of information for forming impressions of others. And because of this, it is also a resource that can be used in managing the impressions we convey to others.

Language-based impressions can occur as a function of many different communication variables, from microlinguistic variables such as phonological variability, to macrolinguistic variables such as dialects and language choice, to extralinguistic variables such as speech rate and volume. Moreover, the effects of these variables on impressions can occur via a number of different processes. This literature is quite vast and only a relatively small sample of these effects will be discussed in this chapter. However, it should be enough to make a fundamental point. Language use and the interpersonal context are related in multiple ways; how we use language is shaped by the social context as we saw in chapter 2, and simultaneously its use helps create that very same context. In this way, the communicative significance of talk extends far beyond the simple transmission of information.

In the first part of this chapter, I review research on social variation, the impact of language variables on impressions mediated primarily by group identification. There are language variables (e.g., accents) that are associated with certain social categories (e.g., social class, ethnicity). These language variables serve to identify a speaker's group membership, and group membership can then serve as the basis for (stereotypic) impressions of the speaker.

In the second, and largest, section of this chapter, I consider stylistic variation. People alter their manner of speaking as a function of the context; they can alter linguistic variables commonly associated with social variation (e.g., accent) as well as many other variables such as speech rate, politeness, and so on. This variability is both an unwitting linguistic reflection of the social context, as well as a means of actively negotiating the meaning of the context. Stylistic variation is thus central to both impression management and person perception.

In the final section of the chapter, I discuss language-based impressions derived from conversation rules. Impressions in this case are based on both an evaluative component of conversation rules (rule violators are negatively evaluated), as well as inferences about a speaker generated in an attempt to make sense of a rule violation.

SOCIAL VARIATION

Much of the field of sociolinguistics has been concerned with the relationship between social and linguistic variables, or more formally, the study of language in relation to society (Hudson, 1980). Thus, sociolinguists have attempted to map how variability in certain linguistic variables (e.g., phonological variability) is related to certain social variables (e.g., ethnicity, social class, group membership). In general, this research has treated language as a dependent variable; linguistic variability is examined as function of social variables. But as we will see, the relationship between linguistic and social variables is reciprocal.

Classic and highly influential research in this vein was conducted by William Labov in the 1960s and early 1970s (Labov, 1966; Labov, 1972a [see also Trudgill, 1974; Milroy & Milroy, 1978]). Essentially, Labov's method involved the collection of discourses produced by speakers, talking about different things, who varied in age, sex, socioeconomic status, religion, occupation, and ethnicity. These corpora were then analyzed for the distribution of linguistic variables as a function of the demographic variables.

Much of Labov's early work investigated the stratification of linguistic variables in New York City. In one simple yet creative study, Labov (1972a) asked department store employees for the location of a particular item known to be on the fourth floor. In this way speakers had to pronounce two words (fourth, floor) with *r*. Labov's interest was in whether speakers pronounced *r* in these words (particularly for the word ending in a consonant—"fourth") as a function of social class, age, and attention to one's speech. The stores he examined varied in status (Saks, Macys, Kleins), as did the age of the respondents. Following the clerk's initial answer, Labov would feign noncomprehension so that the employee had to repeat the phrase, the assumption being that they would then pay closer attention to their pronunciation.

As predicted, Labov found that the pronunciation of *r* increased with social class and attention to speech and decreased with age (but only for the high- and low-class [and not the middle-class] respondents). These results, which were replicated in a larger scale study investigating the stratification of *r* and other phonological variables in New York City, demonstrate the linguistic marking of social class and age. These results also demonstrate intraspeaker variability; respondents were more likely to pronounce *r* when they repeated the words and hence were paying greater attention to their speech. According to Labov (1972a), this illustrates a very general link between class marking and attention to speech: People tend to use upper-class pronunciations when they attend carefully to how they talk.

As in Labov's research, there has been a clear emphasis in sociolinguistics on the linguistic marking of social class. And this research has demonstrated the existence of social class differences in several linguistic variables, including syntax (Lavandera, 1978), lexical choice (Sankoff, Thibault, & Berube, 1978), intonation (Guy & Vonwiller, 1984), and others. But it is not just sociolinguists who are attuned to linguistic variability and its potential meaning. Laypeople are clearly aware of the social class stratification of these variables, as demonstrated by the attention-accent link (Labov, 1972a). But more important, evidence suggests that perceptions of speakers are influenced by this same linguistic variability. For example, in one of Labov's (1966) subjective reaction studies, participants were asked to rate the occupational suitability of people whose speech varied on phonological variables such as postvocalic *r*. Participants showed sensitivity to this phonological variability, and their ratings paralleled the status-phonology relationship he found earlier.

Labov's (1966) research on subjective reactions had been partly inspired by the pioneering research of Wallace Lambert and his colleagues (Lambert, Hodgson, Gardner, & Fillenbaum, 1960). In the late 1950s and early 1960s, they pioneered a technique for examining the effects of linguistic choices on speaker evaluations. The original impetus for this research was a desire to obtain relatively unbiased assessments of attitudes toward differing ethnic groups, in this case French- and English-Canadians in Montreal. So, rather than asking people what they thought of, say, English-Canadians, participants were asked to evaluate people who spoke English. In their research, English- and French-Canadian participants listened to a series of tape-recorded voices, and then indicated their impressions of each speaker on a set of dimensions. Comparing evaluative reactions to speakers of different languages is tricky, of course, because reactions could be influenced by idiosyncratic aspects of the targets' speech patterns (e.g., speech rate, prosody). To control for this possibility, Lambert and colleagues developed what became known as the matched-guise technique; bilingual speakers were recruited to make recordings in both English and French. In this way, the idiosyncratic aspects of individual speakers were held constant across languages.

Although the findings were not completely consistent over dependent measures and sex of speakers and participants, English-Canadian participants tended to perceive speakers more favorably when they spoke English than when they spoke French, an in-group favoritism effect. But French participants displayed the same bias; they too evaluated speakers of English more favorably than speakers of French. In other words, English appeared to be the linguistic standard, and speakers who used it were evaluated more favorably than those who did not.

A plethora of matched-guise studies followed the Lambert et al. (1960) study (see Bradac, 1990; Giles & Coupland, 1991, for reviews). This research has demonstrated clearly that language varieties in a speech community can be ordered on a continuum of prestige, and that evaluations of speakers of these varieties will parallel this ordering. So, for example, in Great Britain received pronunciation (RP) is the prestigious standard, and speakers of that dialect are evaluated more favorably than are speakers of urban varieties such as Cockney and Birmingham (Giles, 1970). Also, nonstandard varieties, in particular nonstandard accents, can be ordered in terms of their strength (i.e., the accents of some people are stronger than those of others). The negative evaluations of speakers on a status dimension who use the nonstandard variety increase with the strength of the accent. Ryan, Carranza, and Moffie (1977), for example, reported that participants rated a Spanish-accented speaker more negatively the more heavily accented the speaker sounded.

But of course things are not so simple. As it turns out, language-based perceptions tend to depend on the specific dimensions that are evaluated. Speakers in this research have been evaluated on a wide range of dimensions (e.g., friendliness, intelligence). Consistent with much other social interaction research, however, perceptions tend to cluster around the two basic dimensions of status and solidarity. Now, the pattern that emerges in many of these studies is that speakers of the standard language variety will usually receive higher ratings on status dimensions such as competence, intelligence, confidence, and so on. But speakers of the nonstandard variety will sometimes receive higher ratings on solidarity dimensions such as friendliness, generosity, and so on (e.g., Ryan, Giles, &

Sebastian, 1982; but see Brown, Giles, & Thakerar, 1985). It is somewhat simplistic, then, to view language varieties as ordered on a simple continuum of prestige. It might be better, following Labov (1972a), to postulate the existence of both overt prestige—the standard variety associated with status—and covert prestige—the nonstandard varieties associated with solidarity.

The effect of linguistic markers on impression formation is further complicated by the fact that these variables are context sensitive, informationally ambiguous, and variable (Brown & Fraser, 1979). Regarding the former, many linguistic effects are limited to specific speech communities. For example, variation in the pronunciation of *r* tends to have less effect on perceptions outside of New York City; people in New York City, but not necessarily elsewhere, have a clear understanding of the social class stratification of this variable. The social meaning of much linguistic variability will depend on the particulars of the social context within which it occurs, a point to be discussed next. Informational ambiguity refers to the fact that many linguistic markers are linked to more than one variable. In Labov's research, for example, pronunciation of *r* marks both social status and level of formality (attention to speech). Ambiguity of this sort exists for many linguistic variables, and it can be exploited as people actively attempt to manipulate the impressions others form of them. Finally, the link between language markers and social categories is (with some exceptions) probabalistic rather than invariant; the probability of any linguistic variable occurring increases with the presence of a particular social category.

Language variables affect not only impressions of a speaker, they also have clear behavioral consequences; people act differently toward a speaker based on how she talks. For example, in a field study, Bourhis and Giles (1976) found that movie theater patrons were more likely to comply with a request made over the public address system when the announcer used a RP style rather than a local nonstandard variety. Language attitudes appear also to have fairly clear implications in educational settings, and several studies have demonstrated that speech style is an important cue in teacher evaluations of pupils (e.g., Seligman, Tucker, & Lambert, 1972). As one might expect, students who use a standard variety are preferred over those using a nonstandard variety (Choy & Dodd, 1976). Language attitudes have also been demonstrated to play a role in medical encounters (Fielding & Evered, 1980), legal settings (Seggre, 1983), employment contexts (Kalin & Rayko, 1980), helping behavior (Gaertner & Bickman, 1971) and more recently, housing discrimination (Purnell, Idsardi, & Baugh, 1999).

How do these linguistic variables affect speaker evaluations? What is the process through which these effects occur? There are several possibilities in this regard (e.g., Cargile, Giles, Ryan, & Bradac, 1994). A speaker's language may activate a social category for the perceiver, with speaker evaluation then being influenced by that category. In this regard, language functions much like any other visible feature (e.g., appearance) that activates a particular stereotype, with the activated stereotype then influencing evaluations. For example, nonstandard language varieties may lead to perceptions that the speaker is from a lower social class, and this categorization may result in negative evaluations of the speaker on certain dimensions. Ryan and Sebastian (1980) found that differential perceptions of standard American and Mexican-American speakers were drastically reduced when participants were informed that all speakers were of middle-class backgrounds. But social class does not always override the effects of language variability; Giles and Sassoon (1983) found that RP speakers were evaluated more favorably than nonstandard speakers, even when social class background was held constant. Importantly, language-based stereotype activation may be largely automatic and out of awareness. Much recent social psychological research on stereotypes has documented their automatic and unconscious quality (e.g., Greenwald & Banaji, 1995), and it seems likely that linguistic variables may often operate in this way.

The social category as mediator view is a bit simplistic. In actual interactions language is only one of many variables that may activate social categories. Other variables may override the effects of linguistic variability, and in fact may affect perceptions of the speaker's language. For example, in a study conducted by Williams, Whitehead, and Miller (1972), participants rated the speech of Black children more negatively (more nonstandard and less confident) than the speech of White children, even though the same (White) voices were used for both the Black and White children. In this case ethnic identification affected speech perception. Along similar lines, Thakerar and Giles (1981) found that when participants believed a speaker to be high status they perceived his speech rate to be more standard than when they believed he was lower in status. Again, one's speech was perceived differently as a function of other characteristics of the speaker.

An important issue here is whether a social category needs to be activated, at some level, for linguistic variables to affect perceptions; such mediation probably need not always occur. A second possibility, then, is that language affects perceptions in a more direct and immediate manner. Certain aspects of speech, in particular extralinguistic variables to be discussed following, may be associated with certain personality characteristics. For example, a relatively fast speech rate may result in perceptions of greater speaker competence. And this effect may occur without the activation of any particular social category.

In some instances, these evaluations may occur without any cognitive mediation whatsoever, they may consist largely of an affective reaction to a speaker's language. Imagine interacting with someone with an unidentifiable accent. Reactions to the speaker may be influenced by the speaker's accent, even though the accent cannot be identified and associated with a particular group. Sometimes such affective reactions may arise because a speaker is perceived to be socially different, she is not a member of one's in-group, and this elicits a relatively automatic negative evaluation.

Language Styles or Registers

Language style refers to a set of linguistic and pragmatic features that are clustered together. Because they are comprised of a cluster of linguistic features, rather than a single linguistic marker, they may be more likely to be noticed by people and play a role in person perception. In contrast to dialects, they are not usually associated with a particular geographical region or social place (Ferguson, 1964), although styles/registers can reflect social variation and hence be associated with certain groups. In this section I discuss powerful versus powerless style and its relation to gender.

A powerless linguistic style refers to a cluster of linguistic features that display hesitancy or lack of assertiveness. Lakoff (1975) published an early, influential paper arguing that these features were markers of women's speech, a female register. Based on her relatively informal observations, Lakoff argued that there are consistent differences between men and women in the use of language—differences that occur at all levels of language use. At the lexical level, for example, woman are believed to use weaker expletives and empty adjectives (e.g., divine). At the syntactic level, there is a presumed tendency for women to use tag questions (e.g., That was a good movie, wasn't it?). Relatedly, it was suggested that woman are more likely to use indirect speech acts and to hedge their assertions. Prosodic differences included a tendency for the declarations of woman to have a rising intonation, thereby giving their declaratives the force of a question.

Empirical evidence bearing on Lakoff's hypothesis has been decidedly mixed. For example, Crosby and Nyquist (1977) reported that in brief same-sex conversations (Study 1), female participants did display a significantly higher overall rate of female linguistic markers than did male participants. But in the same research, no differences in the overall rate of these markers were found in a field study at an information booth (Study 2). In a third field study (Study 3), there were marginally significant differences in the predicted direction.

In terms of research examining differences in specific markers, some researchers have reported no gender differences in the use of indirect speech acts, in terms of both actual use (Rubin & Nelson, 1983; Rundquist, 1992) and in terms of reported use (Holtgraves, 1997c). But others (Carli, 1990) have reported greater use of polite forms and hedges by women than by men. Dubois and Crouch (1975) reported few sex differences in the use of tag questions, but Carli (1990) reported greater tag question use for women participants than for men participants. In what is probably the most well-known study in this genre, Zimmerman and West (1975) reported large sex differences in conversational interruptions; men interrupted women far more often than the reverse. This finding has been replicated by some researchers (e.g., Natale, Entin, & Jaffe, 1979), but other researchers have reported no sex differences for this behavior (e.g., Beattie, 1983; Roger & Nesserhaver, 1987).

The mixed findings regarding sex differences in language use are not surprising given the tremendous difficulty in disentangling sex from other situational variables. The most notable confound, of course, is power. This was one of Lakoff's points; sex differences in language use are not due to sex per se, but due to the subordinate status of women. Clearly, power plays an important role in some of these markers such as the use of indirect speech acts (see chap. 2), and there is research demonstrating that many of these markers are more likely to vary as a function of power rather than as a function of sex (Kollock, Blumstein, & Schwartz, 1985; O'Barr & Atkins, 1980). Consequently, some researchers refer to this cluster of features as a powerless (vs. powerful) style rather than as a woman's (vs. man's) style (e.g., O'Barr, 1982).

As a powerless style, these linguistic features do influence the manner in which a speaker is perceived, and this occurs regardless of the speaker's gender. Speakers who use a powerless style are perceived as less competent and credible and are evaluated less favorably, than a speaker who uses a powerful style (Erickson, Lind, Johnson, & O'Barr, 1978; Newcombe & Arnkoff, 1979). There is also some evidence that a powerless style is less persuasive than a powerful style (Holtgraves & Lasky, 1999).

At the same time, there is some evidence suggesting that the effects of this style vary over speaker sex, a finding consistent with Lakoff's (1975) original orientation. She argued that the use of the female register by women results in their being perceived as relatively less competent and more timid and dependent. Of course, research demonstrates that the use of this style can result in these sort of evaluations (for both men and women). But women have little choice, argued Lakoff. To forgo the female register and "talk like a man" will also result in negative perceptions because one is violating normative expectations regarding how women should talk. Men, on the other hand, are expected to use a more powerful style, and perceptions of their credibility and competence are enhanced when they do. Along these lines, Carli (1990) found that women were more persuasive with men when they used a powerless style—when their language use conformed to expectations about how women should talk—than when they used a powerful style and hence violated normative expectations. But this effect was reversed when the audience was female. This provides some evidence regarding differences in expectations regarding how men and women should talk.

Overall, then, research suggests that a powerless style results in perceptions of lowered competence and credibility, although this effect may be moderated by speaker sex (Carli, 1990; but see Erickson et al., 1978). Note, however, that there is some ambiguity in the meaning of these linguistic markers. Specifically, markers such as tag questions may reflect a lack of certainty and assertiveness and be a result of a subordinate status. However, they may also reflect a more socioemotional orientation, a means of engaging one's interlocutor. And so it has been argued that women's use of this feature may reflect a relatively more socioemotional orientation rather than powerlessness (Fishman, 1980). Like other linguistic (and nonlinguistic) variables, there is potential ambiguity in terms of the meaning of these markers, and this type of ambiguity will be discussed in more detail next.

Extralinguistic Variables

The discussion of social variation so far has focused on linguistic variables—language, accent, dialect, and style. But there are many extralinguistic variables that can influence impressions as well. These are considered to be extralinguistic variables because they involve language delivery rather than anything inherently linguistic. In contrast to social variation, speaker perceptions as a function of these variables are often not mediated by group membership (although they can be). Just like linguistic variables, extralinguistic variability can play an important role in the person perception process.

Consider two examples (for reviews see Furnham, 1990; Scherer, 1979). First, speakers can vary in terms of their lexical diversity. Some people use relatively few words over and over (termed low-lexical diversity), others tend to use a large number of different words (termed high-lexical diversity). Typically, lexical diversity is measured with a type/token ratio (number of unique words divided by total number of words). Evidence suggests that high-lexical diversity is associated with perceived competence and control (Bradac & Wisegarver, 1984), higher status (Bradac, Bowers, & Courtright, 1979) and low anxiety (Howeler, 1972). A related variable, utterance length, appears to be associated with perceived dominance (Scherer, 1979). In short, lexical diversity influences perceptions on the competence/status dimension, but not on the solidarity/liking dimension.

A second heavily researched extralinguistic variable is speech rate. Research indicates that high speech rate is associated with perceptions of speaker competence (Brown, 1980), but only up to a point, after which perceptions of competence do not increase (Street, Brady, & Putman, 1983). Similarly, shorter pauses and response latencies are associated with perceptions of competence (Scherer, 1979). And the effect of speech rate extends to perceptions of credibility, with a corresponding effect on a speaker's persuasiveness (Smith & Schaffer, 1995).

Speech rate can also be a marker of certain personality traits. People who are high in either state or trait anxiety tend to speak more rapidly (Siegman & Pope, 1972), and shorter response latencies appear to be more typical of extroverts than of introverts (Ramsey, 1966). Speech rate can also reflect social variation; Tannen (1984) argues that rapid speech is relatively more characteristic of New Yorkers.

Content Variables

As the preceding discussion makes clear, our perceptions of others can be influenced by how they talk; accent, dialect, and style are all relevant in this regard. But in addition to *how* something is said, *what* people say should also play a role in the person perception process. What people talk about is obviously informative as to the nature of their personality. Some of this may be strategic (as will be discussed in the following), but not all of it. Surprisingly, relatively little research has been conducted on this topic.

Some researchers have designed programs to analyze the content of talk from a psychoanalytic perspective (Bucci, 1997; Gottschalk & Gleser, 1969). These programs are restricted to talk in therapy sessions and hence are rather narrowly focused. A more general research program in this vein was undertaken by Wish, D'Andrade, and Goodenough (1980). Participants were shown videotapes of people interacting and were asked to rate each participant on four bipolar dimensions (solidarity, dominance, task orientation, and emotional arousal). A speech act coding scheme was developed (similar, but not identical, to Searle's (1969) system) and applied to the videotaped interactions. Sizable and theoretically meaningful correlations between ratings and the relative occurrence of certain speech acts were found. For example, perceptions of dominance were positively correlated with the relative frequency of a speaker's forceful requests and negatively correlated with the use of forceless assertions. Perceptions of solidarity were positively correlated with the proportion of utterances that were attentive to the other person and negatively correlated with utterances indicating disapproval.

William Stiles (1978) has developed a speech act coding system that has been used in a number of studies (see Stiles, 1992, for a review). Although originally concerned with therapeutic discourse, his scheme is generalizable to other dyadic interactions. The system is an eight fold scheme based on three binary dimensions: the source of the experience, the presumption about the experience, and the frame of reference. For example, a question involves the speaker's frame of reference and presumption about the experience, with the source of the experience being the other interactant. With disclosures, on the other hand, the frame of reference, presumption, and source of experience all originate with the speaker.

The most general finding in this research program is the clear relationship between roles and utterance type. For example, doctors are more presumptuous (more advisements, interpretations, etc.) than patients during a medical exam (Stiles, Putnam, & Jacob, 1982). The relationship between presumptuousness and role status is quite general and extends to a person's relative status (i.e., a person's presumptuousness varies as a function of with whom she is interacting). So, when a person is higher in status than the other person (e.g., a graduate student interacting with an undergraduate), he will be more presumptuous than when he is lower in status than his interlocutor (e.g., interacting with a faculty member) (Cansler & Stiles, 1981).

More recently, a comprehensive, computerized system for analyzing talk has been developed by Pennebaker and colleagues (Berry, Pennebaker, Mueller, & Hiller, 1997; Pennebaker & King, 1999). Their text analysis program consists of a dictionary of words that is divided into a number of dimensions. At the highest level, these dimensions are grouped into five broad categories: positive emotions (e.g., serenity, optimism), negative emotions (e.g., anger, depression), cognitive mechanisms (e.g., causal thinking), content domain, and language composition. Samples of talk (written or verbal) are analyzed on a word-by-word basis, each word being compared against the dictionary file. Research suggests that people are relatively consistent over time in their linguistic style (i.e., the distribution of words over categories), suggesting that this feature of talk represents an important, stable aspect of personality style (Pennebaker & King, 1999). These categories appear to have some psychological reality for perceivers; perceptions of interactants are related to their linguistic style. Berry and colleagues (1997), for example, asked participants to indicate their perceptions of videotaped interactants who were engaged in brief get-acquainted conversations. Perceptions of the interactants' warmth, competence, and dominance were correlated with variability in their use of positive and negative emotion words, cognitive mechanisms, and other linguisitic categories. Importantly, these effects were independent of other features of the interactants, such as their physical appearance and nonverbal behavior; linguistic variability was a significant and independent predictor of perceptions.

STYLISTIC VARIATION

The picture that emerges from social variation research is that both linguistic variables (e.g., accent, dialect, style) and extralinguistic variables (e.g., speech rate) are socially meaningful; they convey information to others regarding the speaker's identity. But just as clearly, the way we speak is not static. We can alter our speech rate, pronunciation, and style. If bilingual, we might switch languages. As we saw in chapter 2, a speaker's politeness is extremely responsive to the social context. And many of our linguistic constructions are influenced by beliefs about the state of our interlocutors' knowledge (see chap. 5), a situation that is constantly in flux. And so it is with many of the linguistic features discussed so far in this chapter. Not only is there social variation (linguistic differences between people), there is also stylistic variation (linguistic differences within a person). And just as social variation can play a role in person perception, so too can stylistic variation.

For many features of language—in particular language/dialect/accent choices—there is an important connection between social and stylistic variation. According to Labov (1972a), stylistic variation in phonological variability is largely a result of attention to one's speech. The more carefully a speaker attends to her pronunciation, the more likely she is to use a more formal style (i.e., the standard or prestigious variety). And there is some empirical evidence for this. For example, when participants are prevented from monitoring their own speech (by presenting white noise in headphones) their speech becomes less formal (Mahl, 1972).

Hence, class-based social variation parallels stylistic variation based on formality; prestigious pronunciations are formal pronunciations. The situation is similar for language choice. In bilingual settings, speakers can switch languages as a function of the situation, a phenomenon referred to as diglossia (Ferguson, 1964). And in formal situations (e.g., school, government settings), it is the standard or prestige form that tends to be used; in less-formal settings it is the local nonstandard dialect that is more likely to be used (Blom & Gumperz, 1972).

But as Gumperz (1982) has argued, stylistic variation ("code switching" in his terms) is not exclusively a function of the situation. Indeed, it cannot be, for people will switch within a single setting. And people vary widely in terms of the extent to which they switch styles over settings. Code switching does not simply reflect the setting, it also adds to and hence helps create the setting. For example, to switch from a standard variety (or they-code) to a local dialect (or we-code) implicates solidarity with one's interlocutor; it is a means of defining a situation as informal rather than formal.

Gumperz (1982) refers to within-situation shifts as metaphorical switching, and such shifts can have semantic value. Consider the following example (from Gumperz, 1982, pp. 91–92) in which the same message is repeated with a different code:

(1) Father talking to is five-year-old son, who is walking ahead of him through a train compartment and wavering from side to side:
    "Keep straight. Sidha jao (keep straight)."
(2) Adult talking to a ten-year-old boy who is practicing in the swimming pool:
    "Baju-me jao beta, andar mat (go to the side son, not inside). Keep to the side!"

According to Gumperz' analysis, the switch in (1) from the standard to the nonstandard signifies a personal appeal, whereas the reversed switch in (2) signifies a mild warning or threat. This is not trivial. According to Gumperz (1982):

Code switching is thus more than simply a way of contrastively emphasizing part of a message. It does not merely set off a sequence from preceding and following ones. The direction of the shift may also have semantic value. In a sense the oppositions warning/person appeal; casual remark/personal feeling; decision based on convenience/decision based on annoyance; personal opinion/generally known fact can be seen as metaphoric extensions of the "we"/"they" code opposition. (p. 93)

Note the similarity here to Grice's (1975) discussion of conversational implicature. Repetition (as in these examples) violates the quantity maxim, and in so doing may result in a conversational implicature. Additionally, the fact that the repetition occurred with a different code implicates also a particular way in which the message is to be taken (e.g., as a warning rather than a personal appeal). In this way, within-turn style switching can result in a different illocutionary force. But it is also important to note that utterance interpretation as a function of code switching may not be universally agreed upon. Rather, the meaning of any particular code switch may be unique to a particular speech community. Indeed, one of the main themes in Gumperz' work has been on how miscommunication can occur as a result of differing interpretive strategies based on sociocultural differences.

Politeness and Impressions

As discussed in chapters 1 and 2, people have great flexibility in how they phrase any particular remark. One construct that captures much of this variability is politeness, and of course, politeness is extremely responsive to the social context. Hence, it represents a type of stylistic variation.

Brown and Levinson's (1987) politeness theory suggests that a person's amount and type of politeness results from an assessment of various dimensions of the interpersonal context. Greater politeness (e.g., negative or off-record) will be used, for example, if one's interlocutor is relatively high in status. And, there is a fair amount of evidence that these variables do impact the production of politeness (see chap. 2).

Importantly, the relationship between politeness and social variables should be reciprocal. That is, if a speaker's politeness level is a function of her perception of the social situation, then observers (including her interlocutors) can determine her view of that interpersonal situation, or how she views herself in relation to her interlocutors. In this way, one's politeness level is informative about one's (presumed) status and relationship with the other. A person who uses a high level of politeness, or who is very deferential and obsequious, should tend to be perceived by others as being relatively low in status.

And there is some limited empirical support for this notion. Holtgraves and Yang (1990; Experiment 3) asked U.S. and South Korean participants to read vignettes describing interactions between two people. These vignettes were deliberately kept brief and no information about the interactants' status or relationship was provided. Following each vignette was a list of 10 different ways in which one of the interactants could make a request of the other interactant. The requests varied in terms of their politeness; one was bald-on-record (the imperative), two exemplified positive politeness strategies, two were off-record, and five were negative politeness strategies. Hence, the politeness of the requests varied on Brown and Levinson's (1987) politeness continuum. In addition, the five negatively polite forms were ordered in terms of their face-threat implications (Clark & Schunk, 1980).

For each request, participants were asked to indicate their perceptions of the speaker's power relative to the other person and the closeness of the relationship between the speaker and the other person. The results for perceptions of the former were quite clear. Perceptions of the speaker's power varied perfectly and inversely with the politeness of the request; perceptions of speaker power were highest for the bald-on-record requests and lowest for the off-record request, and the negatively and positively polite forms fell between the two extremes. This ordering occurred for both the U.S. and South Korean participants. More impressively, perceptions of power varied perfectly and inversely with the politeness of the five negatively polite forms, and this ordering held for both the U.S. and South Korean participants. So, the "I want you to x" form resulted in perceptions of higher speaker power than the "I'd like you to x" form, which in turn resulted in perceptions of higher speaker power than the "Would you x?" form. These forms involve rather subtle changes in wording, and so they provide relatively strong support for the idea that assumed power is implicated or recoverable from a speaker's politeness.

Perceptions of relationship closeness also varied as a function of request politeness, and the effect was similar for U.S. and South Korean participants. The direction of the results, however, was generally the opposite of that predicted by politeness theory. Although there were some exceptions, greater request politeness was associated with perceptions of greater (rather than lesser) relationship closeness. One likely explanation for this finding is that participants equated closeness with liking (or relationship affect). Hence, the use of greater politeness was presumed to indicate greater liking, and because liking and closeness tend to be equated; greater politeness resulted in perceptions of greater closeness.

An important issue in this process arises from the fact that politeness is determined by at least three social variables: power, relationship distance, and degree of imposition (see chap. 2). Given the existence of multiple determinants of politeness, it is not clear on which dimension(s) a speaker will be perceived as a function of politeness. If a speaker uses a very polite form, for example, will others infer relatively low status, that the act is very threatening, or that the relationship is a distant one? Sometimes information exists regarding one or two of the dimensions such that inferences will be most likely on the unspecified dimension. For example, a boss (high power) making a request to an employee (high distance) with a relatively polite form may implicate, through a high level of politeness, a view that the request is somewhat imposing.

But the existence of multiple determinants allows people to strategically vary their politeness as a means of negotiating and/or altering the interpersonal context; it is, in effect, an important component of impression management. So, a higher power person (e.g., a boss) who moves from negative politeness to positive politeness may be attempting to negotiate a closer relationship. Or, a person in an established relationship may begin to use less politeness as a means of negotiating higher power in the relationship. Or the use of relatively impolite forms in an relationship for which power and distance are established might serve to convey the view that the act (e.g., a request) is not very imposing. And so on. In this way the interpersonal underpinnings of politeness can take on a gamelike quality. If one's bid for higher status (via decreased politeness) is not challenged, the bid has, in effect, been accepted, and the speaker is now defined as the one with higher power in the relationship.

The existence of multiple politeness determinants can also result in interpersonal misperceptions or misunderstandings. A speaker may assume his politeness level reflects one dimension (e.g., closeness), but his interlocutor may assume it reflects a different dimension (e.g., status). So, John might assume he has a relatively close relationship with Mark and accordingly feel free to use positively polite forms (e.g., "How"bout getting me a beer"). But positive politeness represents a relatively low level of politeness, and thus can implicate high speaker power; Mark might view John as making a claim for higher status in their relationship.

Misunderstandings such as this appear to be relatively more likely when people come to an interaction with differing assumptions regarding language use, a possibility that is especially pronounced in interethnic communication. For example, Scollon and Scollon (1981) examined misunderstandings between native Athabaskans and English-speaking North Americans. At a very general level, Athabaskans tend to assume greater distance between unacquainted others than do English-speaking North Americans. As a result, Athabaskans tend to prefer the use of negatively polite strategies in such interactions. In contrast, English-speaking North Americans assume a relatively high degree of familiarity and hence prefer positively polite strategies. Now, positively polite strategies are less polite than negatively polite strategies and hence can implicate either low distance or high speaker power. English-speaking North Americans may assume their politeness implicates closeness; Athabaskans may assume it represents a power grab.

Or consider another example. As will be described in more detail, African Americans may tend to perceive (truthful) bragging less negatively than do European Americans, and this may reflect the former's tendency to prefer positively polite strategies in certain contexts (Holtgraves & Dulin, 1994). So, African Americans may assume bragging reflects solidarity; but their European-American interlocutors may not view it so positively. Again, multiple politeness determinants can result in interethnic misunderstandings.

Accommodation Theory

It is not just languages, dialects, and politeness levels that speakers may alternate during an interaction. Virtually any aspect of speech—speed, volume, lexical diversity, intensity, and so on—can be varied. Some of this within-conversation variability may be noise. But not all of it is. Many such shifts are socially meaningful. Now, it is obvious that people vary their language use as a function of the context. But some aspects of the context are more important than others, and one of the most important and salient features of the setting is one's interlocutor. Much stylistic variation can be attributed to the dynamic interplay between the context that each interactant provides for the other.

One theoretical approach that makes this notion explicit is communication accommodation theory. Originally formulated by Howard Giles (1973), accommodation theory has generated a fairly large amount of research (see Bell, 1984; Giles, Coupland, & Coupland, 1991, for reviews). The basic idea is quite simple. The theory assumes, following Byrne (1971) and others, that similarity results in attraction; we tend to like those most similar to ourselves and to evaluate negatively those most dissimilar to us. The original similarity-attraction paradigm concentrated on attitudinal variables (Byrne, 1971); accommodation theory assumes the same relationship holds for communication variables. Thus, we tend to like those whose speech characteristics are similar to our own. Moreover, a person may sample the speech of his interlocutor and then attempt to alter various aspects of his speech in order to achieve similarity (termed convergence). Importantly, the reverse can occur as well. In certain situations, a speaker may attempt to make her speech different from that of her interlocutor (termed divergence).

Accommodation is thus strategic and dynamic. According to Giles and Coupland (1991): "At one level, accommodation is to be seen as a multiply-organized and contextually complex set of alternatives, regularly available to communicators in face-to-face talk. It can function to index and achieve solidarity with or dissociation from a conversational partner, reciprocally and dynamically" (pp. 60–61). Convergence (and divergence) can occur for a range of speech variables. It represents a strategy whereby ". . . individuals adapt to each other's communicative behaviors in terms of a wide range of linguistic/prosodic/non-vocal features including speech rate, pausal phenomena and utterance length, phonological variants, smiling, gaze, and so on" (p. 63). Accommodation appears to be universal; its existence has been documented in several languages (Giles, Coupland, & Coupland, 1991).

Much of the early research on accommodation focused on the convergence and divergence of language choices. Thus, in bilingual Quebec, French-Canadian speakers who addressed English-Canadians using English (full accommodation) or a mixture of French and English (partial accommodation) were perceived more favorably than speakers who spoke only French (no accommodation; Giles, Taylor, & Bourhis, 1973). Mutual accommodation was seen as well; recipients of accommodative messages were more likely to accommodate in return. Although many early accommodation studies were conducted in laboratory contexts, accommodation has been documented in naturally occurring contexts as well. For example, in a study of John Dean's Watergate testimony, there was a tendency for Dean to accommodate to his interrogators on median word frequency (a measure of formality; Levin & Lim, 1988). And Coupland (1984) documented the phonological convergence of a travel agent to her different clients, clients who varied widely in terms of social class.

The accommodation process can vary in several important ways. For example, accommodation can be upward (toward a more-prestigious variety) or downward (toward a less-prestigious variety). It may involve shifts of varying degrees, and it may occur on many different speech dimensions or on only a few. During the course of a conversation, interactants may converge on some dimensions but simultaneously diverge on other dimensions (Bilous & Krauss, 1988). Convergence may be symmetrical (both interactants converging) or nonsymmetrical (one interactant converges toward the other). And it is possible to converge too much, in which case one's accommodation may be perceived as patronizing (Giles & Smith, 1979).

The primary motive for convergence is generally assumed to be a need for approval from one's current conversational partner. Consistent with this, people scoring higher on a trait measure of need for approval converge more toward their partner than those scoring lower on need for approval (Natale, 1975). Speech divergence, on the other hand, is viewed as a desire to emphasize one's identity with a reference group that is external to the current situation. Such a motive is most likely to be salient when communicating with out-group members and especially when one's social identity has been threatened. For example, Bourhis and Giles (1976) created a situation in which the identity of Welsh speakers was threatened by an English-speaking interviewer who criticized the Welsh language. Speakers subsequently broadened their Welsh accents in their replies (accent divergence).

The impact of accommodation on others' evaluations appears to be mediated by attributional processes. In general, the greater the perceived effort behind convergence, the more positive the resulting evaluations of the speaker (Giles, 1973). Thus, the motive for convergence appears to be critical. For example, Simard, Taylor, and Giles (1976) found convergence to result in positive evaluations if it was attributed to a desire to break down cultural barriers; no increase in positive evaluations occurred if convergence was perceived to be a result of situational pressures. The opposite occurred for nonconvergence. In contrast, if convergence is perceived to be the result of situational pressures, evaluations of a converging speaker may not be positive. So, for example, a salesman who converges to the speech characteristics of a client may not be viewed more positively; his convergence will be viewed as being situationally determined.

The large and growing literature on accommodation is important because it emphasizes the dynamic and contextually sensitive patterning of talk and the effect of that patterning on interactants' perceptions of one another. With accommodation theory, we see how speaker evaluations are not always static—there need not be a one-to-one relationship between a particular way of talking and a particular evaluation. Instead, evaluative reactions sometimes depend on one's talk in the context of the other person's talk and on the extent to which one's talk matches that of the other.

CONVERSATIONAL RULE
VIOLATIONS AND IMPRESSIONS

Language use is rule-governed behavior. There are rules regarding turn taking, changing the topic, answering questions, and so on. Like most rule systems, conversation rules contain an evaluative component; rule violators will tend to be negatively evaluated. So, someone who interrupts frequently, makes abrupt topic changes, doesn't answer questions, and so on will usually be viewed negatively by others. At a very general level, then, our perceptions of speakers vary as a function of the extent to which they conform to conversational rules.

However, more specific impressions may be generated against the backdrop of conversational rules. Rather than a global, evaluative dimension, speakers can be perceived as possessing specific traits and motives depending on the nature of the rule violation. For example, someone who monopolizes a conversation may be perceived as dominant (or extroverted), one who rarely talks as shy (or introverted). As noted above, psychologists are just now beginning to investigate these processes (e.g., Berry et al., 1997).

But as always, things are not so simple. Rules are not straightforward mechanisms for generating impressions; they are heavily context dependent and often require interpretative processes on the part of the perceiver. This can occur in much the same way that addresses interpret a speaker's intended indirect meaning. Speaker perceptions are part of a general pragmatic inferencing process. Two examples—one specific and one more general—can illustrate this point.

Consider, first, how sometimes our impressions of others are based on what they tell us about themselves. Reports of stock market killings, athletic prowess, and hair-raising adventures should prompt impressions of a wealthy, adventurous, athletic person. And they might. But such reports might also affect impressions in others ways, ways that are based on the impact of the communicative content in the context of specific conversational rules. The point is this. Although impressions of others may be affected by what they reveal about themselves or what is revealed about them by others, the act of revealing that information in a particular communicative context can exert a powerful impact on impressions.

Consider again a rule proscribing (at least for European-American residents of the Midwestern United States) modesty during conversational interactions (Berger & Bradac, 1982). To assert one's positive qualities during a conversation can result in perceptions of inconsiderateness and egotism (Jones & Pittman, 1982), an effect that may negate the specific information conveyed (Godfrey, Jones, & Lord, 1986). Thus, a speaker who proclaims athletic prowess may or may not be perceived as relatively athletic but will probably (depending on the context) be perceived negatively on several dimensions. In a similar way, one should not make disparaging remarks about others. To do so results in the speaker being perceived negatively, with no impact on perceptions of the person who is being described (Wyer, Budesheim, & Lambert, 1990).

But positive self-disclosures need not result in negative evaluations. They must be done carefully, of course, and one of the ways they can be done carefully is by being attentive to the conversational context. That is, there may be conversational contexts in which the negative effects of making positive self-statements are lessened. Holtgraves and Srull (1989) examined two such possibilities. One situation is when a positive self-description is in response to a question from one's interlocutor. Because questions demand a response (Schegloff & Sacks, 1973), perceptions of egotism might be lessened (one is simply responding to a question from the other person). Perceptions of egotism are lessened because the discourse context provides an alternative explanation for the positive self-statement; rather than attributing it to the speaker's egotism, it is instead (at least partially) attributed to the conversational context. A second situation is when one's interlocutor is also making positive self-statements. Again, the discourse context (the other's positive self-statements) in a sense obligate one's own positive self-statements. In this research, the effect of these contexts on perceptions of a speaker was clear. Speakers who made positive self-statements in response to specific questions, or when their conversation partner was also making positive self-statements, were perceived as less egotistical, more considerate, and were liked more than speakers who made the exact same statements in the absence of these contexts.

Of course, a person who wants to make positive disclosures need not be passive, patiently waiting for the other to ask the right question. There are many things that can be done to increase the likelihood of the other providing an appropriate context. For example, positive statements can be elicited from one's conversation partner and in so doing create a context in which one's own positive statements are more appropriate. Or, one could attempt to maneuver the conversation to a topic for which one has something positive to say, in which case the likelihood of the other person asking an appropriate question is increased. The point here being that the discourse context is both a source of information in forming impressions of others and a resource to be used in managing the impressions that others form of us.

Conversational rules regarding positive self-disclosures are no doubt culturally specific. The negative evaluations that accrue from bragging in one culture may not occur in a different culture. A good example of this can be seen in differences between African Americans and European Americans in their orientation to bragging, a difference reflecting a broader difference in overall conversational style.

Probably the most well-known research regarding African-American conversational style has been provided by Kochman (1981). He has described several conversational differences between African Americans and European Americans, although most of these differences center on the dimension of emotional expressiveness. In general, African-American communication tends to be emotionally intense, dynamic, and demonstrative; European Americans, on the other hand, tend to be more subdued, modest, and restrained (see also Labov, 1972b). This difference can be seen particularly well in arguments. According to Kochman, the arguments of African Americans tend to be personal, animated, and confrontational; positions are forcefully asserted (when they are in the majority) and in a spontaneous manner (e.g., simultaneous speech is permitted). The arguments of European Americans, in contrast, tend to be more impersonal, dispassionate, and nonconfrontational; deference is paid and the interaction is more orderly and scripted (e.g., simultaneous speech is generally not allowed).

The African-American emphasis on expressiveness also results in a different view of bragging. According to Kochman, as long as the assertions are true, bragging is an accepted and valued feature of African-American communication. In fact, "if the persons who are bragging are capable of demonstrating that they can do what they claim, blacks no longer consider it bragging" (p. 66). Hence, the frequent (and generally true) positive self-statements made by Muhammad Ali were generally not viewed negatively by many African Americans. European Americans, on the other hand, generally take a dim view of bragging, whether truthful or not (Holtgraves & Srull, 1989). Consistent with this, Holtgraves and Dulin (1994) found African Americans to perceive a truthful bragger (but not an untruthful bragger) more positively than did European Americans. Moreover, they were less likely to perceive the positive self-disclosures as bragging, relative to European Americans. These differences in perceptions point to the importance of culture as a moderator of rule-based impressions.

These results demonstrate how impressions of others may be driven not by the content of one's utterances, but rather by the pragmatic implications of those utterances. This is a specific instance of a more general principle that people attempt to make sense of conversational rule violations, and they do so via basic attributional principles. An observer of someone making positive statements will attempt to explain this behavior. And if the discourse context provides an explanation for the behavior, then dispositional attributions of egotism and negative evaluations become less likely.

This general principle can be applied to the operation of Grice's (1975) conversational maxims. The main emphasis with the Gricean framework has been on conveying intended meanings; speakers violate a conversational maxim in order to intentionally convey a nonliteral meaning. If the violation is noted, then recipients should engage in inferential processing as a means of explaining the violation. And some indirect meanings that a speaker intends to have recognized appear to be generated in this way (see chap. 1). But maxim violations might also result in inferences that are unintended. Maxim violations might also serve as the basis for generating inferences about the speaker (intended or otherwise), especially when the recipient is unable to construct an interpretation of the remark that was likely to have been intended by the speaker.

Consider violations of the quantity maxim, or stipulation that one should be appropriately informative. Speakers can violate this maxim by being

underinformative and providing too little information or by being overinformative and providing too much information. An example of the latter would be
saying something redundant, providing information already known to be the
case. In certain contexts, these violations can result in irony (see chap. 1). In
addition, violations of this maxim can generate doubt in the validity of an
asserted proposition. For example, Gruenfeld and Wyer (1992) demonstrated
that under certain conditions, denials of propositions generally believed to be
false can boomerang and increase belief in the denied proposition. In their
research, participants who read a newspaper report denying a proposition generally believed to be untrue (e.g., a story denying that Ronald Reagan is an alcoholic) came to believe the denied proposition to a greater extent than did those
participants not reading the story. Similarly, participants who read a newspaper
story affirming a proposition generally believed to be true (e.g., Republican
congressmen belong to elitist country clubs) believed the proposition to a lesser
extent than those not reading the story.

Why? According to these authors, statements that are obviously true or obviously false represent violations of the quantity maxim; the information they convey is generally known and hence the statements are redundant. Because of their
redundancy, recipients of such statements must construct a scenario explaining
why the statement is being made. One possibility (though certainly not the only
one) is that there must be some doubt about the truth of the affirmed proposition
or some truth in the denied proposition. Why else would such statements be
made? Importantly, these effects are attenuated if attributed to an encyclopedia
rather than a newspaper. The purpose of an encyclopedia is to record archival
knowledge; they are not expected to provide "new" information. Because of this,
the pragmatic implications of uninformative denials and assertions need not be
considered.

In some ways, this effect is reminiscent of Richard Nixon's 1973 "I am not a
crook" speech. During a press conference that year, Richard Nixon proclaimed
his innocence of any financial wrongdoing by denying that he was a crook. By
most accounts he was very defensive and extremely overtalkative during the session. The impact of his denials on public opinion was negative; rather than influencing people to believe he was not a crook, the denials had the opposite effect.
Why? One possibility is that by denying any wrongdoing he was in effect violating the quantity maxim by being overinformative. The reasoning here is somewhat akin to a "methinks he doth protest too much" effect. He must be trying to
hide something, or he would not engage in such vigorous denials.

There is, however, a difference between the Nixon denials and the denials read
by participants in the Gruenfeld and Wyer study. In the latter case, the source of
the denial was a newspaper rather than a speaker making a denial about his own
behavior. In Nixon's case, of course, the denials pertained to the source of the
denial. Obviously Nixon did not intend for his denials to boomerang; his intention
was for people to believe them. So why did his denials boomerang? It appears that

in certain contexts, violations of the quantity maxim can result in the speaker being perceived in a negative way.

To test this, Holtgraves and Grayer (1994) had participants read courtroom testimony in which the defendant sometimes violated the quantity maxim and provided more information than was required by the prosecutor's question. For example, when asked whether he was insured as a driver, the defendant in the overinformative condition replied ("Yes, I've never lost my insurance because of speeding tickets"). In this case, the defendant provided more information (by mentioning speeding tickets) than was required by the Yes-No question. Now, it would be difficult for a hearer to infer an *intended* indirect meaning with this remark. So, in order to make sense of the remark, participants generated inferences about the speaker's motive (e.g., that he was trying to convey a favorable image), personality (that he was nervous and anxious), and guilt (he was judged guilty more often than the defendant in the control condition).

Research suggests that violations of the relation maxim can also influence impressions along these lines as well. For example, Davis and Holtgraves (1984) found that a politician who failed to provide relevant answers to debate questions was perceived more negatively on several dimensions than was a politician whose answers were relevant. Participants noticed the relevance violations and explained them in terms of the speaker's motives (e.g., he was trying to avoid the issues) and personality (e.g., competence).

What these studies suggest is that perceptions of speakers may be part of a general process whereby people attempt to understand the meaning of another's utterances. If a hearer (or overhearer) notices a maxim violation, the overarching question becomes one of understanding why the speaker is making this utterance in this context. Why is he being redundant (quantity maxim violation) or evading the question (relation maxim violation) or being unclear (manner maxim violation), and so on? Numerous studies have demonstrated that people seek to explain why unexpected or unscripted actions occurred; people are more likely to engage in attributional processing when observing unexpected actions (Hastie, 1984). Readers are also more likely to generate causal inferences as a means of explaining unusual events (Singer et al., 1992), a process that represents an attempt to understand why something has been mentioned in a text (Graesser, Singer, & Trabasso, 1994).

Now, given the operation of a cooperative principle and assumption that a speaker's utterances are meaningful, interlocutors should generally attempt to construct an interpretation of a remark that could be viewed as being intended by the speaker. As discussed in chapter 2, interpersonal concerns such as face management can guide this process. But what if an intended meaning cannot be discerned? Then, a variety of nonintended meanings become possible, with most of them involving dispositional inferences regarding the speaker. So, one might infer that a person who fails to answer a question did not understand the question or that he is relatively low in intelligence or that she is engaging in self-presentation, and so on. Which specific inferences will be generated is unclear and unexplored territory. But what is clear is that inferential processing is not limited to the generation of intended, indirect meanings; everything about the speaker is fair game in this regard.

This is not to say that all language-based perceptions are mediated by this type of inferential processing. As noted previously, some linguistic effects are relatively automatic. Sometimes communicators will be perceived as possessing the traits that they use to describe others (Skowronski, Carlston, Mae, & Crawford, 1998); the effects in this case appear to be due to simple associative processing rather than being a result of conversational inferencing.

Of course, all of the weaknesses inherent in the Gricean (1975) approach will apply here as well (see chap. 1). Thus, it is difficult to specify in advance what will constitute a maxim violation and whether or not it will be noticed, and so on. But the general idea, the notion that perceptions of speakers are influenced by a general concern with understanding the meaning of that person's utterances and that those perceptions flow from the cognitive process involved in this search, seems promising.

CONCLUSION

One of the major ways in which we form impressions of one another is through our verbal interactions. It is during the course of our conversations that we get a sense of people, the traits they possess, whether we like them or not, their social associations, and so on. This dynamic, impression formation process is based, in large part, on language use. We evaluate others and infer traits and motives based on their accent, speech rate, conversational topic, responsiveness to our conversational style, inferred reasons for why they violated conversational rules, and so on.

This process is neither simple nor straightforward. Although there may be impression main effects for some communication variables, such effects are likely to be small (e.g., an overall tendency for faster speech to result in perceptions of competence). Instead, linguistic-based impressions are part of a dynamic and contextually sensitive process. The meaning of any linguistic variable will be mediated by characteristics of the speaker and the setting. A powerful, straightforward style may result in positive evaluations if the speaker is male, but negative evaluations if the speaker is female. The use of a less-prestigious dialect may be viewed unfavorably in a formal context, but positively in a less-formal context. Also, certain aspects of linguistic-based impressions will be in the eye of the beholder. Fast speech rate may be viewed positively if it matches one's own rate, negatively if it does not.

If language is potentially informative for others in forming impressions, then language is a resource that can be used for managing our impressions. And so it is. Stylistic (or within-speaker) variation makes most sense as an attempt at impression management, an attempt to place oneself in the most-positive light. Or as an attempt to create more specific impressions (e.g., power and status), or to (re)negotiate the closeness of one's relationship with another.

Stylistic and social variation are obviously related. In fact, stylistic variation presupposes the existence of social variation. Stylistic variation as an attempt at impression management succeeds only insofar as a consensus exists regarding the identity implications of language choices. It is this consensus that is implicated in meaningful social variation (e.g., that RP is the prestigious standard in Great Britain, or that failing to pronounce *r* locates the speaker in the lower classes). Similarly, it is because language use is contextually determined (e.g., one speaks formally in formal situations) that stylistic variation can help to define (rather than just reflect) the context. Switching to an "informal" variety in an attempt to (re)define a situation will work only to the extent that the "informal" variety is typically used in informal settings.

Our talk is rife with social meaning, but in many respects it is only potential meaning. It is meaning that is available to others, but it may or may not be used. For example, some people may be relatively oblivious to the interpersonal implications of their utterances and those of others. And because it is potential meaning it has the feature of deniability. A speaker can always claim that whatever meaning has been recovered by the hearer is a meaning that was not intended. So, attempts to assert one's status by being impolite can simply be denied, as can one's attempt to define a situation as formal by switching to a prestigious variety.

In this way, the types of meaning discussed in this chapter are fundamentally different from the communicative meanings that are intended to be recognized (i.e., reflexive intentions). This is clearly the case for impressions "given-off," those that are in no sense strategically conveyed. But many times it is also the case for impressions "given," or strategic attempts to influence others' impressions of us. We usually do not want others to recognize our intention to convey a particular identity; we want our attempts at impression management to seem natural, sincere, and spontaneous. There are some principled exceptions of course. When visiting a foreign country, we often may want our interlocutors to recognize (and appreciate) our intention to use their native language. But this seems to be the exception.

The manner in which people perceive others—and the strategies that social actors use in order to influence those perceptions—have long been core research areas in social psychology. Yet, with some important exceptions, the emphasis in person-perception research has been on how people encode, represent, combine, and recall information about others. How they get that information in the first place—how they convert raw social stimuli into information that can be used in these processes—has received far less attention. Similarly, research on impression management has been concerned with why and when people engage in impression management; much less is known about *how* people engage in face management.

As this chapter has emphasized, both person perception and impression management are mediated by language use. The information we receive about others usually comes from our interactions with them, just as the stage for our attempts at impression management are those same interactions. And of course, these interactions are largely verbal interactions. So, how we talk, what we say, and how we say it are an important source of information for the person-perception process, just as it is an important resource used for managing the impressions others form of us. Clearly, the study of language contributes substantially to our understanding of these phenomena.

4

Conversational Structure

It is a rare conversation that consists of a single utterance. Of course, a single utterance is not a conversation at all; a minimum requirement for a conversation is that it is comprised of at least two turns of talk. Consequently, our utterances always occur, not in isolation, but in the context of the utterances of other people. Because of this, one's talk is not a result of a single individual—one can't just say whatever one wants whenever one wants to say it—but rather the result of two or more people jointly engaging in talk. What we do as we converse is constrained by what is done by our interlocutors. And of course their contributions are constrained by us.

An amazing and yet obvious feature of conversations is how highly structured they are. People take turns speaking, their utterances generally address the same topic, misunderstandings are often handled quickly and easily, and so on. But equally interesting is the fact that prior to its occurrence, the course of a conversation is completely unpredictable; it is difficult to specify in advance how a conversation will turn out. Structure and order are apparent when viewing a completed conversation, but not predictable at the beginning.

What, then, is the nature of conversational orderliness and structure? How is this accomplished? What are the mechanisms that allow it to be accomplished? Speech act theory and politeness theory really do not help much in this regard.

Now, it is possible to extend these approaches in various ways to account for the sequential properties of talk. Some attempts have been made in this regard, and they will be briefly discussed. But there are other approaches—perspectives that eschew concepts of intention and politeness—that provide some insight into conversational structure. Foremost here is a subdiscipline termed conversation analysis, and most of this chapter will be devoted to research within that tradition.

Conversational structure has important implications for many of the phenomena discussed in previous chapters. Speech acts, for example, are highly contextualized; illocutionary force does not exist independently of the conversational context within which the utterance occurs. Similarly, politeness is often manifested over a series of moves, and face-management processes might be missed if the focus is on single utterances. Of course, the interpersonal implications of language use—its role in person perception and especially impression management—are based on the sequential properties of talk, or how people accommodate to their conversational partner, or negotiate topic changes in order to disclose something positive or avoid conveying face-threatening information. The importance of conversational structure was implicit in the previous chapters; its importance is explicitly recognized in this chapter.

In the first part of this chapter, I provide a brief overview of the genesis and methodological perspective of conversation analysis. This is followed by an extended discussion of the role played by adjacency pairs (e.g., questions and answers) in conversations. Adjacency pairs have a number of interesting properties, and they are capable of accounting for much conversational structure. Then, the systems used for managing turn-taking and repair are considered. In the final section, I discuss the manner in which conversational coherence is achieved, and this will include a brief consideration of some alternatives to conversation analysis.

CONVERSATION ANALYSIS

Conversation analysis is a unique approach to the study of language use. It was developed in the 1960s by the sociologist Harvey Sacks and his colleagues Emanuel Schegloff and Gail Jefferson. Many of Sacks's original ideas were articulated in his lectures and circulated only in mimeo form for a number of years. It is only relatively recently that his lectures have been fully transcribed and published (Sacks, 1992).

Conversation analysis represents a sociological (rather than linguistic) orientation to language; it seeks conversational regularity in terms of the social order rather than in linguistic acts. But as a sociological approach it was quite unlike—and in fact was directly opposed to—most other sociological traditions. Conversation analysis has its roots in ethnomethodology, an offbeat branch of sociology developed by Harold Garfinkel (1967). Ethnomethodology was largely a reaction (both substantive and methodological) to mainstream functionalism. In a functionalist view (e.g., Parsons, 1937), society is an entity that is external to the individual; individuals become socialized and become part of the social order, via the internalization of societal norms. In contrast, Garfinkel adopted a primarily phenomonological perspective (derived from Schutz, 1970) and argued that the social order, rather than being independent of and external to individuals, is continuously created by people as they use language and make sense of their behavior and that of others. Garfinkel thus advocated a shift in emphasis from macrosociological forces to microsociological phenomena, specifically, the commonsense knowledge and reasoning people use as a means of creating a social order (cf. Goffman, 1967).

Ethnomethodology involves a unique methodological stance. A functionalist methodology is primarily quantitative; categories and coding schemes are developed by researchers and then applied to the social phenomenon of interest. For Garfinkel, such coding schemes are not to be trusted because they are based on the interpretive (sense-making) strategies of the researchers who develop them. For Garfinkel, an objective social science was not possible. What is possible, however, is the exploration of the means by which people make sense of their world. It is for that purpose that Garfinkel developed his famous breaching experiments. In these experiments, student experimenters were instructed to enter into interactions with others and violate basic, taken-for-granted routines (e.g., greeting exchanges) and observe the resulting breakdown, which inevitably occurred. These experiments were presumed to illuminate the taken-for-granted knowledge that allows people to engage in social interaction.

Conversation analysis, like ethnomethodology, focuses on the common, everyday competencies that make social interaction possible. Like ethnomethodology, there is a putative rejection of a priori categories and theorizing; the emphasis is on *participants'* (not researchers') sense making. Unlike Garfinkel, however, conversation analysts assume that it is possible to develop a science of social life. And in fact, conversation analysis represents a rigorously empirical approach to social interaction, albeit one that is essentially inductive. Rather than examining rule violations as a means of documenting commonsense understandings (Garfinkel's breaching experiments), conversation analysis seeks to uncover these understandings as they are *revealed* in normal everyday conversational exchanges. A person's understanding of another's conversation turn is assumed to be revealed in the subsequent turn that she produces (see also Clark, 1996a). In this way, an analyst works only from what is available to the interactants themselves—their talk.

The general strategy in conversation analysis is to examine in great detail actual verbal interactions. And they must be actual interactions; contrived examples or speech generated in the laboratory are not acceptable. Actual interactions are audiotaped, with much of the early research relying on recorded telephone conversations. These recordings are then transcribed, keeping as much detail (e.g., overlap talking, pauses, breathiness, word and syllable stress) in the transcription as possible. A fairly standardized transcript system, developed primarily by Gail Jefferson, exists for this purpose. Transcripts are, of course, not entirely neutral, and in the case of conversation analysis they reflect the central concern these researchers have with turn taking and speech delivery (particularly insofar as it is relevant for turn taking).

Working from both the transcript and the actual recording, the analyst then proceeds to examine the interaction for regularities, in particular, patterns in the sequential organization of talk. Again, conversation analysts claim that no a priori concepts or theories are applied to the data at the outset. Instead, the approach is to articulate a category only if the interactants themselves in some way display an orientation to that category. It is thus an ethnomethodological stance; the focus is on how interactants themselves make sense of their activity. If the participants do not display an orientation to a particular conversational occurrence, then the analyst is presumably in no position to claim any particular status for that occurrence. After analysts have identified an interesting conversational phenomenon, they will then collect a number of instances of that phenomenon and ascertain whether these other instances can be described with their account. This, then, is a purely inductive strategy with the aim of providing a formal description of a large set of data.

Despite the emphasis on the accomplishment of interactional work through talk, it is important to note that absolutely no reference is ever made to the internal states (e.g., goals, expectancies, motives) of the interactants. It is an approach that takes talk, and only talk, as the object of study. Thus, many of the internal concepts that lie at the heart of speech act theory (e.g., illocutionary force, intention) and politeness theory (e.g., positive face, negative face) are not relevant, even though, as we will see, many of the phenomena uncovered in conversation analysis can be interpreted within these frameworks. Nor do traditional sociolinguistic variables such as power relations, gender, and formality have an a priori relevance; such variables are relevant only if the interactants themselves display some orientation to them.

The primary aim of conversation analysis is to bring to light the structural properties of talk. Hence, there is an emphasis on conversational context and sequence. The organizational features uncovered with this approach are viewed as resources that interactants use to manage talk, and these resources are available to anyone. In this way, conversational interaction is viewed as a system—a system existing apart from any specific individual. The structural regularities that exist are a means by which the conversational system is maintained. Hence, the focus is on the "system" properties of talk and not on any of its interpersonal or ritual (e.g., Goffman, 1976) properties. In conversation analysis, there really is no meaningful distinction between the conversational system and conversational ritual; the system *is* the ritual.

Research in conversation analysis has, over the past 30 years, documented the existence of a number of sequential properties of talk. This is why conversation analysis is central to a consideration of the structure of conversations; conversation analysis has a near monopoly on investigating this feature of talk. Some of the major findings are described next, beginning with the smallest unit—adjacency pairs—and working outward to the overall structure of conversations.

ADJACENCY PAIRS

People can't say just anything during a conversational exchange; their utterances are constrained in various ways by the context, most notably the utterances of other interactants. If Bob makes a request of Andy, then Andy's subsequent turn at talk is constrained. He cannot, for example, perform the act of greeting Bob. Of course, he might perform a greeting, but if he does so he displays, through his greeting, his orientation to the preceding turn; indicating a lack of understanding, a refusal to comply with the request, a joke, and so on. In other words, the significance of Andy's action, as part of a jointly produced interaction, is constrained by Bob's prior action.

The smallest structural unit exhibiting this quality is termed an adjacency pair [Goffman (1976) used the term *couplet* for a similar unit]. Adjacency pairs figured prominently in early conversation analytic writings (Schegloff & Sacks, 1973; Schegloff, 1968) and continue to receive attention due to their fundamental importance in structuring talk. According to Schegloff and Sacks (1973), adjacency pairs have the following general features.

1. They consist of two utterances, a first-pair part and a second-pair part.
2. The two utterances are spoken by different speakers.
3. The utterances are paired so that a first-pair part must precede a second-pair part.
4. The first-pair part constrains what can occur as a second-pair part.
5. Given the first-pair part, the second-pair part becomes conditionally relevant.

Examples of adjacency pairs include question-answer, apology-minimization, offer-acceptance, greeting-greeting, summons-answer, request-promise, and so on. Adjacency pairs reflect obvious regularities in peoples' talk; people return greetings, answer questions, accept offers, and so on. But the concept, and what it reveals about talk, extends far beyond this simple superficial description.

First, the emphasis is on how people display their understanding of one another's talk and how they ground their conversational contributions (Clark & Schaefer, 1989; see chap. 5 for more detail on Herb Clark's approach to conversational structure). This understanding is observed not through an assessment of the interactants' internal states, interpretations, emotional reactions, and so on. Instead, understanding is to be seen in the talk itself, and this view becomes quite clear with adjacency pairs. The occurrence of an answer in response to a question displays the second interactant's understanding of what was accomplished with the first speaker's utterance, that the first speaker has asked a question. If an answer is not forthcoming, the second speaker, through a failure to answer, displays a lack of understanding of the first speaker's utterance (although this view has problems, as discussed later). It is this emphasis on the structural and sequential regularities as a reflection of understanding that is the hallmark of this approach.

Second, the second-pair part of an adjacency pair need not immediately follow the first-pair part. This is because embedded sequences of talk, termed insertion sequences (Schegloff, 1972) or side sequences (Jefferson, 1972), can occur between the first- and second-pair part. These sequences involve issues raised by the first-pair part and can themselves be ordered as adjacency pairs. Consider the following example from Merritt (1976):

(1)   A: Can I have a bottle of Mich?
       B: Are you twenty-one?
       A: No
       B: No

Rather than providing the second-pair part, B at Turn 2 instead begins an insertion sequence by performing the first-pair part of a second adjacency pair. In Turn 3, A provides an answer to B's question, thereby ending the insertion sequence and denying a condition that would allow B to comply with the request. The second-pair part of the original adjacency pair is then provided by B in Turn 4.

Insertion sequences can become quite lengthy, with adjacency pairs becoming embedded within other adjacency pairs. As a result, the first- and second-pair part of the original adjacency pair might be rather far apart. Consider the following service encounter (simplified from Levinson, 1983, p. 305):

(2)   1 A: How many tubes would you like sir?
       2 B: U:hm (.) what's the price now eh with VAT do you know eh
       3   ....
       4 A: Three pounds nineteen a tube sir
       5 B: Three nineteen is it=
       6 A: Yeah
       7 B: E::h (1.0) yes u:hm (dental click) (in parenthetical tone) e:hjus-
              justa think, that's what three nineteen That's for the large tube
              isn't it
       8 A: well yeah it's the thirty seven c.c.s.
       9 B: Er, hh I'll tell you what I'll just eheh ring you back I have to
              work out how many I'll need. Sorry I did-wan't sure of the price
              you see.

The first-pair part (Turn 1) of the initial adjacency pair is not answered until Turn 9 (and then it is deferred, with an account and apology). Between the first- and second-pair parts of the original adjacency pair are three additional adjacency pairs (Turns 2 and 4, 5 and 6, and 7 and 8) each a question-answer pair dealing with issues raised by the first-pair part of the original adjacency pair. The relevance of these side issues for the original question helps maintain the expectation that the second-pair part will be forthcoming. Clearly, then, adjacency pairs can structure relatively long sequences of talk.

Third, adjacency pairs represent a template for the production of talk. Given the occurrence of a first-pair part, the second-pair part becomes *conditionally relevant* (Schegloff, 1968); it is expected, and if not forthcoming, its absence is noticeable. Thus, greetings usually follow greetings, acceptances follow offers, and so on. But not always. As we've seen, the second-pair part may be delayed with an insertion sequence. And, in fact, the second-pair part may never occur. Adjacency pairs are not to be viewed as statistical regularities; for example, that answers will follow summons 92% of the time (Heritage, 1984). Rather, adjacency pairs are templates for both the production and the interpretation of talk; the conditional relevance of the second-pair part serves as a template for interpreting what follows a first-pair part. The absence of a second-pair part is noticeable and grounds for making inferences about the speaker, for initiating a repair sequence, and so on. For example, failing to return a greeting can result in additional (and louder) greeting attempts and/or inferences that the person is rude or boorish.

There is an obvious similarity here to Grice's (1975) theory of conversational implicature. In Grice's view, flouting a conversational maxim instigates an inference-making process; the recipient will reason about what the speaker really means with the utterance (see chap. 1). Similarly, failing to provide the expected second pair part of an adjacency pair will result in the making of inferences about the person who has failed to perform the expected action. So, not answering a question is both a flouting of the relation maxim and a failure to provide an expected second-pair part, and both serve as grounds for making inferences about the speaker and the meaning of the utterance.

But there are some important differences here. First, the adjacency pair concept has an advantage over Grice's maxims in that it represents a more precise specification of when conversational inferencing will occur (as noted in chap. 1, Grice's maxims are somewhat ambiguous). Second, in conversation analysis the examination of inference making is limited to those inferences that are revealed in a subsequent turn at talk. And quite often inferences are revealed in this way, as when one person comments on the boorishness of another who has failed to return a greeting. But inference making beyond that revealed in talk generally is not considered in conversation analysis. In contrast, the Gricean approach, at least as used by psycholinguists, allows for and in fact focuses on internal inference making.

Adjacency pairs structure action; the first-pair part of an adjacency pair constrains what can follow. But some adjacency pairs are most constraining than others (Levinson, 1983). For example, the greeting-greeting pair is tightly constrained and ritualistic; people generally return a greeting with a greeting, there are few options here. But what about question-answer pairs? There are numerous acceptable responses to a question, acceptable in the sense that the first speaker would display acceptance of the move in subsequent turns. For example, a person can say that she does not possess the requested information, that another person should be consulted, and so on. Although the second-pair part is not provided, the speaker accounts for this, and in this way displays an orientation to the adjacency pair action template. But what about indirect replies? Virtually *any* subsequent utterance (even silence) can serve as an answer to a question in the sense that the recipient will interpret it within an adjacency pair template (see chaps. 1 and 2). The first speaker's subsequent turn at talk may reveal that it has been interpreted in just this way. But are one's interpretations *always* revealed in subsequent turns at talk? Might not some interpretations be made and yet not revealed? If this is so and if any subsequent utterance can serve as an answer to a question, then the explanatory value of the question-answer adjacency pair is decreased.

Preference Agreement

What counts as a second-pair part, then, is something of an issue. The range of utterances that can serve as a second-pair part is quite large and in some instances unlimited. But there is an interesting feature of adjacency pairs that goes some way toward resolving this issue. The feature is this. Not all second-pair parts are of equal status; some second-pair parts are preferred over other second-pair parts. For example, agreements are preferred over disagreements, acceptances over refusals, answers over nonanswers, and so on. The former are referred to as preferred turns, or seconds, and the latter as dispreferred turns, or seconds.

The preferred-dispreferred construct is *not* defined in terms of peoples' attitudes towards others' utterances. Instead, dispreferred turns are defined as turns that are marked (in the linguistic sense) in some way; preferred turns are unmarked turns. The validity of this concept stems in part from the fact that the manner in which dispreferred seconds are marked is remarkably constant over all adjacency pairs (as well as other phenomena such as conversational repair; see as follows). These markings (some of which are described) have been documented for disagreements (Pomerantz, 1984; Holtgraves, 1997b), blamings (Atkinson & Drew, 1979), rejections (Davidson, 1984), and many other actions as well. The preferred-dispreferred construct appears to be a very general one. Table 4.1 displays preferred and dispreferred turns for several types of adjacency pairs.

Dispreferred seconds are marked in a variety of ways. Quite often they are delayed in some way; their preferred counterparts are not. To illustrate, compare the responses to the following two invitation sequences (both from Atkinson & Drew (1979, p. 58):

TABLE 4.1
Preferred and Dispreferred Adjacency Pair Seconds

First-Pair Part	Second-Pair Part	
	Preferred	*Dispreferred*
Assessment	Agreement*	Disagreement
Request	Acceptance	Refusal
Offer	Acceptance	Refusal
Blame	Denial	Admission
Question	Answer	Nonanswer

*Unless the assessment is a self-deprecation.

(3)   A: Why don't you come up and see me some // times?
      B: I would like to

(4)   A: Uh if you'd care to come over and visit a little while this morning
          then I'll give you a cup of coffee.
          B: hehh. Well that's awfully sweet of you, I don't think I can make it
          this morning .hh huhm I'm running an ad in the paper and—and uh I
          have to stay near the phone.

The acceptance (a preferred turn) in (3) is immediate, it actually overlaps with the
invitation. The refusal (a dispreferred turn) in (4) is delayed (hehh). In addition,
(4) illustrates the use of prefaces in dispreferred turns, in this case the inclusion of
a marker (Well) and appreciation (that's awfully sweet of you). The following
(from Pomerantz, 1984) also illustrates the delay and "well" marker of a dispreferred turn, in this case the nonanswer to a question.

(5)   A: An how's the <u>dre</u>sses coming along. How d'they <u>look</u>.
      B: *Well uh* I haven't been uh by there.

Other frequently used prefaces include token agreement (e.g., "Yeah, but . . .")
when disagreeing and apologies when refusing requests. The former is illustrated
here (from Holtgraves, 1997b).

(6)   A: And it's, I think, it's just like murder.
      J: *Yeah, but,* what about, I mean it's an unliked child, you know,
          because how many kids are beaten, because, you know, they . . .
      A: *Yeah, but* you know how many parents are are with well couples
          without children are, dying to have babies.

Frequently, the speaker of a dispreferred turn will provide an account so as
to explain why it is a dispreferred rather than preferred action that is being

performed, as can be seen in (4) and in (7). Dispreferred turns often will be indirect as in (7); preferred turns, in contrast, tend to be direct. Finally, dispreferred turns often will be marked in multiple ways as in (4) and (7). The following (from Wooten, 1981) illustrates the inclusion of a preface, account, appreciation, and indirectness:

(7)   B: She says you might want that dress I bought, I don't know whether
            you do.
       A: Oh thanks (well), let me see I really have a lot of dresses.

The systematic marking of dispreferred turns is a very basic feature of conversational interaction and provides independent criteria for categorizing different second-pair parts. But these markings have another very interesting feature; they illustrate the essentially collaborative nature of conversational interaction. Specifically, the delay or preface or account of a dispreferred turn indicates to the speaker of the first-pair part that the turn in progress is dispreferred. This delay, preface, or account thus provides an opportunity for the producer of the first-pair part, on recognizing that a dispreferred turn is underway, to revise or reformulate the first-pair part before the dispreferred second is completed.

In the following example (from Davidson, 1984), the first speaker, P, reformulates the offer immediately on hearing A's "well" preface.

(8)   P: Oh I mean uh: you wanna go to the store or anything over at the
            Market ⌈Basket or anything?⌉
       A: hhhhhhhhhhhhhhhhhh =
       A: =Well ho ⌈ney I-⌉
       P: Or Richard's?

A speaker of the first-pair part can facilitate this process by building into his turn postpositioned turn components, spaces that anticipate and orient to the possible rejection by the other. In the next example (Heritage, 1984, p. 277), there are two such places where the second speaker could provide a preferred turn (acceptance), once after "anything we can do," and again in his second turn after "shopping for her." In both instances, the acceptance is not forthcoming and H immediately expands or clarifies the offer in lines 3 and 6 in order to make it more concrete.

(9)   1 H: And we were wondering if there's anything
       2 we can do
       3 to help.
       4 S: [Well 'at's]
       5 H: I mean can we do any shopping for her
       6 or something like that?

In the following example (from Levinson, 1983; p. 320), C first provides a brief pause and then a two-second pause, both indicating an orientation to a possible dispreferred second. Consequently, C reformulates following the brief pause ("by any chance") and following the two-second pause ("probably not").

(10)   C: So I was wondering would you be in your office on Monday (.)
           by any chance?
       (2.0)
       C: Probably not
       R: Hmm yes =

People are clearly attuned to possible dispreferred turns, and they structure their utterances to avoid them if possible. In this way, one's turn at talk is impacted by the other as the turn unfolds. If there are indications that the next turn is dispreferred, then the current speaker can quickly change an utterance before it is completed. The speaker of the first-pair part can facilitate this process—increase the likelihood of receiving information regarding the possibility of a dispreferred turn—by building in postpositioned turn components and attending closely to the other's possible reactions. The orientation of people to dispreferred turns and the manner in which this orientation impacts language use illustrates clearly the coordination involved in conversation. More important, it illustrates how conversations are truly collaborative. Turns at talk are not isolated entities; their course can be influenced by the other person as the turns unfold. Conversations are joint products constructed on a moment-to-moment basis.

In conversation analysis, the nonequivalence of preferred and dispreferred turns is assumed to be independent of interactant's internal states; even if one very much wants to disagree with another person, the disagreement will still be often marked in some way. It is as if preference agreement has a life of its own. It is a general feature of the conversation system, a resource used by interactants as they converse. Because of this, no reference is made to the psychological states of the interactants.

But why do conversations have the preference structure that they seem to have? It seems reasonable that preference organization must be motivated in large part by concerns with face, as Brown and Levinson (1987), Heritage (1984), Lerner (1996), and others have argued. Note in this regard that the marking of dispreferred seconds bears a strong resemblance to many of Brown and Levinson's (1987) positive politeness strategies. For example, the expression of token agreement ("Yes, but . . ."), the use of "well" prefaces, mitigators, and indirectness in general are all instance of positive (and sometimes negative) politeness strategies. Although preference organization resides in the talk itself and not the people who produce it, it seems likely that the origin of this preference is the rudimentary respect for face that is required if an exchange is to take place at all (Goffman, 1967). All preferred turns are affiliative; they address positive face wants. If this were not the case, then one would expect an agreement to be the preferred response to all assessments. But this is not the case. If the first turn is a self-deprecation, then the preferred response is a disagreement, and an agreement is the dispreferred response (Pomerantz, 1984). To agree with a speaker's self-deprecation is nonaffiliative and threatens positive face. This preferred/dispreferred reversal illustrates how face concerns may motivate the form that preference agreement takes. Although preference agreement may be viewed as reflecting general properties of the conversational system, these regularities might also reflect interpersonal concerns.

The linking of actions with adjacency pairs provides a means of structuring talk throughout a conversation. Adjacency pairs are a conversational resource, and they are a resource that can be used by people for various conversational purposes. For example, as shown in the next section, adjacency pairs play an important role in the initiation and termination of conversations.

Opening and Closing Conversations

How do people begin a conversation? It seems relatively easy—at least with people we know. But it is not. Consider a few of the issues that must be dealt with in some manner. First, potential interactants must indicate to one another their availability and willingness to enter into a conversation. Second, there must be some recognition of with whom one will be conversing; the parties must recognize each other. Third, a topic must be brought up and sustained. And so on.

These problems are handled neatly and economically with a particular type of adjacency pair termed a summons-answer pair (Schegloff, 1968). A summons—the first-pair part—obliges an answer from the person to whom it is directed. A person who answers a summons has indicated availability for talk; refusing to respond indicates a lack of availability (and may be grounds for making inferences about the person who has failed to respond). If there is some doubt about availability, the summons may be repeated after a short delay. Note that a telephone ring is a summons, and its ring-pause-ring sequence simulates the verbal summons-pause-summons sequence.

Summons-answer sequences are different from other adjacency pairs in that something always follows them; they have implications beyond the two turns of which they are comprised. This is because the person issuing the summons is obligated to respond to the answerer. Thus, the summons-answer sequence, at a minimum, has a three-turn format. A common variation here is for the second-pair part—the answer—to be phrased as a question (e.g., "What is it?") in which case it simultaneously serves as the first-pair part of another adjacency pair, thereby obligating a subsequent move from the other person. In telephone conversations, the answer to a summons (the telephone ring) is most often the first-pair part of a greeting exchange, thereby making a return greeting conditionally relevant.

Telephone conversations, because of the lack of physical copresence, require some sort of identification procedure so that interactants know with whom they are talking (Schegloff, 1979). Mutual recognition is required; both the caller and answerer must identify each other. Consider how this is accomplished. Many times the caller's first turn speaking will be a return greeting, and often this greeting serves to indicate to the other party that she has been identified, as in (11). Also, it is in this slot that a caller may identify herself, if she chooses to do so. But callers frequently do not identify themselves, with the failure to identify serving as a claim that the other should be able to recognize the speaker from the voice sample alone. Examples such as the following (from Schegloff, 1979) are not uncommon:

(11) (ring)
      A: Hell*o::*
      C: *Hi::::.*
      A: oh: *hi::* 'ow are you Agne::s,

Of course if these claims are problematic (i.e., the answerer does not recognize who is calling), then this will usually be indicated quickly with a pause, request for clarification (" 'Who is this?' "), and/or failure to return the greeting, as in the following (from Schegloff, 1979):

(12) (ring)
      A: Hello?
      C: Hello
      (1.5)
      A: Who's this?

If the caller is unsure of the answer's identity, then the caller's first turn will often take the form of a try-marked address term (Schegloff, 1979), as in (13).

(13) (ring)
      A: Hello?
      B: Connie?
      A: Yeah Joanie

In this example, the try-marked term is verified by the answerer. Simultaneously, in that turn the answerer has indicated identification of the caller, thereby preempting the need for the caller to self-identify.

In general, there appears to be a preference for the identification procedure to function without interactants paying explicit attention to the process; other-recognition is preferred over self-identification (Schegloff, 1979). Why? Well, there is the matter of economy—conversational resources (which are scarce) will not need to be used for recognition. This process is possible because simple one-word turns can perform multiple acts. Consider again a prototypical (made up) telephone opening:

(14)   1. Phone rings
       2. Hello?
       3. Hi.
       4. Hi.

This sequence has brought two people in contact, each displaying their availability to talk and indicating their recognition of one another. These minimal units accomplish all of this through their sequential patterning and the fact that multiple adjacency pairs are overlaid on one another. Note also that the interactional work that must be performed at the beginning of a conversation makes multiple acts more likely here. So, Turn 2 is an answer to a summons (adjacency pair 1), a greeting (adjacency pair 2), and a display for recognition. Turn 3 is a return greeting (adjacency pair 2), claim that the other has been recognized, and a display for recognition by the other.

The use of adjacency pairs provides an economical means for beginning a conversation. But it may not be exclusively a matter of economics. There are also strong interpersonal reasons for this system, just as there are for the structure of preference agreement. Mutual, implicit recognition is obviously more economical than explicit identification, but it is also a marker of relationship closeness (positive politeness). To begin a conversation with each person recognizing the other without any explicit identification process implicates a relatively high degree of familiarity between the parties. Again, conversational structure reflects both system and interpersonal processes.

Closing a conversation presents obstacles similar to those involved in opening a conversation, and these also must be handled with care. The final portion of a conversation is usually a terminal exchange (e.g., bye-bye). Again, an adjacency pair is being used, and again the second-pair part serves to indicate the speaker's awareness of what is being accomplished by the first speaker. But one can't just end a conversation. This can happen, of course, but when it does it is often marked with an account of some sort (e.g., "I hear the baby; I've got to run."). The general tendency is to gradually close down the conversation. And, as with openings, there are both economical and interpersonal reasons for this.

First, people may still have topics that they want to talk about. To simply end a conversation with a terminal exchange would prevent participants from having the opportunity to mention some topic that had not yet been talked about. A device that provides an opportunity for this possibility is a preclosing move, or more accurately, a possible preclosing (Levinson, 1983). A preclosing (e.g., "well", "So . . . ," "OK") occupies an entire turn and serves as a "pass," indicating that the speaker has nothing new (at this point) to add. Sometimes the preclosing will be initiated by mentioning the initial topic or reason for the call ("Well, I just wanted to see how you were doing"), a move that serves to frame the encounter as a separate unit (Sacks & Schegloff, 1979). A preclosing breaks with a prior topic, thereby suspending any rules regarding topical coherence and allowing the next speaker to bring up an entirely new topic. And she may do just that, with the conversation then proceeding for a number of turns. Or, she may acknowledge the preclosing with an acknowledgment of her own (e.g., "Yeah," "OK, so . . ."). This serves to indicate an understanding of the first speaker's move and acceptance of it, and hence permission to initiate the terminal exchange. Thus, the prototypical (made up) closing looks something like (15):

(15) A: OK
     B: OK
     A: Bye
     B: Bye

A second motivation for the negotiated manner in which conversations are brought to a close is interpersonal. Simply ending a conversation can be offensive to the other person. It represents a threat to the positive face of the other person, because it is a dramatic severing of the momentary bond constituted by the current exchange. Preclosings and adjacency pair terminations allow this predicament to be handled mutually, so that neither interactant feels particularly threatened by the closing of the talk. Things can go wrong, of course. One may preemptively end an exchange. But to do so is impolite and grounds for inferences of brusqueness on the part of the person who does so. Note also that the interpersonal variables discussed in chapter 2 may play a role here. There has been little research in this vein because conversation analytic researchers purposefully exclude consideration of such variables. But one might reasonably expect, for example, a higher status participant to be more likely to unilaterally end a conversation, and to do so with greater impunity, than a participant who is relatively lower in status.

Presequences

Adjacency pairs represent a fundamental, if not *the* fundamental unit of conversations. They capture, in a very basic way, the interlocking nature of a stretch of talk. In its simplest and most basic form an adjacency pair represents two contiguous turns at talk. But they can be expanded, as we've seen, with the inclusion of an insertion sequence. Adjacency pairs also underlie longer sequences of talk, sequences that display many of the same properties of adjacency pairs. Levinson (1983) refers to these as presequences, and they have a number of interesting properties.

We have already seen how adjacency pairs are used in preclosings to negotiate the termination of a conversation. Another common type of presequence is a preannouncement, a tightly structured set of adjacency pairs that prefigure an extended turn (for the telling of a story, news, gossip, etc.) by one of the interactants. Preannouncements can be viewed as two superimposed adjacency pairs, with the second part of the first pair simultaneously functioning as the first-pair part of the second pair. Consider the following exchange (reported in Levinson, 1983, p. 349):

(16)   D: Heh, you'll never guess what your dad is lookih-is lookin' at.
       R: What are you looking at?
       D: A radar range.

Turn 1 is a check on the newsworthiness of the potential announcement and is the first part of the first adjacency pair. Turn 2 both validates the newsworthiness (the second part of the first adjacency pair) and requests that the information be told (the first part of the second pair). Turn 3 provides the announcement and is the second part of the second adjacency pair.

Note the interlocking nature of the sequence, with Turn 2 orienting both backwards to the prior turn and forward to the subsequent turn. The sequence structures a stretch of talk, and not just the presequence but the talk that will follow. Preannouncements are a means of securing an extended turn at talk (see turn taking following). They are also motivated by a general preference for not communicating information that is already known by one's interlocutors; preannouncements thus serve as a check on the Gricean (1975) maxim of quantity (do not be overinformative).

Other presequences include prerequests and preinvitations, both of which display the same structure. Position 1 is a check on the precondition for the act to be performed, and Position 2 provides an answer regarding that precondition. Position 3 is the prefigured act (i.e., request or invitation), contingent on the preconditions holding in Position 2. Finally, Position 4 is the acceptance/compliance. Examples of a preinvitation and prerequest, respectively, follow.

(17)   (From Atkinson & Drew, 1979, p. 253)
       A: Whatch doin'?
       B: Nothin'
       A: Wanna drink?
(18)   (From Merritt, 1976, p. 357)
       C: Do you have hot chocolate?
       S: mmhmm
       C: Can I have hot chocolate with whipped cream?
       S: Sure (leaves to get)

Prerequest sequences provide an alternative approach to the issue of how best to characterize indirect requests (as discussed in chap. 1). Following Levinson (1983), this analysis proceeds as follows. In general, a prerequest sequence is utilized to check on the potential obstacles that would prevent the recipient from complying with the request (see also Gibbs, 1986; Francik & Clark, 1985); their use is motivated by a desire to avoid an action that would be followed by a dispreferred second. Thus, the first position of the sequence is usually an attempt to assess the likelihood of the request succeeding, as in (18). In this way, the first speaker can avoid making a request that would be likely to result in refusal (a dispreferred second). Alternatively, Position 1 may elicit an offer from the other interactant, a preferable situation insofar as it eliminates the need to even make the request. In this view, the issue of whether or not indirect requests have literal and indirect forces does not arise. Rather, the turns in a prerequest sequence simply have literal meanings that prefigure a set of alternative responses. But note that face management is the likely motivation for a prerequest sequence, just as it is for indirect requests.

Adjacency Pairs and Speech Act Theory

The conversation analytic view of adjacency pairs is a view of language use as action, and more importantly, as joint action. As an action-based view of language, it both shares certain features with speech act theory, and extends it in important ways. In speech act theory the emphasis is on illocutionary force, or the action that the speaker performs with an utterance. In conversation analysis the utterances making up adjacency pairs are also viewed as actions. But with adjacency pairs, unlike speech acts, the emphasis is on *joint* (rather than individual) action. A single individual cannot perform an adjacency pair, it must be performed by two different people who are orienting to each other's actions. In contrast, the emphasis in speech act theory has been on the action performed with a single utterance by a single individual (though see Searle, 1990). But does not the successful performance of a speech act require some ratification by the recipient that the intended act has been performed? If I say "I bet $5 the Yankees win the series" and you ignore me, have I successfully placed a bet (even if all the preconditions for betting are met)? One of the most important features of adjacency pairs is the emphasis on the second-pair part as an indicator of the recipient's understanding (or lack thereof) of the act performed with the first-pair part.

But note that the speech act and adjacency pair concepts are not incompatible; for some adjacency pairs, the felicity conditions underlying the performance of the first-pair part link up quite nicely with the felicity conditions underlying the second-pair part (Clark, 1985). Consider, for example, the request-promise adjacency pair depicted below.

First-pair part (Request)	Second-pair part (Promise)
Bob: Can you type my term paper?	Tom: I'll do it tonight.
Preparatory: Bob believes Tom is able to type the term paper.	Tom is able to type the term paper.
Sincerity: Bob wants Tom to type it.	Tom intends to type the paper.

Propositional Content: Bob predicates   Tom predicates a future act of Tom.
a future act of Tom.

Essential: Utterance counts as an   Utterance counts as an obligation
attempt to get Tom to type   to type the paper.
the paper.

Each of the felicity conditions underlying the request has a complimentary felicity condition underlying the promise.

TURN TAKING AND REPAIR

One of the most amazing features of conversations is how orderly they are. Usually, one speaker speaks at a time, and speaker transitions occur with little or no overlap. Moreover, this orderliness occurs regardless of the number of speakers, the size of the turns, the topic of the conversation, and so on. How is this possible?

In a seminal article, Sacks, Schegloff, and Jefferson (1974) proposed a model to account for turn-taking regularity. In general, their model can be viewed as a system for allocating in the fairest and most economical manner a scarce conversational resource, turns at talk. There are two components in the model. The first is termed the turn-constructional component, a feature that specifies what constitutes a turn. Turns can vary in length, from a single word or partial word to a complete utterance, but they all have the characteristic of projectability; once begun, it generally becomes known what type of turn is underway and what it will take to complete it. In general, projectability is assumed to be determined by the intonational and syntactic properties of the turn. That talk has this feature can be seen by the fact that sequentially appropriate starts by the next speaker occur after single-word turns with no significant gap. Interactants apparently have the ability to identify the end of a turn (termed a transition-relevance place).

The second component of the model is the turn allocation component, or the techniques used for the allocation of turns within a conversation. Turn selection is accomplished by either "self-selection" or "current speaker selects next speaker." This process is governed by three rules along the following lines:

1. If at the first possible transition point, the current speaker uses the "current speaker selects next" technique, he selects the next speaker who is then obligated to take the turn at that point (as with adjacency pairs).
2. If, at the first possible transition point, the current speaker does not use the "current speaker selects next" technique, then the "self-selection" technique becomes operative allowing the first speaker to hold the floor.
3. If, at the first possible transition point, the current speaker does not use the "current speaker selects next" technique, then she may, but need not, continue unless another self-selects.

These rules are ordered such that Rule 1 takes precedence over Rule 2, and Rule 2 over Rule 3. They are also cyclical such that if Rule 3 applies and current speaker continues talking, then Rules 1 through 3 reapply at the next transition relevance place.

This model allows for variation in turn size and number of parties. In other words, it is managed both locally (not specified in advance) and interactionally (it arises out of the interaction process itself). These rules certainly describe some of the most basic facts about turn taking. To wit, usually only one speaker speaks at a time (thus, some rule system is being followed), but when overlap does occur, it occurs at places that would be predicted by the rules. For example, overlap most frequently occurs as competing first starts (Rule 2 is operative), and at possible transition relevance places (supporting the idea of a turn constructional unit).

There is some debate about the nature and significance of these turn-taking rules. For example, are people generally aware of them? No. Similar to the rules of grammar, they are, for the most part, outside of conscious awareness. Are they causal, then, in the sense that grammatical rules are causal? Searle (1992) argues that they are not. In fact, he argues that they are not rules at all, having no intentional component. Turn taking is clearly patterned and systematic (it is not random), but not because people are following these particular rules. In other words, these rules might *describe* turn-taking regularity (but so could any number of other rule systems), but they do not *explain* it.

Conversation analytic theorists maintain, however, that these rules are more than merely descriptive. Schegloff (1992a) argues that although the rules may not cause or bring about actions, the rules are displayed or discoverable in the action. That is, as people converse, they display an orientation to these rules, they are sensitive to their violation, and they undertake actions designed to get the turn-taking system back on track.

This, then, is an ethnomethodological conception of rules; rules are discoverable in the actions of people. But because of this, it is very difficult to empirically test this model. For example, according to the model, turn taking should occur at transition relevance places, and transition relevance places are assumed to be identifiable in advance (turns project to their completion points). But people sometimes start talking before another has finished. To account for this, it is actually claimed only that people are orienting to *possible* transition relevance places, rather than actual ones (Schegloff, 1992a). If stated in this way, this aspect of their rule system is not really falsifiable. But, then, producing a falsifiable model was not really the developers' intent.

It should be noted that there are alternative approaches to turn taking (e.g., Argyle, 1973; Duncan & Fiske, 1977; Kendon, 1967). Many of these approaches are based on the idea that turn taking is regulated via a signaling procedure. Speakers are assumed to signal their intent to relinquish a turn; other participants are assumed to signal their intent to occupy the next turn. The signal most frequently invoked here is gaze. For example, a speaker will signal that he intends to relinquish the speaker role by returning his gaze to the next speaker (Argyle, 1973). This position is undermined somewhat by the fact that turn taking seems to be quite orderly even when signaling via gaze is eliminated, as in telephone conversations. Although it is clear that gaze does play a signaling role in conversational exchanges, signals alone do not seem capable of explaining the orderliness of turn taking.

Repair

One of the ways in which people are said to display their orientation to the turn-taking system is by how they repair the system when it momentarily breaks down. Consider, for example, instances of overlapping talk. This might seem to indicate a failure on the part of the turn-taking rule system. But, as Jefferson (1986) has shown, overlapping speech is itself quite orderly. In the first place, much overlapping talk does not occur at random points in a conversation, but instead at transition relevance places. Moreover, when overlapping talk does occur, the repair system is quickly engaged; either one speaker will rapidly drop out, or if this does not happen, an allocation system will kick in whereby the speaker who upgrades the most (e.g., increased volume) wins the floor. Regardless of how this is settled, the overlapped turn will then be repeated by the remaining speaker.

The notion of repair has received considerable attention from conversation analytic researchers, an attention that is warranted by the fact that the conversation repair system appears to be generalizable over conversational problems (e.g., mishearing, misunderstanding, incorrect word selection, etc.). Conversational repair, like turn taking, preference structure, and adjacency pairs, is part of a conversational system, a resource that is available to conversationalists. In another important paper, Schegloff, Jefferson, and Sacks (1977) outlined a number of important features of this system. First, they made a distinction between the repair itself and the initiation of the repair. The latter, termed a next-turn repair initiator (NTRI) refers to phrases (e.g., "huh?"), questions (e.g., "What do you mean?"), repetitions of the preceding turn, nonverbal gestures, and so on that may serve as prompts for the undertaking of a repair.

Second, repairs and repair initiations can be undertaken either by the speaker or by the other interactant. These two distinctions result in a fourfold scheme of repair types: self-initiated self-repair, self-initiated other repair, other-initiated self-repair, other-initiated other repair. Finally, repairs can be classified in terms of when they occur. Repairs can occur in the turn that is problematic (Position 1 repair), in the transition space or turn following the problematic turn (Position 2 repair), or two turns after the problematic turn (Position 3 repair). Note that turns need not be adjacent here; insertion sequences may separate them. Repairs later than the third position are extremely rare (but see Schegloff, 1992b on fourth-position repairs) and for good reason. The system is structured so that trouble will be repaired as quickly as possible in order to decrease the likelihood of subsequent organizational problems (e.g., the difficulty involved in backtracking in order to deal with an earlier problem).

In addition to early repair, the system clearly favors self-repair over other repair. In other words, conversational repair displays a preference structure, with the least-preferred options being marked in various ways. The most preferred is self-initiated self-repair in first or second position, followed by other-initiated self-repair in Position 2, and finally, other-initiated other repair in Position 2 (Levinson, 1983). Note that the structural preference for early repair increases the likelihood of self-repair (early repair can only be undertaken by the speaker). If self-repair does not occur, the recipient will often provide a brief delay, thereby providing the speaker one last opportunity to repair. Finally, even when other repair is possible, there is a preference for the recipient to use a NTRI and hence only initiate a repair, allowing the speaker to perform the actual repair to correct the problem. In the following example (from Schegloff, Jefferson, & Sacks, 1977, p 370), the recipient B delays her response for one second, thereby providing A an opportunity to self-correct. When this fails to occur, B then initiates repair, which A undertakes.

(19) A: Hey the first time they stopped me from sellin' cigarettes was this morning.
      (1.)
      B: From selling cigarettes?
      A: From buying cigarettes.

Conversational repair, like the other structural regularities discussed in this chapter, is generally viewed by conversation analytic researchers as constituting a conversational system, a system designed to facilitate communication. Again, there are also strong interpersonal reasons for the form that repairs take. Both self-repair and early repair are more efficient than other repair and later repair. But self-repair also minimizes or eliminates both the negative and positive face threat that can be implied when correcting another person. And early repair (Position 1 or 2), because it can only be undertaken by the speaker, can also be interpreted in this way.

Extended Turns at Talk

During the course of a conversation people will sometimes hold the floor for an extended period of time, telling jokes and stories and gossip, and so on. Like openings and closings, taking the floor for an extended period of time presents certain problems for interactants, and again, these problems are both system oriented and interpersonally oriented.

First, to hold the floor for an extended period of time requires a temporary suspension of the turn-taking system. Everyone involved must understand that an extended turn is underway, such that bids for the floor at transition relevance places are put on hold until the extended turn is completed. This does not mean that others cannot speak during the extended turn; they do participate in various ways, particularly in terms of providing feedback and demonstrating appreciation. Then, once an extended turn is complete, the turn-taking system must be reengaged. That this routinely happens suggests that interactants can tell when a story is complete. Stories appear to have the feature of projectability, just like single turns at talk.

Second, conversation turns can be viewed as a scarce resource, and thus an extended turn at talk represents a monopoly of this resource. Consequently, an extended turn at talk will often involve a justification of some sort. Accordingly, speakers often attempt to make a story relevant in some way for the conversation. Of course, this is an issue for any turn at talk (see as follows), but it is particularly important for stories because of their potential extended duration. There appears to be a distinct preference for the introduction of stories at points in the conversation where they would fit (Schegloff & Sacks, 1973). Stories, it seems, are usually "locally occasioned," triggered by something in the conversation or the environment (Jefferson, 1978; Schenkein, 1978).

So, the potential speaker of an extended turn needs to make it clear that a story is underway, and hence that the turn-taking system is temporarily suspended, that the story is in some way connected with their conversation, and so on. Interactants must align themselves into the teller and recipient roles (Sacks, 1992) and mutually agree that a joint project is underway (Clark, 1996a). Often this is accomplished with some version of a preannouncement, as discussed earlier. Preannouncements are a set of adjacency pairs that prefigure an extended turn. Frequently they deal with the issue of whether the recipients have heard the story, joke, or gossip. In general, there is a concern about not telling people things they already know (e.g., Sacks & Schegloff, 1979), a concern that makes sense in terms of attempting to hold the floor for an extended period of time. A crucial point here is that interactants must *mutually* agree to the extended turn. Lack of agreement (e.g., that the recipient has already heard it) will short-circuit the attempt, as in the following example (from Clark, 1996a, p. 347):

(20)   C: Did I tell you, when we were in this African village, and *—they
           were all out in the fields,—the*
       I: yes you did, yes—yes*
       C: babies left alon,—
       I: yes

An extended turn is usually followed by a response sequence, including moves designed to show appreciation of the story (e.g., commenting on its significance), the joke (laughter), the gossip (e.g., indignation), and so on. Structurally, such moves are designed, in part, to move the conversation forward. For example, in some conversations the telling of a story by one person occasions the telling of a story by another person (Jefferson, 1978; Ryave, 1978); the conversation consists of a round of stories. Generally, the stories that people tell will bear some relationship to each other. Sometimes they will be on the same topic and share a common referent (e.g., stories about bosses). Other times, they may be topically different, but related in terms of the significance or point of the story (Ryave, 1978).

Finally, note how the structural features of extended turns also have implications for the interactants' face. Holding the floor for an extended turn is presumptuous; it presumes the speaker has a right to this scarce resource and thus threatens the face of the other interactants by restricting their opportunity to speak (their freedom is threatened). The alignment procedures used to take an extended turn (e.g., justifying the turn) are probably motivated, in part, by face-management concerns. The response sequence following an extended turn also activates interpersonal issues. Consider, for example, reactions to jokes. Obviously, one is supposed to laugh, but the timing of one's laughter can be problematic (Sacks, 1974). Timing is crucial here, as inferences of stupidity may result if laughter is delayed.

CONVERSATIONAL COHERENCE

The tendency of stories to be related reflects a very general feature of conversations. This is that most conversations appear to cohere on a topic or a set of topics. Interestingly, conversations are generally not planned in advance, and hence, conversational coherence is an emergent property. Obviously, people can bring agendas and topics they want to talk about to a conversation, but the specific manner in which these things will get talked about emerges on a turn-by-turn basis as the conversation unfolds. In other words, one cannot specify in advance what people will say during the course of a conversation. So, what happens? How is it that (reasonably) coherent conversations are usually achieved?

The notion of conversation topic is ambiguous; there is really no agreed-on definition regarding the manner in which utterances can be viewed as being related. There is, of course, a large literature on text grammar dealing with the manner in which sentences within a discourse are related or connected to each other (e.g., Givon, 1989; Grimes, 1975; Halliday & Hassan, 1976). This research has dealt with both referential coherence (the manner in which referents are referred to again in a discourse) and topical coherence (the manner in which a set of sentences in a discourse can be said to be "about" a common topic), as well as the manner in which coherence is linguistically realized. There is also a large and influential literature within cognitive psychology dealing with the cognitive operations involved in the comprehension of narrative or expository text. The emphasis in this research is on the inferential processing required of readers in forming a coherent representation of a text (Gernsbacher, 1990; Graesser et al., 1994; Kintsch & van Dijk, 1978).

Certain aspects of discourse comprehension and text grammar (e.g., the given-new distinction) are relevant for understanding conversational coherence. But in the end, conversational coherence is a very different animal than cohesiveness in a text. This is because conversational coherence is achieved by two people (rather than a single writer) interacting in real time in a specific context. Coherence is something that is created on the spot and may be visible only to those involved in the conversation (due to the use of elliptical expressions, etc.).

In one sense conversational coherence is not really a problem at all. If conversational relevance is assumed (Grice, 1975), then all conversation utterances will be heard by participants as being somehow relevant to what has gone before (e.g., see Sperber & Wilson, 1986). Thus, regardless of how incoherent and off-the-wall a contribution might seem, the recipient will usually interpret the utterance as if it was relevant.

Still, conversationalists do seem to be oriented to some sort of topic continuation rule. For example, many times people seem to position their topic introductions so that a connection with prior turns can be made by others. This type of topic shading allows a prior topic of talk to serve as a resource for the raising of a new topic, such that the new topic will be heard as relevant to the prior topic (Schegloff & Sacks, 1973). Sometimes shifts of this sort will be marked in various ways, as with embedded repetitions (e.g., "Speaking of the dean, I heard that . . .") and disjunct markers (e.g., "Oh, that reminds me . . .") (Jefferson, 1978). Sometimes topics discussed earlier will be reintroduced, and these reintroductions will often be marked as well (e.g., "Anyway . . . ;" "Like I was saying . . ."; Keenan & Schiefflin, 1976). And when completely new topics are introduced, they too are quite likely to be marked, for example, with disjunct markers (e.g., "One more thing . . . ;" "Incidentally . . .").

Experimental evidence in support of a topic continuation rule also exists. For example, Vuchinich (1977) recorded the conversations of two students in a get-acquainted session. One of the students, however, was actually an experimental confederate who, at various times during the conversation, produced abrupt, incoherent topic shifts that were not marked by the speaker in any way. The other (real) participants displayed their orientation to a topic continuation rule in their responses. The unmarked shifts often resulted in the initiation of a repair sequence: "Huh?" "What?" "Why are you saying that?" Also, such shifts often resulted in a noticeable gap, with a mean latency of 2.8 seconds versus a mean latency of .6 seconds following a cohesive turn.

Participants were probably attempting, with the pause, to give the speaker an opportunity to make the relevance of the contribution clear. Noncohesive turns were also more likely to result in topic termination than were cohesive turns. Finally, in postexperimental interviews all participants indicated they had been aware of the topic shift, even when their conversational responses did not display an orientation to the shift.

Conversation coherence is an extremely elusive construct. It is one of those things that no one can define, yet everyone can recognize. People agree quite highly, for example, regarding how to segment conversations into topics (Planalp & Tracy, 1980). Yet no one has really been able to define conversational coherence in a formal manner, and it has stymied researchers in conversation analysis, artificial intelligence, linguistics, philosophy, and so on. This is clearly an important and wide-open avenue for future research.

Researchers in disciplines other than conversation analysis have investigated various aspects of conversation structure, including conversation coherence. Most notable in this regard is a set of topics and techniques referred to as discourse analysis. Although there is some overlap between discourse analysis and conversation analysis, methodologically they are quite different (Levinson, 1983). Unlike their conversation analytic counterparts, discourse analysts will undertake the detailed examination of stretches of talk using a variety of sources of information (e.g., the social context, talk occurring later in the conversation, conversationalists' possible motivations) that are not part of the talk itself. Discourse analysis is rather eclectic (unlike conversation analysis) and includes a wide variety of approaches and techniques that have yielded important findings regarding conversation and written discourse (e.g., see van Dijk, 1998).

Much of this research has examined conversational structure within a particular conversational activity. Thus, there are studies of the organization of classroom talk (Sinclair & Coulthard, 1975), therapy talk (Labov & Fanschel, 1977), arguments (Jacobs & Jackson, 1982; Rips, Brem, & Bailenson, 1999), marital communication (Gottman, 1979), and so on. Although some of the research emphasizes how genre determines structure (e.g., the structure of talk in a classroom is heavily influenced by the situational context), other research programs have implications beyond the specific verbal activity examined. Two examples will be considered briefly here: Labov and Fanschel's (1977) work on therapy talk and the artificial intelligence approaches of Schank (1977) and Reichman (1985).

Labov and Fanschel's Therapeutic Discourse

Labov and Fanschel's detailed analysis of 15 minutes of a psychotherapy session is a prototype of discourse analysis and notable for its attempt to incorporate within speech act theory both interpersonal and sequential considerations. These researchers assume that utterances involve the simultaneous performance of multiple acts, a specific speech act, and depending on the context and type of speech act, an interpersonal act (or acts).

Talk is viewed as being structured both vertically and horizontally. Vertical structure involves the relation between utterances and actions and is described in terms of rules of production and interpretation. There are, for example, rules for interpreting indirect requests, and these are quite similar to the rules described in chapter 1 for performing indirect requests (e.g., Gordon & Lakoff, 1975). Another rule specifies when and how assertions function as questions. Specifically, an assertion made by the speaker about a topic known only to the hearer will be interpreted by the hearer as a request for confirmation about the topic in question. Some of the proposed rules deal with interpersonal acts. For example, a request that is repeated will be interpreted as a challenge to the recipient's competence. This is obviously similar to a face-management view of requests. But with a difference. The challenge in this case comes not from the request so much (although a single request can also function as a challenge if it involves an act that the recipient should have performed) but from the fact that the request is repeated. Thus, the threat made to the recipient's face emerges over a sequence of moves.

Horizontal structure involves the relation between chains of utterances and the actions they perform, and these are described in terms of sequencing rules. It is the actions (what is done) that are structured via these rules rather than the utterances themselves (what is said). Thus, understanding the structure of conversations involves both rules of interpretation (utterance → action) and sequencing rules (action → action). This is in direct contrast to conversation analysis, where the exclusive focus is on the surface meaning of utterances (or what is said).

Consider, again, a repeated request. An interpretation rule specifies that a repeated request will be heard as a challenge to the recipient's competence. According to sequencing rules, the options open to the recipient are either to acquiesce to this characterization or attempt to defend against it. Or consider an indirect request (the result of a specific interpretation rule). One can comply with the request, of course. But there are other possibilities. Sequencing rules, for example, allow people to put off requests by requesting additional information, relaying the request to someone else, challenging the requester's right to make the request, and so on. Importantly, these means of putting off requests are related to the conditions presupposed in the request itself (e.g., the recipient's ability), as well as to the interpersonal underpinnings of the act (e.g., the speaker's right to make the request). In this way, one gets sequential chains of speech acts based on the meshing of the felicity conditions and the interpersonal implications of the act.

Labov and Fanschel's research demonstrates the role of interpersonal actions in structuring talk and, hence, how those implications are revealed in a stretch of talk. Note that in contrast to politeness theory (chap. 2), the emphasis here is on a sequence of talk rather than a single utterance. On the other hand, the results of this research are limited and involve only a very restricted set of actions, primarily requests and the responses to them. The methodology itself can be criticized for being overinterpretative; the researchers use information in their analysis that was not available to the interactants themselves (e.g., Levinson, 1983). In fact, whether these rules and categories have any psychological reality is an open question. In many ways, this represents an important but unfulfilled approach to conversation structure.

Artificial Intelligence Approaches to Conversational Structure

For a number of years, researchers in artificial intelligence have attempted to simulate human language use. Much of this research has been concerned with modeling sentence comprehension. But some researchers, Roger Schank and Rachel Reichman in particular, have been concerned with modeling larger stretches of talk.

Schank (1977), for instance, has attempted to model conversation coherence with a set of production rules that specify what counts as an appropriate response to a prior utterance. These rules exist for both objects and actions. An example of an object rule is as follows: if an utterance introduces a new object, then one appropriate response is to ask where the object came from. If a person says "I just bought a new car," an appropriate reply would be "Where did you get it?" An example of an event rule is: if a person describes an event, then one appropriate response is to ask what happened next. So, a reasonable reply to "I was arrested last night" would be something like "Did you spend the night in jail?"

Shank's approach is intuitively reasonable, but obviously of limited value. It specifies some properties of concepts that can explain how two utterances about that concept are related. But it does not appear to be an exhaustive set of rules. Also, the approach is completely asocial (the interpersonal implications of utterances are ignored) and deals only with adjacent turns (the relation between nonadjacent turns is ignored).

A broader and somewhat more promising approach was developed by Rachel Reichman (1978, 1985). Although similar to other artificial intelligence approaches to modeling task-related conversations, her model is a general one and presumably relevant for any conversational activity. The most important feature of her model is the treatment of conversations as having a hierarchical structure. This assumption allows for capturing an aspect of conversational structure that is largely missed in the major approaches discussed so far (i.e., speech act theory, politeness theory, conversation analysis).

In Reichman's model, conversation utterances can either embellish and continue what has previously been said, or they can begin a new communicative act. The latter are referred to as conversational moves, and they are often marked with cue words specifying their discourse function such as support (e.g., because . . . ; like when . . .), restatement or conclusion (e.g., so . . .), interruption (e.g., by the way . . .), indirect challenges (e.g., yes, but . . .), direct challenges (e.g., No, but . . .). And so on. Now, conversations consist of a sequence of utterances, but this temporal sequence represents only a surface structure. At a deeper level, conversations consist of a hierarchically structured set of "context spaces," or a group of utterances referring to a single episode or issue. All context spaces contain the utterances (and inferences if necessary) that define the context space, as well as slots specifying context type, context function (the method used to perform the move and its relation to the context space), context status (whether the context space is active [or current]), and so on.

The underlying structure of a conversation is specified by the set of relations existing between the context spaces. It is assumed that conversational structure is based on a set of discourse rules in much the same way that sentence generation is based on a linguistic rule system. The overarching rule here is Grice's (1975) maxim of relation (be relevant), which underlies the possible relations that can exist between context spaces. Relevance can be achieved in various ways. One can contribute to the same topic, or one can introduce a new concept, idea, and so on as long as it bears some sort of structural relation (e.g., supports, contradicts, illustrates, etc.) to the active context space. It is important to note also that an utterance can be relevant for a context space occurring earlier in a conversation, rather than the currently active space (although a surface marking of this relation would be required).

Reichman's model does reasonably well at modeling certain types of talk; whether it describes how humans actually produce and comprehend conversational utterances is unknown. It does seem that her model applies best to certain types of conversations, in particular arguments in which speakers take extended turns to develop their points; in certain respects her model parallels the work of others on the structure of arguments (Jacobs & Jackson, 1982). Also, like Schank's approach, there is no concern with the interpersonal features of talk and how such features might structure conversations.

CONCLUSION

That conversations are structured is obvious; how this structure comes about is something of a mystery. Capturing the manner in which conversation turns are sequentially related has proved to be a very difficult task (Slugoski & Hilton, in press). Currently there does not exist a grammar of conversation in the sense that there exists a grammar for individual sentences. Clearly, a linear sequence (or finite state grammar) is not appropriate, given the possibility of embedding, side sequences, topic recycling, and so on. Conversations appear to be too contextualized and idiosyncratic to allow for a formal grammar.

But researchers working within the discipline of conversation analysis have made some headway with this issue. Like speech act theory, conversation analysis views language use as action. Unlike speech act theory, the actions performed with talk are not characterizable in terms of interactants' abstract intentions. Intentions are irrelevant. Language use is action (and it is social action) in the sense that its occurrence has implications for what follows—implications for one's own actions and those of one's interlocutors.

This emphasis on sequential implicativeness is one of the most, if not *the* most, important contribution of conversation analysis. And as such it represents an important correction to the primarily single-utterance-based approaches (speech act theory and politeness theory) covered so far. In converation analysis, an utterance performs an action based not so much on any inherent characteristics of the utterance itself but on its placement in a sequence of utterances. For example, an answer cannot be defined in terms of syntactic, phonological, logical, or semantic features—only by its placement in a sequence of utterances.

The principle of sequential implicativeness has implications for many of the phenomena discussed earlier in this book. The adjacency pair construct, for example, provides an important addition to Grice's (1975) ideas regarding conversational implicature. According to Grice, violation of the cooperative principle results in conversational inferencing. But as we've seen, what constitutes a violation of the cooperative principle is somewhat ambiguous. With adjacency pairs, the impetus for conversational inferencing is clearer—failure to provide an expected second-pair part. More importantly, when this happens, the failure to provide the expected part is usually marked, and these markings might play a role in comprehension, facilitating recognition of a nonliteral meaning. For example, when people provide an indirect reply to a question, the nonliteral meaning of the reply can be recognized more quickly if it is marked with a "well" preface or if it is preceded by a delay (Holtgraves, 2000). In this way, a dispreferred marker provides the recipient with evidence that she should search for an ulterior meaning. And because dispreferred turns are often face threatening, they may guide the recipient to a face-threatening interpretation of the utterance. The structure of adjacency pairs and marking of dispreferred turns specify more clearly how the conversational inferencing process described by Grice (1975) might actually work.

Preference organization also reveals the essentially collaborative nature of talk, a point that will be discussed in more detail in the next chapter. People orient to possible dispreferred seconds, and any signal that one is forthcoming can prompt the speaker to alter the act being performed in midturn. Speakers, in formulating their utterances, build in opportunities (e.g., brief pauses) for others to provide such signals. This responsiveness to feedback from others suggests the speech act view of an intention giving rise to the performance of an act may be too simple. The act that is ultimately performed may, on occasion, be a function of the interactants' joint communicative intentions.

Although not considered by conversation analysts, certain features of conversational structure have clear implications for the interpersonal causes and consequences of language use. Presequences in general, and prerequest in particular, demonstrate how politeness can be conveyed over a series of moves rather than within a single turn. Moreover, many of the interpersonal variables discussed in chapters 1–3 are probably related to various features of conversational structure. Consider, for example, the relationship between status and topic changes. Changing a topic can be tricky business and is often undertaken with a series of bilateral moves that gently transition the conversation from one topic to another. But if the conversationalists differ in status (think boss-employee), then the higher-status person is probably more likely to undertake unilateral topic changes (Weiner & Goodenough, 1977). And if status is roughly equal, undertaking a unilateral topic change might be a means of making a claim for a higher status. Similarly, dominance can be claimed or established by interupting others (Ng, Bell, & Brooke, 1993). These effects can be extended to intergroup behavior; topic changes and interruptions become more frequent when interacting with outgroup members (Ohlschleget & Piontkowski, 1997). In this case, attempts at conversational control provide interactants with a means of achieving social distinctiveness. On the other hand, continuing with a topic raised by one's partner, being responsive to her talk, can signal liking and affiliation (Davis, 1982).

Options in structuring talk are a resource that people can use to achieve various social goals. In this way, many social psychological phenomena—intergroup behavior, self-presentation, relationship maintenance, and so on—are played out in our conversations. It is not just cognitive processes that undergird our conversations (e.g., keeping track of what is being talked about), but also our interpersonal goals and concerns.

Despite its contributions to our understanding of talk, there are several ways in which the conversation analytic approach is limited. First, in conversation analysis, much of what occurs in a conversation, at least at the surface level, is explained with a limited set of concepts such as adjacency pairs, preference organization, a turn-taking system, and conversational repair. These concepts are part of the conversational system, a system existing independently of the people who use it. It is thus a system readily adaptable for use by anyone, in any context, with any number of participants.

But why does this conversational system exist? The underlying motivation is generally assumed to be economic; the system allows for efficient communication. And no doubt the turn-taking and repairs systems are models of communicative efficiency. But efficiency alone cannot explain the form that conversations take. As we've seen, virtually all of the structural regularities uncovered by conversation analytic researchers are amenable to a face-management interpretation. Talk would look very different if its structure evolved independently of face concerns. It would be fast and explicit and more efficient than it already is. Because acts could not be face threatening, indirectness would probably not exist, moves would not be necessary to open and close conversations, a clear preference structure would not exist, and so on. Unfortunately, the interpersonal underpinnings of conversational structure have not been investigated heavily. But it does seem likely that conversational structure is, in part, interpersonally motivated, a reflection of conversationalists' attempts to manage face, negotiate power, establish relationships (or dissolve them), present a specific identity, and so on.

Second, one of the hallmarks of conversation analysis is the exclusive focus on talk and only talk. No internal concepts—no thoughts, motivations, intentions—are brought to bear on the analysis. In so doing, the researchers are using only that which interactants have available to them as they engage in a conversation. But are our utterances the only thing we respond to when interacting with others? Do we produce and interpret utterances based only on linguistic input? Clearly not. Language use is nothing if not contextualized; we produce and interpret utterances based on various features of the context including our shared knowledge (see chap. 5). Conversation analytic researchers would reply that context is obviously important in their analyses, and that when it is important interactants will display that importance in their talk. No doubt this is true. But contextual effects can be quite subtle and impact comprehension in ways that may not be apparent in the interaction itself (Holtgraves, 1994).

Is it reasonable to assume, then, that our utterances display our understanding (or lack thereof) of our interlocutors' remarks? Clearly, utterances display an orientation to other utterances, both those occurring previously and those yet to come. Yet not *everything* is revealed in talk. We don't always communicate everything we've inferred, noticed, or thought about regarding another's utterances. For example, in Vuchinich's (1977) experiment in which one conversationalist produced an abrupt, unmarked topic change, all participants reported noticing the shift, but for a subset of them this awareness was not noticeable in their conversational behavior. Thus, our interpretations of others' talk, our sense of what they mean or intend, may remain covert. We sometimes misunderstand one another, and these misunderstandings might never be revealed (e.g., Weizman & Blum-Kulka, 1992). So, as an approach to talk and only talk, conversational analysis is a reasonable approach. But it is obviously not a psychological model of how people produce and comprehend utterances.

Third, conversation analysis takes a unique methodological stance toward the study of conversation. In addition to eschewing all internal concepts, there is the putative rejection of all a priori concepts and theorizing—a presumably pure inductive strategy. But of course the regularities that emerge are not completely free of the analysts' a priori categories. Some conceptual stance must be adopted if any sense is to be made of conversational interaction. For example, the terms that conversation analysts use—rejection, acceptance, and so on—reflect their conceptions of what constitutes those terms.

Conversation analytic researchers have also demonstrated little concern with the representativeness of the conversations on which their analyses are based. Talk is analyzed if it is available; there is no attempt to randomly sample instances of conversational interaction. Therefore, the generalizability of their findings is not known. And it seems likely that there will be cultural variability in many of the regularities that they have uncovered. Take the turn-taking requirement that only one speaker speaks at time (Sacks et al., 1974). Is this universal? Probably not. Reisman (1974) notes, for example, that in Antigua this requirement is relaxed considerably. The initiation of a turn by a speaker is not regarded as a signal for the current speaker to relinquish a turn. According to Reisman, conversations in Antigua have an almost anarchic quality.

Despite these limitations, conversation analysis has brought to light many of the subtle patterns underlying the organization of talk. And it should be noted that the conversation analytic approach is not necessarily incompatible with more traditional, experimental methodologies. Some scholars have called for the merging of these different research traditions (e.g., Robinson, 1998). And fairly impressive attempts have been made in this regard (e.g., Clark, 1996a; Roger & Bull, 1989). Clark (1996a), in particular, has energetically pursued the examination of the psychological properties of conversational structure informed by conversation analytic research. His research is discussed in more detail in the next chapter.

5

Conversational Perspective Taking

One of the most social aspects of language use is the fact that it involves perspective taking. Take the use of a simple directive such as "Close the door." Successful use of this expression will require the recipient to take the speaker's perspective in order to recognize the intention (what speech act is being performed), what door is being referred to, whether the door should be shut right now or later, and so on. And the speaker must have some awareness of the perspective the recipient is likely to take if the utterance is to be understood as intended. In this regard language use is clearly a collective endeavor; one's actions, and the meaning of those actions, are closely intertwined with the actions and interpretations of others.

Language use and perspective taking are linked in a reciprocal manner. Successful language use affords people the chance to take another person's perspective; it allows individuals existing in private worlds to achieve a measure of intersubjectivity, to create a temporarily shared social world with others (Rommetveit, 1974). In other words, perspective taking is an affordance of language use. But at the same time, language use *requires* perspective taking. To understand and be understood requires some attempt to take the perspective of one's interlocutor(s). In order to construct an utterance that will be understood by a recipient, the speaker must try to adopt the hearer's perspective, to see the world (roughly) the way the hearer sees it, and to formulate the remark with that perspective in mind.

For the recipient to understand the speaker's utterance requires the same thing; she must try to adopt the speaker's perspective and view the world (roughly) the way he does, and interpret the remark with that perspective in mind.

Perspective taking is thus fundamental for language use. In fact, many theorists have argued that it is *the* fundamental task in language use (Brown, 1965; Clark, 1985; Krauss & Fussell, 1991a, 1991b; Mead, 1934; Rommetveit, 1974). It is a process that occurs for all aspects of language use, from phoneme identification to referent identification to speech act recognition, and so on (Krauss & Fussell, 1996). All of the phenomena discussed in previous chapters depend, to varying degrees, on perspective taking. So, how is this accomplished? How do people manage to take another's perspective? How good are people at doing this? Are there systematic errors in this process? In this chapter, I consider these and other issues involved in perspective taking and its relationship to language use. Much of this will compliment and overlap research covered in previous chapters. I first discuss the role of coordinating perspectives and the mutuality that this entails. Then, research on perspective taking and referent identification is reviewed. Finally, the role of perspective taking for phenomena other than referent identification is considered.

THE NATURE OF PERSPECTIVE TAKING

People are not born with the capacity to take another's perspective; in the beginning we are all egocentric. For Piaget (1926), a child's egocentric perspective is the defining feature of the preoperational stage. The development of perspective taking is a fundamental achievement marking a child's move to the concrete operational stage. For G. H. Mead (1934), this ability to take another's perspective was a requirement for the development of a "self." Reciprocal role taking, or taking the perspective of others toward one's self, was the mechanism through which the self (or Me) was achieved. And the process through which this occurred was communication. Obviously, perspective taking is a fundamental ability with important cognitive and interactional implications.

But even for adults, perspective taking is not easy, nor is it ever perfect; the totality of one's perspective is entirely unique. We each have unique perceptions and ways of categorizing the world (Kelly, 1955), our own history and store of memories, and so on. Now, even though each person's total perspective is unique, there is some overlap in our perspectives; we share certain perceptions and categories and memories and experiences with others. The trick for people is to determine what is shared, or what part of their unique perspective coincides with the perspective of another. To do this people must coordinate their perspectives. According to Herb Clark (1996a), it is coordination that is the essence of successful communication. Coordination, of course, is not limited to language use; it is required for any joint human activity. Driving an auto, ordering a pizza, buying a newspaper from a vendor, all require coordination to succeed. It is Clark's view that language use is the prototype of coordinated joint action. There is really nothing more social than language use.

Now, there are many different features of another's perspective that might be relevant (Schober, 1998). Most fundamental here is another's perspective regarding a particular referent. Are we talking about the same object, event, experience, or what? As we will see, most research has focused on this aspect of perspective taking. However, much more is involved. The expressions used to identify a referent can also convey the speaker's attitude toward that referent, and so a consideration of the recipient's attitude toward that object might influence the referring expression that is chosen. There are also issues of perspective taking involved in the identification of illocutionary force and speaker intention; perspective taking may be crucial here as well. These different features of perspective taking will be subsumed under the global term *knowledge,* with knowledge referring to what a person knows, believes, infers, recognizes, and so on. Knowledge in this sense will encompass both procedural and declarative knowledge.

Common Ground and Mutual Knowledge

Although perspective taking is necessary for successful communication, it is not necessarily sufficient for successful communication. I might adopt my addressee's perspective, but if my addressee does not realize I have done so, she may fail to comprehend my message. For example, if I want to find out from my wife if she has seen one of our sons, and I say to her "Have you seen him?" the referent for "him" is ambiguous. But let's say that just a few minutes earlier we had been talking about one of our sons. If I take her perspective into account, then I might reasonably believe that she will recognize that "him" refers to the son we had just been talking about. But she may not make that judgment unless she has reason to believe that I am in some sense taking her perspective into account in formulating my utterance. If she doesn't do so, then she is not justified in inferring that "him" refers to the recently talked about son. In other words, there has to be some sort of mutual perspective taking.

Mutual perspective taking is captured most clearly in the concept of common ground. Common ground has been discussed by a number of theorists (e.g., Stalnaker, 1978), but it has been treated most extensively (and in psychological terms) by Herb Clark and colleagues (Clark, 1992, 1996a; Clark & Carlson, 1981; Clark & Marshall, 1981). At a relatively simple level, common ground for two people refers to the sum of their mutual knowledge, beliefs, and suppositions, in other words, what they mutually know. Successful language use requires an accurate assessment of what is in common ground. If I say to my wife "Have you seen him?" and the referent for "him" is in our common ground, then identification of whom I'm talking about will not be problematic. But there are two tricky issues here. First, how do people establish what is in common ground? Second, how is common ground represented?

One ubiquitous source of common ground is convention (Lewis, 1969). Conventions are behavioral regularities that have evolved as a means of solving coordination problems. Obvious examples include driving on the right side of the road (in the United States), waiting in line at a store, and so on. Much of language is conventionalized. Word meanings, syntax, and phonology are all conventions. We arbitrarily and conventionally call the four-wheel vehicles we drive cars, not jars, bars, or anything else. This is what the linguist de Saussure (1916) referred to as *l'arbitraire du sign*. When conversing with someone who speaks English, I know that he will know English grammar, the meaning of many words and expressions, and so on. Linguistic conventions may be represented in terms of both procedural knowledge (e.g., grammar, conversational rules) and declarative knowledge (e.g., word meanings).

But conventions alone are not sufficient for successful language use. Consider the word *web*. It has at least two conventional meanings—a set of interlocking computers or the silken material spun by a spider. So, which meaning is intended by a speaker when using this word? Conventionality only gets one so far; people have the capacity to produce and understand words in nonconventional ways (Clark & Gerrig, 1983). So, interlocutors must reach some on-the-spot mutual understanding of the meaning of words such as *web*. Imagine that we had just been discussing computers and the latest advances in the Internet, and I say something like "I use the Web in a lot of my classes." Obviously, the context disambiguates the intended referent of *web,* and interactants will frequently treat the immediate context as common ground.

Clearly, common ground depends on more than just convention. But what else is involved? Historically, common ground is related to the concepts of mutual knowledge (Schiffer, 1972) and common knowledge (Lewis, 1969). Mutual (or common) knowledge must be distinguished from shared knowledge. Shared knowledge refers to knowledge that is possessed by all interlocutors; whether interactants are aware of each other's awareness of this state is not relevant. For a state of mutual knowledge to exist, however, there must be mutual awareness of the existence of this knowledge. According to Schiffer (1972), for persons A and B to mutually know *p* requires that:

1. A knows *p*
2. B knows *p*
3. A knows that B knows *p*
4. B knows that A knows *p*
5. A knows that B knows that A knows *p*
6. B knows that A knows that B knows *p* ad infinitum

Mutual knowledge in this sense is reflexive; people must be aware of what they know that others know; and others must be aware of this awareness, and so on.

Obviously such a view is not plausible psychologically, involving as it does an infinite number of steps in order to verify mutuality (Clark & Marshall, 1981). Peoples' reasoning (with the possible exception of spies and others involved in intentional subterfuge) would rarely (if ever) extend beyond the first few steps. This mutual knowledge "problem" can be dealt with in a number of ways. The approach taken by Clark (1996a; Clark & Marshall, 1981) is to argue for the existence of heuristics that allow common ground to be inferred based on certain pieces of evidence. The mutuality of common ground in this view is based on interactants' awareness of the fact that the evidence giving rise to it is shared. Now, the strength of such evidence can vary, and accordingly belief regarding what is in common ground can vary also. Clark and Marshall (1981) suggested that the following categories of evidence are used by people in formulating beliefs about common ground.

1. *Physical copresence.* (Perceptual copresence in Clark, 1996a). If two people are physically together and attending to (roughly) the same aspects of their environment, they can assume that what they are attending to is in their common ground. In other words, the basis for information regarding common ground is shared. If Andy and Bob are both watching a football game, then the specifics of the game can be taken to exist in common ground for Andy and Bob. This state exists because Andy and Bob are mutually aware of each other's presence in the football game environment. And because of this, Andy can say something like "They should've tried to keep the drive going" and be certain that Bob will know to whom "they," "the drive," and so on refers. Obviously one's environment is constantly changing, as well as the specific aspects of the environment to which one is attending. Hence, there is a temporal dimension to physical copresence. It can be immediate (what they are currently focused on), prior (what they had been attending to earlier in the interaction), and potential (what they could, but have not yet, focused on).

2. *Linguistic copresence.* During the course of a conversation, people will introduce information, which, if understood, will then constitute part of their common ground. This information can then be referenced by the interactants with some assurance that the intended referent will be identified. So, if Andy and Bob are talking and Andy introduces the topic of last night's football game, he can then say something like "They should have gone for the touchdown in the fourth quarter," and Bob will most likely know exactly what he is talking about. Note that linguistic copresence is symbolic; the entities being talked about are not actually present, but are instead represented linguistically. Physical copresence, on the other hand, relies on natural evidence—the entities are physically present. But in both instances mutuality of knowledge is derived from each interactants' awareness that the information giving rise to common ground is shared.

3. *Community membership.* People belong to many different communities based on variables such as age, gender, occupation, location, hobbies, and so on. The identification of a person as belonging to a particular community

allows one to make reasonable assumptions about what that person knows. Take, for instance, members of the community of speakers of English. If I identify someone as a member of that group, I can assume of them (and them of me) knowledge of English grammar, word meanings, and so on. If I identify someone as having been raised in Indiana, I can reasonably assume that certain bits of information (that basketball is the favorite sport, that the Indy 500 is run in May, and so on) will be in our common ground. I can refer to these things and reasonably expect to be understood.

The major types of definite reference reflect these three sources of common ground (Clark & Marshall, 1981). For example, deictic expressions (e.g., *this, that, you*) depend on physical copresence. Thus, a speaker can say "That should have been a foul" and have the intended referent for *that* recognized only if both interactants are watching the same game. Similarly, the referent for *this* in "This is lovely" can be identified only if the interlocutors are attending to the same object. Anaphora, on the other hand, relies largely on linguistic copresence. In a conversation about last night's game, Bob can say "That should have been a foul" and expect the referent for *that* to be identified if earlier in the conversation they had been discussing this particular incident. Similarly, the successful use of pronominal reference depends on who has been talked about so far. Finally, the use of proper names depends on community membership. I can refer to the Bulls or the Chiefs or to Mark McGuire when discussing sports and assume that these entities will be identified based on the membership of my interlocutor in the group of people who follow sports.

The use of heuristics for assessing common ground makes sense; obviously people do not engage in an infinite number of reasoning steps in order to assess what is mutually known. And, basing common ground on evidence that is "shared" finesses the problem of infinite regress in establishing mutuality.[1] Still, there are some unresolved issues with this view. For example, it seems unlikely that people will retain everything during the course of a conversation, and participants may differ in what they remember. Thus, what is assumed to be shared may not be. Similarly, even when physically together, the perspectives that people take may not be identical; there are multiple perspectives that a speaker might adopt (Schober, 1998).

The community membership heuristic can present particular difficulties for interactants. All members of a group do not have identical knowledge, and establishing whether a person belongs to a particular group can be problematic at times. For example, if I find out that a person is a psychologist, there are a

---

[1]Note that this solution requires mutual knowledge to include self-referential statements (e.g., I am aware of a situation and aware of my awareness). Self-referential statements are inconsistent with certain traditional approaches to logic.

number of assumptions I may make that will impact my conversation with him, that will allow me to use certain terms I believe he will understand. But the psychologist category is extremely broad and encompasses tremendous variability in terms of orientation (e.g., therapist vs. researcher) and hence what is "known." In what subcategory do I place my interlocutor? And if group membership is correctly identified, clearly not every member of a group has identical knowledge; obviously, errors regarding common ground will still be made.

Heuristic-based assessment of common ground is not perfect; errors are inevitable. What happens, of course, is that these errors are often brought to light and repaired during the course of a conversation. Hence, common ground should be viewed as something that is fluid, negotiable, and tentative, rather than being fixed and absolute. How this occurs will be discussed in some detail next.

There are alternative approaches to mutual knowledge that should be noted here, alternatives that deemphasize the importance of mutual knowledge as a prerequisite for successful communication. Sperber and Wilson (1986) are quite explicit in this regard. They argue that what underlies communication is mutual manifestness rather than mutual knowledge. A proposition is manifest if a person is capable of representing it mentally (it need not be currently represented as is the case with mutual knowledge). A speaker is responsible for ascertaining the extent to which a proposition might be manifest for a hearer, but not with whether the hearer is aware of this awareness (i.e., the mutuality of mutual knowledge). Then, it is assumed that the hearer can work from the utterance and context to infer the identification of any ambiguous referents (as well as the speaker's intention). In other words, propositions attain the state of mutual manifestness via an inductive reasoning process, a process similar to that proposed by Grice (1975) for inferring speaker meaning.

In this view, then, perspective taking, like conversational relevance, is something that is assumed rather than always followed. People do not always produce literally relevant utterances, yet we assume relevance and interpret accordingly. Similarly, people don't always assess common ground, yet we assume that they do and act accordingly. In short, as hearers, we assume a speaker has taken an appropriate perspective in phrasing a utterance, and as speakers we assume the hearer will adopt the relevant perspective in interpreting an utterance. A conceptually similar perspective was developed by Rommetveit (1974) who argued that intersubjectivity is a state that is achieved (to varying degrees) through language. In other words, a mutually shared perspective is a result of communication, rather than being a precursor to successful communication. It should be noted that these views are not necessarily at odds with the perspective articulated by Clark. As we will see next, Clark has recently emphasized the negotiated and interactive moves through which common ground is achieved on a moment-to-moment basis, a view that implies that perspective taking is simultaneously a cause and effect of language use.

EMPIRICAL RESEARCH ON PERSPECTIVE TAKING

Most of the research on perspective taking has been conducted by psychologists and has focused on referent identification. There are several important issues here. The most fundamental one is whether speakers actually do attempt to take the hearer's perspective into account when formulating messages. And if they do make the attempt, how good are they at gauging another's perspective? Are there any systematic errors in this regard? And if perspective taking does occur, to what extent does it facilitate communication? Finally, *how* do people coordinate perspective taking during the course of an interaction?

Do Speakers Attempt to Take the Hearer's Perspective?

Do speakers attempt to take their recipient's perspective into account when formulating a message? Informal observation suggests that they do. The form of explanation that I give to my five-year-old will be different from those that I give to my seven-year-old, and that explanation will be different from one I would give to my wife. And these differences are based on what I assume my interlocutor "knows." Along these lines, DePaulo and Coleman (1986) demonstrated that speakers who were giving instructions to another person varied their explanation as a function of the presumed competence and knowledge of their interlocutors. Specifically, the instructions given to six-year-olds were clearer and simpler than those given to adult native speakers. Moreover, talk addressed to mentally retarded adults, or to adults who spoke English as a second language, were similar to the talk directed to six-year-olds. Participants apparently attempted to estimate the knowledge and competence of their partners based on group membership, and used these estimates to fine-tune their messages for their respective audiences. Children, too, appear to be sensitive to variations in the knowledge possessed by their interlocutors (Shatz & Gelman, 1973).

A field study conducted by Kingsbury (1968; cited in Krauss & Fussell, 1991a) demonstrated how people try to estimate and take into account others' knowledge when giving them directions. Kingsbury asked randomly selected Boston pedestrians for directions to a department store. In doing so he spoke either with a local dialect, a rural Missouri dialect, or a local dialect but prefaced his request with the statement that he was from out of town. As one would expect, people gave longer and more detailed directions when Kingsbury informed them he was from out of town; someone from out of town cannot be presumed to possess knowledge of the local terrain. Speakers obviously took that into account, adopted the requester's perspective, and gave directions that were longer and more detailed. Interestingly, the same thing occurred when Kingsbury spoke in a nonlocal dialect (but did not announce that he was from out of town). Apparently, people categorized him, on the basis of his dialect, as someone relatively unfamiliar with Boston, and they formulated their message based on what they assumed a person from out of town would know. This is a nice demonstration of how people utilize linguistic information (in this case dialect) in an attempt to adopt that person's perspective.

At a much more general level, the operation of Grice's (1975) conversational maxims entails perspective taking. Consider, for example, the quantity maxim, or stipulation that one's conversational contribution should be as informative as required. Obviously, adherence to this principle requires an assessment of what one's interlocutor "knows"; one can't be appropriately informative without an assessment of the recipient's knowledge. And people are sensitive to this; the explanations they give others vary as a function of what they believe their audience knows (Slugoski, Lalljee, Lamb, & Ginsburg, 1993).

The fact that people give different explanations and directions to different audiences is equivocal support for perspective taking. People vary their talk for many reasons, and it can be difficult to demonstrate unambiguously when it is perspective taking that is impacting message formulation (Keysar, 1997). The development of a laboratory referential communication task by Robert Krauss and his colleagues (e.g., Krauss & Weinheimer, 1964) contributed greatly to the examination of this question.

In a series of experiments Susan Fussell and Robert Krauss used this referential communication task to investigate the structure of messages formulated for different audiences. In one study (Fussell & Krauss, 1989a), participants were asked to describe innominate "nonsense" figures under one of two conditions: so that other participants would be able to use the descriptions to identify the objects or so that the participant herself would be able to later use the description to identify the object. Consider how these two tasks differ. When a participant is formulating a message for herself, common ground for speaker and eventual hearer (the initial speaker) is almost identical (it is not completely identical because one's mental state changes over time). That is, the speaker "knows" roughly what she will "know" later when using the message to identify the object. But this is not the case when formulating a message for another participant. In this case, one cannot know in advance everything the other person will know; common ground is less than perfect. Accordingly, the speaker must encode more information in the message, rather than relying on common ground. This is exactly what occurred. Messages constructed for use by others were far longer than messages constructed for use by oneself. Moreover, the messages differed in terms of the extent to which they employed literal (e.g., lines, angles) or figurative (e.g., spider on a dime) terms. Literal terms can be easily understood by others; they are part of common ground (everyone knows what a circle looks like). But this may not be the case for figurative descriptions, terms that may not be familiar to others. Participants were quite sensitive to this distinction, using more literal and fewer figurative terms in their descriptions for others than for themselves.

Not only did participants vary their descriptions as a function of the intended audience, the success with which the descriptions allowed the objects to be identified also varied as a function of the speaker's perspective. Participants were asked to identify objects based on descriptions from three different sources: descriptions they had previously provided for themselves, descriptions other participants had provided for other participants, and descriptions other participants had provided for themselves. As one would expect, participants were most successful when using their own personal descriptions, next most successful when using descriptions participants had designed for use by other participants, and least successful when using descriptions other participants had provided for their own personal use. These results demonstrate clearly the impact of perspective taking on whether a referent is correctly identified; when perspective taking was not involved (i.e., messages designed for one's own use but which were later used by someone else), people were not very good at identifying the intended referent.

Taking the perspective of oneself versus the perspective of another represents a very basic self versus other distinction. Do more fine-grained distinctions occur? Is there variability in perspective taking (and message formulation) as a function of the characteristics of the intended recipient? In a second study, Fussell and Krauss (1989b) used the same method but asked participants to construct messages that would be used by a friend of theirs (rather than simply another student). Later, participants were asked to identify objects based on descriptions provided by their friend or descriptions that had been generated by a different participant for his friend (and hence not specifically tailored for this participant). Participants were more successful using messages formulated for them by a friend than they were with messages that had not been formulated specifically for their use. Again, speakers attempted to take into account the perspective of an intended message recipient, and this had a corresponding impact on referent identification.

The Fussell and Krauss (1989b) study demonstrates how people who know each other can use their common ground to generate more successful communications. If two people are very well acquainted with each another—if they are intimates with a long history together—then their common ground is quite large (relative to the common ground between people who are relatively unacquainted). And because of this, our intimate couple can rely on and use that shared knowledge in communicating with one another; they need not make everything explicit in their talk. They can use elliptical expressions and gestures that might make little sense to an outside observer, but because of their shared perspective are quite understandable for them. An interesting study conducted by Kent, Davis, and Shapiro (1978) illustrates this quite nicely. They had pairs of people engage in conversations. Some of the pairs were well-acquainted friends, and some were strangers. The conversations were transcribed, with each utterance typed on a single index card. These cards were shuffled and then given to other participants who were asked to reconstruct the conversation. These participants were far more successful at reconstructing the dialogues of strangers than of friends. Strangers need to make almost everything explicit in their talk—and hence it is available in their utterances. Such is not the case with friends, where much is left unsaid because it is shared knowledge.

How Good Are People at Taking Another's Perspective?

The results of the Fussell and Krauss (1989a, 1989b) studies suggest that people attempt to take the perspective of their audience into account when generating a message and that doing so improves communication. Even so, referent identification was not always successful in these studies. When participants designed a message for another participant, the recipient successfully identified the referent only 60% of the time (Fussell & Krauss, 1989a). This suggests that perspective taking is far from perfect, and there are several reasons why this is so. The most basic reason is simply that it takes more effort to formulate a message from a perspective other than one's own (Schober, 1998). This reflects a very pervasive tendency that is not limited to communicative situations. In general, when people attempt to estimate others' opinions and beliefs, they tend to overestimate the extent to which others are similar to them. This effect, originally termed the false consensus effect (Ross, Greene, & House, 1977), has now been demonstrated for a number of different attitudes and behaviors (Miller & Prentice, 1996; Nickerson, 1999). Although there is some debate about the precise mechanisms responsible for the effect, its existence demonstrates how difficult it is to accurately take another's perspective and that attempts to do so are constrained by one's own perspective. In other words, it reflects an egocentric perspective. This effect is particularly strong for members of one's in-groups (Mullen, Dovidio, Johnson, & Copper, 1992). We tend to assume members of our in-groups are more similar to us than they really are; perspective taking based on community membership may be particularly susceptible to the false consensus effect.

There is research demonstrating that the false consensus effect operates in communication settings. Fussell and Krauss (1991, 1992) asked participants to both identify various objects (public figures, landmarks, tools) and to estimate the percentage of others (e.g., an average student) who could correctly identify the objects. In general, estimates of others' ability to identify objects correlated quite highly with others' actual ability to correctly identify the objects ($r = .95$; Fussell & Krauss, 1991). Now, this relationship may be a result of either truly accurate perspective taking (participants' ability to identify objects was almost perfectly related with participants' judgments of object recognizability) or a result of a false consensus effect (participants who recognized the objects judged that others would be able to do so; those who could not identify the objects judged that others also would not be able to identify them). It appears to be a result of both. Accurate perspective taking occurred because the correlation between identifiability estimates and actual identifiability was roughly the same for objects that participants could and could not name. At the same time, the results also demonstrate a false consensus effect. Even though the correlation between actual and estimated identifiability was roughly the same for the named and unnamed objects, participants were far more likely to estimate that others could identify an object if they themselves could identify the object than if they could not identify it. In other words, if I know what this is, others will probably know as well; if I don't, they won't.

Finally, it should be noted that in these studies, participants' estimates of object identifiability affected their messages. For example, participants provided less identifying information for objects believed to be easily recognizable by others; when identifiability was estimated to be low, speakers included more information. Hence, regardless of their accuracy, speaker beliefs about the recipient's knowledge influenced their choice of referring expressions.

In general, then, communicators attempt to take the perspective of their audience into account when formulating a message. Their success at doing so, however, is limited. Perspective taking sometimes reflects an egocentric bias, and people base their judgments of others' mental states on their own mental states. Accordingly, some have argued that accurate perspective taking is relatively rare, and that people generally assume (unless receiving information to the contrary) that others know what they themselves know and act accordingly (Steedman & Johnson-Laird, 1980; see also Johnson-Laird, 1982).

One model that makes explicit the (at least initial) egocentric nature of perspective taking is Keysar's perspective adjustment model (1998; Keysar, Barr, Balin, & Paek, 1998). Importantly, this model focuses on the addressee and the role of perspective taking in message interpretation (Keysar et al., 1998), as well as the speaker and the role of perspective taking in message formulation (Horton & Keysar, 1996). Keysar's model assumes that addressees first interpret a remark without considering the speaker's perspective, and hence the initial, default interpretation is an egocentric interpretation. Interactants do not consider common ground; instead, any available information is used regardless of whether or not it might be mutually known. These egocentric interpretations are assumed to be fast and effortless and what the processing system does best. But people are not completely unaware of the importance of common ground, and they sometimes do take it into account. This occurs during what Keysar refers to as an adjustment process, a process that attempts to correct the initial egocentric interpretation. Unlike the initial egocentric interpretation, the adjustment process is slow and effortful.

Keysar has provided support for certain aspects of this model. For example, he has demonstrated that the interpretation of some referring expressions are initially egocentric and based on information known only to the hearer (i.e., information that is not in common ground). In two experiments, Keysar and colleagues (Keysar et al., 1998; see also Keysar, Barr, Balin, & Brauner, 2000) had participants (addressees) respond to questions from a speaker about objects referred to with either articles (Experiment 1) or pronouns (Experiment 2). The crucial manipulation was that on some trials the addressee was made aware of an object to which the expression could be referring. But this information was privileged and known only to him and not to the speaker, and the addressee was made aware that this was the case. This privileged information was used, however, because on the trials for which it was available, response latencies were significantly longer, relative to the control trials. Thus, the initial interpretation was an egocentric interpretation; it was based, in part, on information known only to the addressee, and with the addressee aware that this was so. The referential ambiguity was resolved, however, as addressees generally corrected (the adjustment process) and correctly identified the intended referent (although there were more errors when referential ambiguity existed).

Speakers are no less immune to an initial egocentric perspective. In a modified referential communication task, Horton and Keysar (1996) found that participants failed to use common ground when generating descriptions under pressure; instead, they used privileged information. This did not happen when time constraints were not imposed. This suggests that a speaker's initial message formulation was egocentric, a formulation that was later revised (when there was no time pressure) to incorporate the recipient's perspective.

One of the important points demonstrated in this research is that it is possible for research on common ground to confound mutual knowledge with self-knowledge. By definition, all mutual knowledge is self-knowledge (but not the reverse). In order to demonstrate the use of mutual knowledge, it is necessary to construct situations (as Keysar did) in which certain aspects of self-knowledge and mutual knowledge conflict (Keysar, 1997).

So, perspective taking is not guaranteed; it is imperfect, variable, and effortful. Because of this there may be important individual differences in perspective taking, some people staying with their initial egocentric perspectives, and others adjusting their perspectives. Webster & Kruglanski (1994) have identified a personality dimension that may be important in this regard. Specifically, people who have a high need for closure tend to prefer to settle for an initial assessment rather than entertaining additional hypotheses and potential ambiguity; those low in need for closure are more comfortable with ambiguity. The former, then, should be less likely than the latter to modify an initial egocentric perspective. Using a referential communication task, Richter and Kruglanski (1999) found exactly that: high need for closure participants produced messages for others that were shorter and more nonliteral than those produced by low need for closure participants. It appears the former failed to take into account the perspective of their audience, that their audience might not comprehend their nonliteral descriptions. Individual variability in perspective taking is an important avenue for future research, particularly because it has implications for communication success. High self-monitors (Snyder, 1979), for example, given their social skill and motivation to monitor the reactions of others, might be particularly good at perspective taking.

Overall, then, initial perspective taking is far from perfect. Instead, it is best viewed as imperfect and tentative, a hypothesis about what is in common ground (Krauss & Fussell, 1991a). Speakers and hearers seem to have an awareness of its importance, yet they err in its estimate. But common ground is not static; it represents a set of propositions that will be constantly in flux. The accessibility of internal information changes, people forget some things and other things come to mind, the environment changes, attention shifts, the conversation continues to unfold, and so on. Thus, what is in common ground changes on a moment-to-moment basis. Importantly, talk itself serves as a means of establishing exactly what is in common ground and for keeping track of common ground as it changes. If one's perspective is initially egocentric, one impetus for subsequent adjustment is feedback from one's interlocutor. As a speaker, one can use a tentative referring expression, and then modify and/or elaborate on it, depending on the other person's reaction (Krauss & Fussell, 1991a, 1991b). A complete understanding of common ground and perspective taking, then, requires a consideration of how they operate in interactive settings. And a fair amount of research has illuminated some of these properties.

CONVERSATIONAL INTERACTION
AND COMMON GROUND

A very basic property of referent identification in interactive contexts was first demonstrated in the classic experiments conducted by Krauss and Weinheimer (1964, 1966). In these experiments, participants were asked to communicate, over a number of trials, about a set of nonsense figures. A key finding in this research was that the referring expressions that participants used to identify these figures became shorter over trials. For example, a figure described on the first trial as "looks like a martini glass with legs on one side" would be described on subsequent trials as "martini glass with legs," "martini glass," and eventually "martini." This gradual shortening makes sense in terms of common ground. Once an object has been introduced and is in common ground, participants could rely on their common ground (linguistic and physical copresence) for identifying the figures; they did not need to provide complete descriptions for successful identification to occur.

Importantly, this tendency to gradually shorten referring expressions over time was far more pronounced when partner feedback was available than when it was not. The presence of feedback allowed for verification of common ground; with no feedback, direct acknowledgment for what was in common ground was lacking (although participants obviously assumed its existence, albeit more tentatively than when feedback was available). As one would expect, the availability of feedback generally improves communication success, even if the feedback is very general. For example, Traxler and Gernsbacher (1992, 1993) had participants write descriptions of figures that would allow another person to identify them.

Some of these writer-participants were subsequently informed as to how many of their descriptions had been understood. All writers then rewrote their descriptions. Participants who received feedback produced more effective communications on subsequent trials; there was no improvement for participants who did not receive feedback.

Grounding

Why is feedback important? How does it contribute to successful communication? What is the nature of conversational feedback? These questions have been explicitly and extensively investigated by Herb Clark and his colleagues (Clark, 1996a; Clark & Brennan, 1991; Clark & Wilkes-Gibbs, 1986; Clark & Schaeffer, 1989; Schober & Clark, 1989). The view developed in this approach is that interlocutors must *ground* their respective contributions to an exchange. That is, they need to make their contributions part of their common ground, and for an exchange to proceed, interactants must mutually believe that a contribution has been grounded. It is not enough for one of the participants to believe a contribution has been understood; all participants must believe that this has occurred.

Clark (1996a; Clark & Wilkes-Gibbs, 1986) argues that contributing to a conversation can be viewed as involving two steps: a presentation phase and an acceptance phase. The presentation phase refers to a conversational contribution (an utterance, phrase, etc.) that must be evaluated in terms of its mutual understandability. The acceptance phase, then, refers to the evidence provided by the other interlocutors regarding their understanding of the contribution. Interactants attempt to provide, in various ways, evidence of their understanding of a contribution so that the conversation can continue; the current contribution now forms part of the interactants' common ground.

What constitutes evidence for the acceptance of a contribution? Many approaches (e.g., Stalnaker, 1978) have assumed that the absence of negative evidence (i.e., an indication that the other person has not understood; e.g., huh?, what?) is sufficient for the acceptance of a contribution. But there is a problem with interpreting the absence of negative evidence, a problem that is nicely illustrated in a study conducted by Chen (1990; cited in Krauss & Fussell, 1996). He asked participants to communicate in a standard referential communication task. In contrast to other instances of this procedure, on certain trials the two participants had different sets of stimuli (unbeknownst to the participants); on other trials the stimuli for the participants were identical. Chen coded a number of verbal and nonverbal behaviors. As one would expect, positive back-channel responses indicating understanding were far more frequent when both participants had the same stimuli. What he did not find, interestingly enough, was an expected high rate of negative evidence when participants had different stimuli. Rather than providing negative evidence regarding their lack of understanding on these trials, participants simply withheld back-channel responses. In other words, the absence of negative evidence is ambiguous and can be misleading.

One of Clark's main arguments is that the absence of negative evidence is not enough; people ultimately seek positive evidence of understanding. Positive evidence is the evidence an interactant provides demonstrating that a contribution (or part of a contribution) has been understood. According to Clark, this is accomplished in several ways. There is, first of all, *direct acknowledgment* of understanding, or back-channel responses (Yngve, 1970). These include continuers (uh, huh, yeah, etc.) indicating that one is passing up the opportunity to repair a turn, and hence that the contribution is understood (Schegloff, 1982), assessments of a contribution (wow, really? no kidding? etc.; Goodwin, 1986), and many gestures such as head nods. Note that direct acknowledgments do not generally occupy a separate turn at talk, but instead often overlap with the contribution of the other interactant.

A second form of positive evidence is the occurrence of a subsequent turn that displays, through its orientation to the prior utterance, an understanding of that utterance. In other words, the occurrence of a relevant response signals, via the fact that the response is relevant, that the speaker has understood the prior speaker's utterance. This, of course, is one of the major principles in conversation analysis: A recipient displays understanding of a prior turn with a subsequent turn (Sacks et al., 1974). So, an acceptance, answer, and refusal following an offer, question, and request, all indicate the second person's understanding of the first pair part of the adjacency pair.

The occurrence of a relevant response is both an acceptance (of the prior turn) and a presentation for the other interactant; the other interactant must now provide evidence regarding the acceptance of this contribution. This is an important feature because it makes grounding manageable. Because a relevant response functions as both an acceptance and a presentation, the need for an infinite number of steps to ground the contribution is not necessary. If one had to indicate acceptance of a turn, and the other had to indicate acceptance of that acceptance, a conversation would obviously never go anywhere.

The third and most basic form of positive evidence is continued attention to the current speaker. Obviously, the likelihood of understanding and accepting a contribution decreases with the lack of attention on the part of the intended recipient. Thus interactants enact various moves to indicate that attention is being paid. Speakers may, for example, begin a turn and then wait until the other indicates attention before attempting to complete the turn; they can then either finish the turn or repeat the part that had been presented (Goodwin, 1986). There are numerous attention-getting devices that interactants can use to secure and verify that attention is being paid, and many of these are nonverbal (e.g., gaze).

Collaboration

Grounding is particularly important for the identification of referents, especially in task-based dialogues; what one says about a referent will make little sense unless the referent is identified. And it seems likely that this understanding must be mutual; it must be grounded. Now, grounding is not always a simple matter of presentation and acceptance. There are potential problems that can arise in the identification of referents. People recognize this and collaborate in the grounding process so that they mutually agree that a particular item is now in common ground. Grounding is not a one-sided affair with one person presenting and the other person accepting. Rather, both the speaker and hearer mutually orient to potential grounding problems. Clark and his colleagues (1996a; Clark & Brennan, 1991; Clark & Wilkes-Gibbs, 1986) have identified several techniques interactants use for accomplishing this. Consider the following sample of techniques.

1. *Alternative description.* A technique that is frequently used to ground the referent is for the recipient to provide an alternative description of the referent. The alternative description represents both a tentative acceptance and a presentation that the first speaker can now accept (or not). The following example illustrates this technique (from Clark and Brennan, 1991, p. 136):

A: Well, that young gentleman from—((the park)) .
B: Joe Joe Wright you mean? - - *(- - laughs)*
A: *yes, (laughs) yes*
B: ((God)), I thought it was old Joe Wright who (('d)) walked in at first

Speaker B provides an alternative description at Turn 2, seeking confirmation of this description with a rising intonation. Speaker A then confirms in Turn 3.
2. *Indicative gesture.* People can present their tentative identification of a referent by, for example, pointing to it. The act of pointing thereby serves as a presentation that can be accepted (or not) by the first speaker.
3. *Referential installments.* Rather than presenting a complete contribution, a speaker can check on the recipient"s ability to identify a referent by treating the referent as an installment; if it is accepted, the remainder of the contribution can then be presented. A special construction in English—termed left-dislocation—exists for just this purpose. Left-dislocation involves the presentation of a referent, followed by a comment on the referent (e.g., My car, it's on the blink vs. My car is on the blink). What's interesting about dislocation in actual conversations is that it is usually followed by an intervening remark from the other interactant (indicating either acceptance or not) or an unfilled pause (the lack of negative evidence providing positive evidence for the dislocated referent). Then, the remainder of the turn (the comment on the referent) is completed.
4. *Trial references.* Occasionally, speakers may be uncertain of the object to which they want to refer. A technique to handle this is to invite collaboration and begin the grounding process by using a try marker (rising intonation following the referent) followed by a pause. The other interactant can then either accept or reject understanding of this potential referent, as in the following example (from Clark & Brennan, 1991, p. 138):

A: So I wrote off to . Bill, . uh who ((had)) presumably disappeared by this time, certainly, a man called Annegra?

B: Yeah, Allegra.

A: Allegra, uh replied, . uh and I . put . two other people [continues]

Speaker A is uncertain about the name Annegra and so presents it with a try marker. Speaker B accepts the contribution (Yeah)—she knows to whom A is referring—but corrects the name to Allegra, a correction that A accepts in the next turn.

An additional, overall feature of communication that illustrates its collaborative nature is what Clark terms the principle of least collective effort. This principle is in the spirit of other proposals regarding a tendency for people to minimize their communicative effort. Such a tendency is reflected in Grice's (1975) maxim of quantity, or stipulation that one should not say more than is required. Similarly, a tendency uncovered in conversation analytic research is for people to "overassume" what their interlocutors know and "undertell" (i.e., assume the recipient can assess the relevant information) (Sacks & Schegloff, 1979). For example, people prefer to have others identify them rather than identifying themselves on the telephone (Schegloff, 1979); they both overassume (i.e., that the recipient can identify them) and undertell (i.e., they don't identify themselves).

But Clark argues that rather than trying to minimize individual effort, people attempt to minimize their *collective* effort. The principle is stated as follows:

> In conversation, the participants try to minimize their collaborative effort—the work that both do, from the initiation of each contribution to its mutual acceptance. (Clark & Wilkes-Gibbs, 1986)

This principle is consistent with a number of findings. For example, participants in one of Fussell and Krauss' (1992) experiments were asked to provide brief descriptions of objects so that others could name them. Interestingly, on initial trials speakers often provided relatively brief descriptions, for example by naming but not describing the object. This strategy makes sense in terms of collective effort. If the recipient can identify the referent, then little overall effort has been expended. If she can't identify the referent, then she can provide feedback allowing the original speaker to customize a message designed specifically for her. Why provide a full detailed message at the outset when the detail provided may be of little help to this particular addressee? It may be a waste of time. It is more efficient, collectively, to wait for information allowing one to construct a tailor-made message.

The manner in which people undertake conversational repair also illustrates this tendency (see chap. 4). Interactants apparently have a relatively strong preference for repairing their own utterances (self-repair) rather than allowing another to do so (other-repair). Similarly, people tend to initiate their own repairs rather than letting others initiate a repair sequence (Schegloff et al., 1977). Why? Well, self-repair will require fewer turns than repairs initiated by another. So, although the effort may be greater for the person making the repair, collectively the amount of effort is minimized. The preference for other-recognition rather than self-identification in telephone openings can be interpreted in the same way; other-recognition eliminates the turns required for mutual recognition of the involved parties (Schegloff, 1979).

The approach to perspective taking developed by Clark and colleagues is unique. They have demonstrated quite clearly the collective nature of referent identification. In this way, our view of perspective taking has been expanded. For example, prior research has demonstrated the importance of recipient feedback for referent identification. But with Clark's research, we now have some idea of how and why feedback from others is important. No longer can perspective taking by viewed as static and one sided. Instead, people work together in order to mutually establish what is in common ground. Which is why when pragmatic errors occur, it is *both* interactants who are blamed (Kreuz & Roberts, 1993).

Second, earlier theories of referent identification were largely ahistorical, or based on principles operating independently of an interaction. The best-known proposal in this regard suggested that a referring expression would simply be the most concise term that would allow the recipient to identify the referent (Brown, 1958; Olson, 1970). Interactants should thus choose expressions that conform to Grice's maxims of quantity (informativeness). But such a view ignores the collaborative, and hence historical, nature of referent identification, how the process of grounding referents can override the principle of informativeness. For example, people will sometimes continue to use referring expressions that they have used previously, even though the expressions are more informative than required (Brennan & Clark, 1996). Moreover, the presentation of referring expressions changes over the grounding process; hedges will be used if identification is uncertain, but these will quickly drop out once the term is grounded (Brennan & Clark, 1996). And of course grounding is partner specific; the referring expressions a person uses with another may be unique to that person (Brennan & Clark, 1996; Wilkes-Gibbs & Clark, 1992). Again, the expressions that are used depend on the history of the interaction.

As important and influential as Clark's collaborative model has been, there are two features of it that are somewhat problematic. First, there is obvious overlap between Clark's approach and conversational analysis. In conversation analysis the emphasis is on talk as an indicator, and as the *only* indicator, of people's mental states. As noted in chapter 4 this can be problematic because people's understanding, or lack thereof, need not always be revealed in their utterances. Clark has reformulated this as a psychological model, and so internal states are inferred from behavior other than talk (e.g., how participants perform in a matching task). Still, it is assumed that grounding occurs; thereby short shrift is given to potential misunderstandings that may not be revealed during an interaction.

And second, like conversation analytic research, there is a disregard for the role of interpersonal processes in the structure of conversation. Consider, first, the manner in which interlocutors ground a reference. One way to accept a contribution is with a direct acknowledgment (e.g., back-channel response). From the current speaker's perspective, these indicate understanding of the present contribution and provide permission to continue with that contribution (or introduce something else). But should these always be taken at face value, as indicating actual acceptance? The problem is that on occasion such acknowledgment may be motivated by a desire to appear knowledgeable and to avoid the appearance of incompetence, rather than reflecting actual acceptance and understanding of a contribution. Although little studied, this tendency no doubt occurs and may reflect face management concerns, or a striving to project competence.[2] For example, during tutoring sessions, students occasionally indicate understanding of concepts when their comprehension is lacking (Person, Kreuz, Zwaan, & Graesser, 1995). The point, then, is that positive evidence for grounding a contribution may be misleading; there may be other motivations (e.g., face management) behind their occurrence that should be considered.

For direct acknowledgment there is an additional ambiguity. Direct acknowledgment can be taken as indicating that one has understood a contribution. But from the contributor's standpoint, it might also be taken as indicating agreement with what is being said. Back-channel responses are ambiguous in this sense; they can indicate understanding, agreement, or both.

Another technique for indicating acceptance of a contribution is to provide a relevant response to that contribution. But there is a problem here, one that was noted in the discussion of conversation analytic research (see chap. 4). The problem is identifying, unambiguously, the occurrence of a relevant next turn. Given the occurrence of a question, especially one that is sensitive or face-threatening, virtually any subsequent turn can be construed as relevant by the recipient via the operation of a Gricean inference process. But, of course, the person may not actually be communicating an indirect meaning at all; he may simply have failed to understand the question. Now if this occurs, it may motivate a repair sequence later, and so it will show up in the talk exchange. But it might not; people do misunderstand each other on occasion. Again, there is a potential problem in viewing language use as revealing completely a speaker's understanding.

Finally, the third mechanism for indicating acceptance—giving attention—also contains potential ambiguities. Clearly, people sometimes feign attention, in which case there is no clear understanding of the contribution. And does real attention by itself indicate understanding? Evidence that one is attending to another need not mean that one is understanding the contribution. Attention

---

[2]Strictly speaking, this motivation would not fit well in the Brown and Levinson model, although it is represented in other approaches to face management (e.g., Lim & Bowers, 1991).

would seem to be necessary but not sufficient for acceptance. There is also cultural variability in terms of how one indicates attention. For some groups, directly gazing at the speaker indicates attention; for other groups this is not the case (LaFrance & Mayo, 1978). There is a cultural dimension to the grounding process, a dimension that is infused with meaning; to gaze directly at another is sometimes threatening.

Overall, then, interpersonal motives may drive much of the regularity that is observed in conversational grounding. Consider some additional examples. People appear to prefer positive evidence rather than a lack of negative evidence for grounding their contributions. Why? One possibility may be face management; negative evidence is face threatening and hence avoided. Or consider the principle of least collaborative effort. Support for this principle comes from the fact that people prefer self-repair to other repair (Schegloff, Jefferson, & Sacks, 1977), and they prefer other recognition to self-identification in telephone openings (Schegloff, 1979). It is true that these preferences lessen collective effort. But there are also good interpersonal reasons for their use. To initiate repair of another's utterance imposes on that person. Hence, self-repair avoids the imposition created by other repair and avoids threatening the other person's negative face. And other identification in telephone openings displays closeness with the other (I know you well enough to recognize you), in effect, a positive politeness strategy.

PERSPECTIVE TAKING, ATTITUDES, AND SPEECH ACTS

Most of the research on perspective taking has focused on referent identification. But perspective taking is required for all levels of language use, and in this section I consider briefly its role in attitudes and speech act identification.

Clearly, perspective taking plays a role in referent identification. However, referent identification cannot be the only factor affecting the choice of a referring expression. There are a multitude of expressions that can be used to refer to an object, thought, emotion, and so on that would allow the referent to be identified. Thus, many times a speaker's referring expression might also reflect an attitude toward the referent (Schober, 1998). For example, with my family I can refer to our dog as "Miles" or "that dog," and with either term be assured that they will know what I'm talking about. What might influence my choice of one term over the other is my current view of him. If I want to complain about him I might say "That dog is driving me nuts," with the use of "that dog" rather than his name conveying my present displeasure with him; "that dog" implies a greater distance between us than "Miles." I will be most likely to do this if I believe my audience will view my use of this expression in this way. In other words, coordinated perspective taking is required.

Many of the same issues that arise with perspective taking and referent identification arise also with attitudes toward a referent. Unfortunately, much less is known about this process. One of the most basic issues, of course, is whether speakers take the attitude of their audience into account when formulating a message. In other words, does attitudinal perspective taking occur and influence our choice of referring expressions? Research conducted by Higgins and Rholes suggests that it does. In an important early study, they (1978; see also Sedikides, 1990) gave participants behavioral descriptions of a target person and then asked them to describe that person so that he could be identified by the message recipient. Participants also received, in an offhand manner, information that the recipient either liked or disliked the target person. Participants clearly tailored their messages to be in line with the recipient's attitude; their messages were more positive if they believed the recipient liked the target than if they believed he was not liked. This effect occurred for both ambiguous and unambiguous behavioral descriptions of the target. For unambiguous behavior (e.g., the target was athletic), the effect demonstrates participant selectivity in what they chose to include in their descriptions. But the more interesting effect occurred for ambiguous information, thereby revealing how participants labeled the behavior. For example, if participants had been told that the target tended to rarely change his mind, the behavior could be labeled as either stubborn or independent. If participants believed the recipient liked the target, they were more likely to describe him with an evaluatively favorable label (independent), relative to participants who believed the recipient did not like him, and who were more likely to describe him negatively (stubborn).

This can be taken as a demonstration of attitudinal perspective taking and its impact on the choice of referring expressions. It should be noted, however, that there is no direct evidence of perspective taking in this study. It is possible, for example, that participants simply initially adopted the recipient's attitude toward the target person (rather than having an initial perspective that they then altered). Although not demonstrating a change in perspective, it does demonstrate some sensitivity to the attitudes of one's interlocutor, and how that sensitivity may be revealed in language use.

In addition, the type of message that participants fashioned affected their own subsequent memory for and impressions of the target (a "saying is believing" effect). If they believed the recipient liked the target and hence conveyed a positive description of him, their own later impressions and memory were more positive than if they had formulated a less-positive message. This represents an interesting long-term impact of perspective taking on one's own internal representations, an effect conceptually similar to that demonstrated in the "cognitive tuning" literature (Zajonc, 1960). In that research, participants received information with the expectation that they would either communicate the information to another person, or that they would be receiving additional information. When participants had the former expectation, their representation of the information was more distorted and polarized than if they expected to receive additional information. The point is that their internal representation of the information was influenced by considerations of perspective taking (i.e., attempting to formulate a clear, concise, and coherent message for another person).

There is also interesting variability in terms of the extent to which people vary their message as a function of the recipient's attitude. For example, motivation to modify one's messages may vary as a function of the recipient's power and the speaker's personality characteristics. Speakers who are high on authoritarianism are more likely to modify their message if the recipient is relatively high in power; speakers low on authoritarianism do not demonstrate this tendency; in fact, they are more likely to produce messages in the direction opposite of the recipient's (Higgins & McCann, 1984). Speakers who are high self-monitors are more likely to construct a message in line with the recipient's attitude than are low self-monitors (McCann & Hancock, 1983). In both of these studies, message modification influenced subsequent memory and impressions of the target.

In one sense, this tendency to alter one's communications as a function of the recipient's attitude reflects basic impression management (Schlenker, 1980) or self-presentation (Goffman, 1967) processes. All self-presentation and impression management involves perspective taking; to perform an action with the goal of conveying a particular impression implies a belief that one's audience will interpret the action as intended. Of course successful self-presentation entails not having one's intention to self-present recognized (Schlenker, 1980; Jones, 1964). And so it is with language use. For example, in the Higgins study, participants did not believe that their audience knew that they knew their audience's attitude toward the target person. If they had, they very well may not have modified their messages to be in line with the recipients' view. For if they had done so, the recipient might have discounted their message due to a belief that the message was being modified for them. What is involved here is shared knowledge rather than mutual knowledge; if it is mutual knowledge, then the game is up. And there is some persuasion research consistent with this idea. For example, people take into account the possibility that a speaker might be tailoring her message for a specific audience, and as a result, they "correct" their estimate of her true opinion (e.g., Newtson & Czerlinski, 1974).

Obviously, impression management underlies much of the manner in which people use language (see chap. 2 and 3). We talk differently as a function of various features of the setting, and our motivation to do so is often in the service of impression management. An implicit part of this process is perspective taking, an estimate that the audience will perceive a particular linguistic form as representing a particular attitude. Now, much of this is probably conventional; particular meanings are conventionally associated with the use of particular forms. For example, direct speech is conventionally associated with high speaker power (Holtgraves & Yang, 1990). The point here is simply that just as perspective taking is fundamental for linguistic meaning (e.g., referent identification), so too is it fundamental for nonlinguistic meaning (e.g., speaker attitudes).

Perspective Taking and
Speech Act Recognition

Language use can be viewed as having an action dimension; one is attempting to do something with one's utterances. Now, as discussed in chapter 1, the manner in which this is accomplished (or even if it is necessary) is not well understood. But if one assumes that recovery of a speaker's intention plays a role in language use, then perspective taking must be involved in this process. We have, then, another level of analysis for which perspective taking must be considered.

Perspective taking is often implicit in treatments of speech acts. But it shouldn't be. As with referent identification, a speaker must have some sense that his interlocutor will recognize his illocutionary point, and the only way this can occur is if the speaker has some evidence that the recipient will recognize his intention from his utterance. What evidence? Well, as with referent identification, one source is convention. Just as many word meanings are fixed by convention, thereby allowing a speaker to anticipate how they will be interpreted, so too is the illocutionary force of many utterances fixed by convention. In speech act theory (Searle, 1979), it is the essential condition that specifies a conventionally accepted dimension of force (illocutionary act) for an utterance in a particular context.

What about indirect speech acts? What is the role of perspective taking in their use? Here, too, conventionality plays a role, as many indirect speech acts (especially requests) are conventional. Thus, "Can you take out the garbage?" is conventionally recognized as a means of requesting another to take out the garbage.

But not all conveyed, indirect meanings are conventional; some require an inference process for recognition. For this to occur successfully requires some coordination of perspective. For example, how is it possible for a speaker to utter "It's cold in here" with the intention of having the recipient recognize the utterance as a directive? Conversely, how does the hearer recognize this intention? For this to come off, there must be coordination in terms of the recognition that an indirect meaning is being conveyed. If this is signaled via a maxim violation, then both interactants must believe that each other is aware of the maxims and how they work. This might very well be conventionalized, the Gricean maxims serving as general pragmatic principles of communication that all competent speakers of a language can be assumed to possess. The second stage of the inference process—the generation of a specific nonliteral meaning—obviously requires coordinated perspective taking as well. But here the Gricean model is incomplete; there are no general principles (other than face management; see chaps. 1 and 2) that might serve as a conventional means for generating and interpreting specific indirect meanings.

Do interactants coordinate in this way? Obviously they must; we routinely convey and recognize indirect meanings. There is also some evidence that people are sensitive to their interlocutor's ability to comprehend literal expressions. Recall that in the Fussell and Krauss study (1989a) participants were less likely to use figurative descriptions when describing objects for people that they did not know; participants probably realized that a figurative description may not be correctly recognized by someone with whom they share little common ground, and so they were more literal.

But as with referent identification, there is evidence suggesting that such perspective taking is far from perfect. Instead, people demonstrate (at least initially) an egocentric bias. For example, people demonstrate a transparency of meaning effect (Keysar & Bly, 1995), or a tendency to believe that the idiomatic meaning of certain expressions is more transparent than the meanings really are. A person who has come to believe that an expression has a particular meaning may assume others will arrive at the same meaning, and in this way fail to consider the possibility of alternative interpretations of the expression.

Similar results have been found for the interpretation of potentially sarcastic expressions (Keysar, 1994). Participants in these studies tended to endorse interpretations of utterances that would be based on information unavailable to the intended addressee. For example, when indicating how they thought an addressee would interpret Mark's utterance regarding a recent dining experience ("Marvelous, simply marvelous"), participants were likely to infer a sarcastic reading if they knew Mark had a negative dining experience, even though the addressee had no knowledge of Mark's dining experience. In other words, participants generally failed to correctly take the addressee's perspective into account when interpreting utterances. Instead, they used their own egocentric perspective.[3] What about the speaker? Even though hearers and overhearers are somewhat egocentric initially, do speakers consider the perspective of their audience? There is no clear evidence here. However, it may be that speakers and hearers diverge, in consistent ways, in their interpretation of remarks with potential indirect meanings, each taking an egocentric perspective and interpreting the meaning from their own respective frame of reference.

In preliminary research, we asked participants to interpret the meaning of indirect replies from either the perspective of the person making the reply (the speaker) or from the perspective of the recipient of the remark (Holtgraves, 2001). Now, if interactants coordinate their perspectives in using indirect expressions, then speakers and recipients should agree on the meaning of these replies. But this is not what happened. Instead, when taking the perspective of the recipient, participants were more likely to interpret indirect replies as conveying negative

---

[3]There is some debate about whether Keysar's (1994) results truly reflect a transparency of intention. Gerrig, Ohaeri, and Brennan (2000) argue that his materials were biased toward sarcastic readings; in their research they found sarcastic interpretations to be just as likely when no information was provided as when participants were given negative information. But such a finding does not really explain why participants interpreted utterances differently as a function of privileged information (Keysar, 2000). At this point, the issue is an open one.

(face-threatening) information than when they took the speaker's perspective. When taking the speaker's perspective, participants were more likely to interpret the replies as simply avoiding the topic. What this demonstrates is an interesting lack of speaker-hearer coordination in the use of indirect remarks. Each is being somewhat egocentric; the speaker is failing to consider how the hearer might interpret the utterance as conveying negative information, and the hearer is failing to consider how the speaker might simply want to avoid the topic. A person's conversational goal or agenda may blind them to the possibility that their interlocutors have different goals or agendas (Russell & Schober, 1999).

CONCLUSION

Successful language use requires a speaker to have some sense of how a recipient will view his utterance. The speaker needs to have some idea that the recipient will be able to identify the referents, recognize his intention, perceive his politeness, and so on. So the utterance is designed with the recipient in mind, following the principle of audience design (Clark & Murphy, 1982). Research suggests that people are sensitive to what they believe their interlocutors "know"; they clearly vary their talk as a function of with whom they are talking. We talk differently to children than to peers, to friends differently than to strangers, and so on (DePaulo & Coleman, 1986; Fussell & Krauss, 1989a, 1989b; Kingsbury, 1968).

Simple perspective taking is not enough, of course. Some sort of mutuality or intersubjectivity is required. A speaker needs to have some sense that his interlocutor is aware of the perspective being taken, that she knows that he is designing his utterance with her in mind. And he needs to know that she knows that he knows, ad infinitum. This infinite regress can be finessed, however, through the operation of evidential heuristics, mutual orientation to evidence for the existence of common ground.

Demonstrating the use of mutual knowledge in language use is not easy. For example, does the fact that we talk differently to various others really reflect the assessment of mutual knowledge? Language variation might simply be the result of what the speaker knows, regardless of any belief about whether this is mutually known (Keysar, 1997). I might speak differently to another psychologist than to my neighbor because I estimate the knowledge of the former to be different than that of the latter. But this does not necessarily mean that I believe that what I know is mutually known to my interlocutors and myself. The point is not that common ground fails to play a role in language use, only that experimental demonstrations require an unconfounding of what is known to an interactant with what is mutually known to a set of interactants.

There is an additional methodological problem involved in perspective taking that is worth noting. Participants in many language experiments are asked to adopt a rather unusual perspective; they are asked to adopt the perspective of a fictional person and to interpret or produce utterances from that person's vantage point. But it is an experimenter who is asking them to do this, and so they must also take the experimenter's perspective in asking them to perform this task. There is, in effect, another layer here (participants taking the experimenter's perspective as they take the perspective of the hypothetical person), a layer that is absent in nonlaboratory interaction. Whether laboratory results generalize to non-laboratory conversations is unclear (see chap. 6 for a discussion of participants' interpretations of experimenter communications).

Although perspective taking is clearly an important aspect of language use, it is far from perfect. Young children, for example, are egocentric in their use of language. This tendency eventually drops out but it does leave a residue: Adults too (at least initially) are somewhat egocentric in their perspective taking. According to Keysar (1998), both speaker and hearer initially use privileged information in the formulation and interpretation of an utterance; they work from their own perspective. But this is only an initial stage, and it is very brief. If people are motivated (Richter & Kruglanski, 1999) and have adequate resources (Horton & Keysar, 1996), they quickly adjust and attempt to take into account the perspective of their interlocutor and to make an initial assessment of what is mutually known.

Even though people may be motivated to adopt another's perspective, doing so is extremely difficult. Just exactly how does one establish what is in common ground? An initial assessment of another's perspective is probably guided by the heuristics suggested by Clark (1996a). Interactants' mutual awareness of the immediate context, the conversation as it unfolds, and their membership in various groups can be used to infer what is in common ground. But by themselves these heuristics are not sufficient. For example, people tend to assume that others, particular members of one's in-groups, are more similar to them than they really are, a false consensus effect (Nickerson, 1999). Because of this, estimates of common ground based on community membership will produce errors.

Perspective taking is best viewed as being imperfect, tentative, and hypothetical (Krauss & Fussell, 1991a); we have ideas about what is common ground, but those ideas are subject to change. What happens is that people collaborate, through their talk, and jointly establish what is in common ground (Clark, 1996a). If one's initial perspective is in error, then one's interlocutor may provide feedback to help correct that perspective; if one's perspective is adequate, then one's interlocutor may provide evidence that this is so. In this way interactants display to one another, through their talk, their understanding, or lack thereof, of what is in common ground. Talk itself, then, is the site for the establishment of common ground; people simultaneously seek and provide evidence for the grounding, or understanding, of their respective contributions. Most important, this is an essentially collaborative process. Establishing what is in common ground is not a solitary activity; it requires the cooperation of all parties that are involved.

Note that many of the structural features described in chapter 4 play a role in this process. Adjacency pairs, for example, structure talk and in so doing allow people to ground their conversational contributions. If a person answers a question, the answer can be taken by the other as demonstrating an understanding of the question, that the question has been grounded. Providing a relevant response indicates that one has successfully comprehended the others' prior utterance. Of course, this system is not perfect; the evidence for grounding that people provide can be ambiguous and misinterpreted. For example, failing to provide a relevant response can indicate a failure to comprehend the prior utterance, or it might reflect an attempt at face management (see chap. 1 and 2).

Although most of the perspective taking research has focused on referring expressions, perspective taking should play a role in all levels of language use, including the interpersonal level and the level of speech acts (or illocutionary force). Just as the coordination of perspectives is necessary for successful referent identification, so too it would seem to be required for successful speech act recognition. This should be particularly true for the use of figurative language and indirect speech acts. When common ground is high, people can use figurative expressions with some assurance that the nonliteral meaning will be comprehended; when common ground is low people tend to stick with the literal (Fussell & Krauss, 1989a).

One of the reasons perspective taking is so important for nonliteral meaning is that Grice's (1975) cooperative principle and conversational maxims depend on perspective taking. Grice's conversational maxims state that one's contributions should be relevant, informative, clear, and so on. But how does one decide if a contribution is the right level of informativeness? Or that an utterance is appropriately relevant? It can only be appropriately relevant and informative relative to some standard, and to be successful that standard needs to be based, in part, on estimates of the recipient's knowledge. Clearly perspective taking is required here.

Finally, consider the likely role played by perspective taking in the interpersonal aspects of language use. Politeness, for example, can be conveyed successfully only if interactants mutually recognize how it can be conveyed, and this requires a coordination of perspective; a lack of coordination in this regard can result in cross-cultural misunderstanding (see chap. 2). Or consider how errors in estimating another's knowledge can have interpersonal implications; a speaker who underestimates the knowledge of the interlocutor may be perceived as patronizing or as boring. For example, Al Gore's slow, deliberate speech to some audiences during the 2000 presidential campaign resulted in many perceiving him as underestimating his audience, and hence patronizing them. The process of conveying an identity through one's talk will require grounding, the responses of the other serving as evidence that one's proffered identity has been confirmed or challenged (Goffman, 1967). In fact, grounding in this case might be quite intricate and complex, as interactants' views of their identities and the situation may conflict.

Although people strive to communicate effectively, they are not always successful. Communication is imperfect; misunderstandings frequently occur, and they can occur at all levels of language use (e.g., Coupland, Giles, & Weiman, 1991). Recipients misidentify referents, fail to discern a speaker's intention, take offense when none was intended, and so on. Why? What are the sources of communicative misunderstandings? No doubt there are many. But clearly errors in perspective taking, or failing to attempt to take another's perspective, can be critical in this regard. Perspective taking has been shown to be related to successful interactions and friendship formation (Noller & Venardos, 1986; Selman, 1981). The related concept of empathic accuracy has proven to be important and beneficial in a number of interpersonal contexts (Ickes, 1993). Perspective taking is critical for successful intercultural communication; failing to realize the operation of different language rules can result in misunderstandings (see chap. 3). But *why* is perspective taking so important for relationship satisfaction? *How* does it contribute to relationship development? It seems likely that these effects will be mediated by language use, that perspective taking will influence communication in a positive way, and that it is these communicative effects that impact relationship satisfaction and interaction success. The manner in which perspective taking plays out in interactions and affects relationships is a fertile ground for future research.

To use language successfully, one must understand another's understanding (Kelly, 1955) and achieve a measure of intersubjectivity (Rommetveit, 1974); perspective taking is critical and one of the features of language use that mark it as a social action. Perspective taking and language use are reciprocally related; language use both requires perspective taking to some degree, but it also allows for perspective taking. Perspective taking, then, is an excellent example of how language use and social psychology are intimately related, how language use is ultimately a social experience.

6

Language and Social Thought

The idea that language shapes the manner in which we perceive and think about our world is an old one. It is one that just seems to make a lot of sense, as anyone who has tried to learn a second language can attest. Language can be regarded as a tool used in the service of thought (Semin, 1998), and it is a necessary tool that allows us to impose some order on the influx of stimuli impinging upon us. But many times the type of tool one uses can impact the results that one obtains. And so it is with language. The nature of one's language, the words available, the structure of the grammar, the pragmatic rules for conversing, all might affect how we perceive and think about our world. Such effects might be especially strong in the social domain because of the ambiguity involved in perceiving people.

But this is controversial. Language and thought are so interwoven as to make the empirical examination of their relationship most difficult. In psychology, the idea that language affects thought has had its most popular realization (somewhat unfortunately, as we'll see) in what has become known as the Whorf-Sapir hypothesis. In the first part of this chapter, I provide a brief overview of this hypothesis and some of the early research designed to test it.

The Whorf-Sapir hypothesis is a rather narrow look at the language-thought relationship, and one that carries excess baggage. A broader approach to the problem can be articulated, as some researchers (e.g., Chiu, Krauss, & Lau, 1998;

Hardin & Banaji, 1993; Hunt & Agnoli, 1991) have recently suggested. The basic idea is that language, and especially language use, can influence the manner in which people process information in specific situations, rather than determining in an absolute manner how people think in all situations. This idea has been demonstrated in several areas of research, three of which I review in this chapter: language use, implicit causality, and reasoning and pragmatics. In this way, many of the phenomena discussed in prior chapters—speech act production and recognition, politeness, impression management, perspective taking, and so on—may have additional social psychological consequences.

EARLY TESTS OF THE WHORF-SAPIR HYPOTHESIS

The idea that language affects thought is most closely associated with what has generally been referred to as the Whorf-Sapir hypothesis (which will be shortened here to the Whorfian hypothesis). Benjamin Whorf (1956) is generally given credit for articulating this view, though it is a (more extreme) view consistent with ideas espoused by Edward Sapir (1921) and others. Whorf was a very atypical contributor to the linguistics and anthropology literature. He was trained as a chemical engineer at Yale where he took classes from Sapir. He then spent his career (he died young, at age 44) as a fire prevention engineer for the Hartford Fire Insurance Company. His ideas regarding language and thought were derived from his lifelong interest in, and study of, Native American languages and culture.

It was Whorf's contention that cognition is malleable and conditioned by language; our experience and representation of the world is a function of the language we speak. According to Whorf:

> We cut nature up, organize it into concepts, and ascribe significance as we do, largely because we are parties to an agreement to organize it in this way—an agreement that holds throughout our speech community and is codified in the patterns of our language. The agreement is, of course, an implicit and unstated one, but its terms are absolutely obligatory; we cannot talk at all except by subscribing to the organization and classification of data which the agreement decrees. (1956; pp. 213–214)

Consider an example. There are distinct linguistic differences between English and Hopi in the manner in which time is handled. English allows for both real plurals (e.g., 10 dogs) and imaginary plurals (e.g., 10 days). The latter, of course, cannot be objectively experienced at the time one uses the term; in a sense it is metaphorical. In contrast, the Hopi language allows for real plurals but not imaginary ones. Thus, the phrase "He stayed 10 days" would have to be translated into something like "He left after the 10th day." Moreover, the English three-tense system does not have an exact parallel in Hopi; temporal relations are marked, but only in a relative rather than absolute sense. It was Whorf's contention that the English language objectifies time in a way that the Hopi language does not. Because of this, people who speak Hopi are presumed to experience time in a way that is very different from those who speak English.

It has been argued that there are two ways of interpreting Whorf's ideas regarding the relationship between thought and language. The first, often termed linguistic relativity, suggests that cognitive variation parallels linguistic variation; structural differences in language are associated with nonlinguistic cognitive differences. In this view, the direction of causality is not specified. Thought may influence language, language may influence thought, or they might influence each other. Regarding this issue, Whorf (1956) stated: "How does such a network of language, culture, and behavior come about historically? Which was first: the language patterns or the cultural norms? In the main they have grown up together, constantly influencing each other" (p. 250).

The other thesis, usually termed linguistic determinism, asserts that cognitive differences among language communities are *caused* by the language differences among those communities. Stated simply, language determines thought. Now, there is some dispute about whether Whorf should be interpreted as adopting this position (Alford, 1981); Whorf's quote suggests linguistic relativity rather than determinism. But his quote continues as follows: "But in this partnership the nature of language is the factor that limits free plasticity and rigidifies channels of development in the more autocratic way. This is so because a language is a system, not just an assemblage of norms" (1956, p. 250). So, there is some ambiguity surrounding the interpretation of Whorf's writings. Regardless, it is determinism for which Whorf has been held accountable and for which early research designed to test his ideas was directed.

Whorf's ideas were fascinating, speculative, and ultimately controversial. Unfortunately, early attempts to empirically evaluate his ideas were ambiguous and open to alternative interpretations. One of the earliest tests of linguistic determinism was conducted by Carroll and Casagrande (1958), who sought to evaluate whether language differences between English and Navajo (Navajo emphasizes structure to a greater degree than does English) were reflected in cognitive differences. Navajo children who were dominant in either Navajo or English performed a classification task. They were shown a pair of objects that simultaneously varied in color and form (e.g., a yellow rope and a blue stick). They were then asked to choose which member of the pair most closely resembled a comparison object that matched both members of the pair on some dimension (e.g., a blue rope). Which member of the pair chosen was assumed to reflect the dimension used for categorizing the object; the choice of the blue stick would reflect color, the choice of a yellow rope, form. Consistent with the English-Navajo language differences, the Navajo-dominant children were more likely to classify on the basis of form (70% of the time) than were the English-dominant children (40% of the time).

However, when Carroll and Casagrande examined the classification of a different set of non-Navajo children (middle-class, English-speaking children from Boston), they found an even higher incidence of classification based on form. So, although the predicted effects occurred for the English-dominant versus Navajo-dominant children, the fact that the non-Navajo children were even more likely to classify on the basis of form contradicts the hypothesis. These ambiguous results have resulted in this study being cited by some writers as providing support for Whorf's hypothesis and by other writers as disconfirmation of Whorf's ideas.

Other early research examined perceptions of, and memory for, color. The logic here was straightforward. According to Whorf, language underlies the categories used for partitioning the "kaleidoscopic flux" of incoming perceptual stimuli. Because linguistic communities differ in the manner in which the color spectrum is lexicalized, there should be corresponding differences in perceptions of and memory for colors. Some early research was consistent with this idea. Brown and Lenneberg (1954), for example, examined the relationship between color codability and memory. Colors that were the easiest to code, as indicated by high coder agreement and the need for relatively few terms, were easier to recall. Hence, the availability of color terms in the lexicon affected the ease with which colors could be remembered. Cultural differences in color codability and subsequent memory have been demonstrated as well (Lantz & Stefflre, 1964; Stefflre, Castillo Vales, & Morley, 1966).

But other studies, in particular those of Rosch (1973; Heider, 1972; Heider & Olivier, 1972)[1] and Berlin and Kay (1969) provided what was regarded as evidence that strongly disconfirmed the hypothesis. Rosch (1973), for example, examined color memory in the Dani, an aboriginal people in Papua, New Guinea. The Dani language has only two color terms, black and white. In this study, Dani participants were shown color chips and then later tested for their recognition of the presented chips. Participants performed better for chips representing primary colors, even though their language had no words for those colors. Rosch then taught participants arbitrary associations between color chips and nonsense syllables. Consistent with the memory results, participants learned the associations more easily for the primary colors. Obviously, there was something about the color spectrum that affected their performance, and that something was independent of their language.

Berlin and Kay (1969) provided further support for the idea that it is the color spectrum itself that affects color perception, independent of the language that a person speaks. First, they noted that there is an underlying logic to the assignment of color names. A few languages (e.g., the Dani's) have only two color terms, and when this occurs those two terms are always black and white. When a language has three color terms, the third term is always red. The next three terms added are always yellow, blue, and green. Second, they found that people from different

---

[1]Heider and Rosch are the same person.

linguistic communities agree on the best (or prototypical) example of any color category, even though they may disagree on defining the boundaries. Like Rosch's research, these results were interpreted by many as indicating that there is an underlying physiological basis for color perception, and that the perception of color is thereby independent of language. Although these results and interpretations have been questioned (see following discussion), they played a very significant role in persuading people that the Whorfian hypothesis was without merit.

Lucy and Schweder (1979) questioned the prevailing interpretation of these studies. They argued that Rosch's results reflected the fact that the primary colors used in her studies were simply more distinctive than the other colors. They showed English-speaking participants three colors (two that were identical and a third that was slightly different) and asked them to indicate which two colors were the same. Participants performed significantly better at this task for the primary colors, a result that did not depend on language because there was no labeling involved. In other words, primary colors appeared to be more distinctive than other colors, and it is this distinctiveness that could explain Rosch's results.

Additional support for (at least) linguistic relativity was provided by Kay and Kempton (1984). Participants in this research were shown triads of color hues and asked to choose which of the three hues differed most from the other two. The colors consisted of eight hues along a continuum of greenish-blue to bluish-green. Participants were speakers of English (who possessed lexical items for green and blue) and speakers of Tarahumara (who did not). Clear between-language differences emerged in this study. English speakers, but not Tarahumara speakers, demonstrated categorical perception; they exaggerated the distance between hues that were close to the boundary between blue and green. Thus, a portion of the color spectrum was perceived differently as a function of whether lexical items existed for the colors blue and green.

A second experiment tested this logic further. If it is the existence of the lexical items that results in exaggerating the perceived distance between blue and green, then if the relevance of the color names is eliminated, the effect should disappear. This was accomplished by showing three hues, two at a time. The hue that was common to both presentations was described as blue (or green) on the first presentation and green (or blue) on the second presentation. By calling the chip both blue and green, the relevance of the lexical items was eliminated and so were the differences between English-speaking and Tarahumara-speaking participants.

The demonstration of categorical perception is important—it provides evidence that lexical items can influence perception in some ways. Conceptually similar results have been demonstrated with speech perception. For example, speakers of English clearly discriminate sounds that vary continuously from pure /r/ to pure /l/; Japanese speakers do not. This perceptual difference has a parallel in the differences between the English and Japanese languages; the former discriminates between these two sounds, the latter does not (Miyawaki et al., 1975).

Importantly, this perceptual difference appears to be acquired; it is not demonstrated by infants (Werker, 1991).

Early tests of Whorf's hypothesis clearly yielded mixed results. There was some supportive evidence (e.g., Brown & Lenneberg, 1954). But critics focused on the studies demonstrating that color perception was pretty much the same the world over, despite linguistic differences in color terms. As a result, Whorf's hypothesis was generally viewed (by psychologists at least) as being disconfirmed (e.g., Clark & Clark, 1977). However, just because color perception is independent of language (and it is by no means clear that it is completely independent) does not mean that other perceptual and cognitive domains are independent of language. It is to those other domains that we now turn.

Reasoning

One plausible way language might affect thought is in terms of the development and use of the basic building blocks of cognition (e.g., schemas). So, for example, number schemas provide a means of communicating about abstract properties regarding a set of objects. But languages differ in terms of the manner in which numbers are lexicalized. English, for example, has a relatively regular system for naming numbers, with the exception of the teens (11–19 are irregular compounds). Chinese, on the other hand, is a completely regular system for base-ten numbers (e.g., 11 is 10 and 1). This difference has consequences: English-speaking children have greater difficulty learning to count in the teens than do Chinese children (Miller & Stigler, 1987).

The most interesting (and controversial) research in this vein has been provided by Bloom (1981), who investigated cross-linguistic differences in counterfactual reasoning. In English and most Indo-European languages there are linguistic devices for expressing counterfactual statements. Thus, in English many counterfactuals take the form of the past tense, or "were to," in the first clause and the use of the subjunctive in the second clause; for example, "If it *hadn't* rained we *would have* played ball." There are apparently no parallel constructions in Chinese. Hence, counterfactual statements such as these are difficult to express in Chinese, and the closest translation would be something like "It rained yesterday, so we did not play ball." The two expressions are not equivalent.

Bloom explored the possibility that English-Chinese language differences have a corresponding impact on the ability to reason counterfactually. In some studies, he had participants read counterfactual paragraphs containing a negated premise regarding a target (e.g., Brier couldn't read Chinese), as well as implications of the premise had it been true (e.g., Brier would have discovered the relevance of Chinese philosophical works for his own investigation). Participants were then asked to choose an answer that described the target's contribution. All but one of the presented answers described implications that could not occur given the negated premise; the other answer was that none of the other answers were correct. The latter was the correct counterfactual response (as long as participants also explained why). American participants were far more likely to endorse the correct counterfactual answer (98% in the weak counterfactual version; 96% in the strong counterfactual version) than were Chinese participants (6% in the weak counterfactual version; 46–63% in the strong counterfactual version).

In a related but simpler study, Bloom presented the following example to American and Taiwanese participants:

"If all circles were large and this small triangle △ were a circle, would it be large?"

Again, far more American participants (83%) chose the counterfactual response (i.e., yes) than did the Taiwanese participants (25%).

On the basis of these data, Bloom argued that the existence of counterfactual devices in English (but not in Chinese) allows speakers of the former language to more easily and accurately engage in counterfactual reasoning than speakers of the latter language; it is clearly a demonstration of linguistic relativity in the realm of reasoning. Note, however, that these results do not mean that speakers of Chinese never engage in counterfactual reasoning. Many of the most basic and universal features of human experience—regret, hope, etc.—all require thinking in this realm. Hence, a reasonable interpretation of these results is that it is more difficult for Chinese speakers to reason counterfactually than it is for English speakers.

Bloom's claims have not gone unchallenged (e.g., Au, 1983, 1984; Cheng, 1985; Liu, 1985). The most frequent criticism of his research is that the Chinese translations he used were less idiomatic than the English versions. When Au (1983) used more idiomatic translations, she found virtually no difference between English and Chinese speakers in counterfactual reasoning. It should be noted, however, that the Chinese participants in her study were Chinese-English bilinguals, and so their reasoning could have been performed in English. This is an important avenue for future research; reasoning differences get at the heart of linguistic determinism. More sophisticated, alternative measures of reasoning would also be helpful. For example, although counterfactual reasoning is possible for speakers of Chinese and English, it might be easier for the latter than for the former, and reaction time differences might reflect this fact (e.g., Hunt & Agnoli, 1991).

Perhaps the most interesting manner in which language might influence thought is in terms of person perception. Many behaviors are ambiguous and can be described in multiple ways. For example, Bob's behavior might be described as friendly by some and flirtatious by others. But any behavior description will be constrained by the lexical items available in one's language. Thus differences among languages in terms of available personality constructs might result in differing impressions of people.

There is pretty compelling evidence that this is so. Hoffman, Lau, and Johnson (1986) presented Chinese-English bilinguals with personality descriptors. Two of the descriptions were consistent with a one-word label in English (but not Chinese) (e.g., artistic type), and two were consistent with a one-word label in Chinese (but not in English) (e.g., *shi gu;* a person who is worldly, experienced, reserved, socially skilled, and devoted to family). Participants were randomly assigned to read the descriptions in either Chinese or in English, and then five days later their impressions of and memory for the target were assessed. Participants demonstrated schematic processing of the descriptions when the language they used provided a label for the description; their impressions were more congruent with the label, and they were more likely to endorse nonpresented traits consistent with the label. In other words, participants formed a more stereotypical representation of the description when the language they used contained a relevant personality construct than when it did not. This study demonstrates that thinking about people can be influenced by the language that one uses. Note, however, that this is not a strong Whorfian effect; people using any language can form a representation of another person. However, the nature of that representation (e.g., the ease with which it is formed) may vary among languages.

Person perception, unlike color perception, is a realm for which language-thought effects would seem to be relatively likely. There appears to be a physiological basis for color perception, and this may reduce the role of language in the perception of color. Person perception, on the other hand, is a far more ambiguous enterprise; people may differ in terms of how they label the behavior of others. And so it is in this domain that linguistic influences might be most pronounced. Of course, this does not mean that person perception is completely subjective. The fact that the five-factor personality taxonomy (the "Big Five") appears to replicate in different cultures (John, 1990) suggests that there is an underlying, universal order to our perceptions of others' personalities. Still, person perception is clearly more ambiguous than color perception, and hence more likely to be linguistically influenced.

The role of language in person perception may explain some well-known social psychological phenomena. Consider the fundamental attribution error, or tendency to explain the behavior of others in terms of internal dispositions and to ignore the role of situational variables. This effect appears to be limited to Western cultures; it does not occur, for example, in India (Miller, 1984). Why? Well, one possibility is that the English lexicon has a relatively high number of personality descriptors, thereby increasing the likelihood that the behavior of others will be thought about in dispositional terms. Languages (e.g., as in India) that have fewer dispositional terms available make it relatively more difficult to interpret other's behaviors in terms of traits. However, these languages may have available a greater number of situational descriptors; hence, the situation is more likely to be invoked when explaining the behavior of others.

Issues and Recent Research

As this brief review suggests, tests of various versions of Whorf's hypothesis have yielded conflicting findings. Of course, many of these results are not directly comparable because researchers have investigated different aspects of thought (perceptions, memory, reasoning) and done so in different domains (color, people). Although these ambiguities have caused some to proclaim the death of Whorf's hypothesis (e.g., Clark & Clark, 1977), others have been less critical. Recently there has been a clear resurgence of interest in these ideas by psychologists (e.g., Chiu, Krauss, & Lau, 1998; Hunt & Agnoli, 1991; Hardin & Banaji, 1993), anthropologists and linguists (e.g., Gumperz & Levinson, 1996), and others.

Of course, the idea that all thought is conditioned by language is absurd, and so a less-extreme view, a view that language influences (rather than strictly determines) thought is usually espoused (e.g., Hunt & Agnoli, 1991). Some (e.g., Foss and Hakes, 1978) have argued that a weaker version of the hypothesis cannot really be tested because it postulates qualitative rather than quantitative cognitive differences. But others (e.g., Hunt & Angoli, 1991) have suggested that this is not an insurmountable problem; the language-thought relationship can be quantified by testing for effects relative to some standard psycholinguistic effect.

Linguistic relativity, of course, is antithetical to much of the universalist thinking that has dominated linguistics and cognitive psychology for the past 25 years. The universalist position (e.g., Pinker, 1994) suggests that there is really only one human language, albeit one with thousands of different manifestations. So, although there is tremendous variability among languages in terms of surface features, the deep structure is believed to be essentially the same. In this view, language is viewed as something of a late-in-the-game appendage to our basic cognitive apparati, and if this is so, then obviously language could not play a role in determining the nature of our thoughts. It is important to keep in mind that language and thought exist at different levels, and although there may be basic levels of thought that are universal and independent of language (e.g., categories such as male-female), this may not be the case for all levels of thought. This is especially so for social cognitions, a domain of our thinking most likely to be interwoven with language. If languages differ only in terms of surface structure, whether or not those differences influence thought is an empirical question rather than grounds for rejecting linguistic relativity completely.

It is also important to note that in addition to between-language differences, there are also within-language differences; languages provide options (e.g., active vs. passive) for its users. This has led some (e.g., Kay, 1996) to argue that linguistic relativity is impossible because it means that speakers of a single language must possess conflicting views of their world. Similarly, Clark (1996b) argues that languages are exceedingly flexible in the manner in which meaning is conveyed. For example, people can quite easily generate new expressions on the spot and be understood by others (Clark & Gerrig, 1983). Because of this, Clark argues that meaning should be viewed as residing not in words but rather in the communicative uses to which words are put. Such linguistic flexibility would obviously attenuate the effect of language on thought.

But the fact that there are within-language options need not be completely detrimental to a relativistic view. After all, languages differ in the options that they provide. Rather than being absurd (à la Kay), it might be the case that intralanguage options do influence thought, albeit in a way somewhat different than that envisioned by Whorf. For example, Slobin (1996) argues that rather than framing the issue in terms of the impact of language on thought, we should instead view the issue in terms of thinking for speaking. During the course of language acquisition, children develop particular ways of thinking in order to use the language they are acquiring. In this way cognition (at least at a very basic and fundamental level) may not vary over language communities, but the thinking required to use a particular language could vary. Many of the aspects of thinking that might be affected in this way are derived from language (e.g., voice, definiteness), rather than being general categories of thought that exist independently of language. As a result, Slobin argues that speakers of different languages may have a "different on-line organization of the flow of information and attention to the particular details that receive linguistic expression" (1996, p. 78). This suggests that it is the use of language, rather than language per se, that affects thought. It is this possibility that is considered in detail in the next section.

LANGUAGE USE

Research testing linguistic relativity has generally treated language as an abstract system; the relationship between the linguistic system and a parallel cognitive system is examined. But the language-thought relationship can be viewed in broader terms. Specifically, thought can be viewed as being influenced by language *use* rather than being affected by the existence of language as an abstract system (Chiu, Krauss, & Lau, 1998). These effects would then be specific to a particular occasion of talk. This may not reflect linguistic determinism as envisioned by Whorf, but it does represent a specific way in which language can affect cognitive processes. Rather than making cross-linguistic comparisons, the comparison of interest now becomes the effect of using language versus not using language. Such effects might be referred to as indirect effects; it is not the language itself, but rather its use, that influences thought. There is a wealth of psychological research consistent with this view.

For example, many studies have demonstrated how verbal labels influence the manner in which people encode, represent, and retrieve information. One of the earliest studies in this regard was conducted by Carmichael, Hogan, and Walter (1932). They gave participants identical figures to memorize, but with different labels randomly assigned to the figures. For example, one figure was described as a dumbbell for some participants and as a pair of glasses for other participants. Later, when participants were asked to draw the presented stimuli, their drawings were consistent with the label they had received (e.g., those receiving the dumbbell label produced a figure closely resembling a dumbbell; those receiving the glasses label, a pair of glasses).

Recent research has demonstrated that the effects of verbal labels on visual memory are complicated, and that the use of labels can both hinder and facilitate subsequent memory. The phenomenon referred to as verbal overshadowing (Schooler & Engstler-Schooler, 1990) is an example of the former. Participants in these experiments were presented visual stimuli (e.g., a videotape of a bank robbery, color chips) and in some conditions were asked to verbally describe what they had seen (e.g., the face of the robber, the color chips). Participants asked to describe the stimuli displayed poorer memory for the stimuli than participants who had not verbalized descriptions of the stimuli. The authors suggest that the act of verbalizing the stimuli created a verbal representation of the stimuli (in addition to a visual representation). This verbal-based representation then interfered with the visual representation, making subsequent recognition of the stimuli more difficult.

Bahrick and Boucher (1968) demonstrated that verbalization of stimulus labels can hinder visual recognition, but actually facilitate verbal recall. In this study, drawings of common objects were presented to participants, some of whom were asked to verbalize a label for the objects. Later, participants' visual recognition and verbal memory for the presented objects was tested. Those who had labeled the objects had relatively poor visual recognition (a verbal overshadowing effect), but enhanced verbal memory for the objects; linguistic encoding facilitated memory for the verbal representation, but interfered with the visual code.

In a similar way, the mislabeling of a visual stimulus can bias subsequent memory for that stimulus. In a well-known study Loftus (1977) showed participants a film of an accident involving a green car. Later, participants were queried about the film and asked about either a blue car or a car for which no color was mentioned. Participants memory was influenced by the car label; those asked about the "blue" car recognized the car as being more blue than those asked about the car without a color label. For the latter participants, the colors were normally distributed around the true color of the presented car. Note the similarity here to the results of some of the early color tests of the Whorf hypothesis (Lantz & Stefflre, 1964). In the Loftus case the *use* of a particular color term affected subsequent memory; in the Lantz and Stefflre study it was the existence of the color term that influenced memory.

Language use does not always hinder subsequent visual memory. It can, for example, facilitate subsequent visual memory if there is a high degree of correspondence between the visual and verbal representation (Klatsky, Martin, &

Kane, 1982). More important, verbal labels can provide a means of organizing a large stimulus set, an effect demonstrated by Santa and Baker (1975). Participants in this study were shown shapes paired with either nonsense labels or meaningful words. Subsequent memory for the shapes was superior for the meaningful words than for the nonsense words. In addition, recall of shapes paired with words were clustered around the word categories, an effect that did not occur for the nonsense words. Verbal labels provided an organizational framework for the presented visual material.

The role of verbal labels in organizing incoming stimuli has been clearly demonstrated with written materials. Take, for example, the classic studies conducted by John Bransford and colleagues in the early 1970s. In one of these studies (Bransford & Johnson, 1972), participants were asked to read an ambiguous paragraph (about washing clothes) either with a title, without a title, or with a title that was presented after the passage had been read. Participants who had received the title before reading the passage recalled far more of the material than did other participants. The presentation of the title provided a means of organizing and creating a coherent representation of the passage.

Verbal labels may play a role in processing many different types of information. Schemas, for example, can be activated with a verbal label and influence the manner in which subsequent information is encoded and represented and the process by which it is retrieved. Numerous studies have demonstrated that role schemas (e.g., Cohen, 1981) and event schemas (or scripts; e.g., Schank & Abelson, 1977) can function in just this way. For example, being told that someone is a "waitress" can influence what we notice and remember about that person when we interact with her (Cohen, 1981). Verbal labels serve as a means of directing attention to a subset of incoming information, an effect that is reminiscent of Allport's (1954) description of the role of language in prejudice.

Of course, these effects are not due to language per se; they result from the chunk of knowledge (or schema) that is activated by a lexical item. But in general it is the use of language that activates that structure. The importance of language use is not limited to models of schematic processing; representations in other high-level models of cognition (e.g., exemplar models, associative models) are labeled with lexical items.

One verbal activity with important cognitive consequences is storytelling (McAdams, 1993; Pennington & Hastie, 1988; Schank & Abelson, 1995). For example, the construction of a story involves the glossing over of details (everything can't be included in a story) and the forcing of a sequence of events into a storylike structure. Consequently, the representation that remains is a function of the act of verbalizing a story (Schank & Abelson, 1995). A recent study by McGregor & Holmes (1999) illustrates this well. They had participants tell a biased story about a relationship conflict as if they were a lawyer for one of the characters. Later, participants' memory for and judgments of the targets were assessed. In all studies there was clear evidence of a storytelling effect. Specifically, subsequent judgments were biased in the direction of the story that participants told. Note that this effect is independent of any motivational influences; participants were randomly assigned the particular story perspective that they adopted. The effect also occurred after a delay of 40 weeks, a time when memory for most of the original details was lost, and it occurred when participants were provided the unbiased information (the complete transcripts they originally used) immediately before making their judgments. The effect is due, in part, to selective memory; people tend to recall story-consistent information. But the effect occurs even when differential memory is controlled or is nonexistent. In this case, the story skeleton or gist serves as a heuristic that is used for making judgments of the people.

Another verbal activity with important cognitive consequences is the giving of reasons for one's decisions. Research demonstrates that verbalizing reasons for a decision can influence various aspects of the decision-making process, including the quality of the decision itself. For example, Wilson and Schooler (1991) asked participants to judge the quality of different brands of strawberry jam (Experiment 1) or to indicate their preferences for different college courses (Experiment 2). In both experiments, participants who had been asked to analyze the reasons for their decisions made less-optimal decisions than did those who did not verbalize their reasons.

Apparently, analyzing reasons causes people to attend to nonoptimal criteria, which then produces poorer decisions. But why? The generation of reasons appears to be a biased activity that is influenced by the ease of language use. Reasons that are the easiest to verbalize—the easiest to put into words—are the ones most likely to be articulated. Other reasons that may have played a role, yet are more difficult to verbalize, will tend not to be mentioned. For example, in a study conducted by Wilson et al. (1993), participants rated a set of posters that were either humorous (easy to verbalize features) or artistic (difficult to verbalize features). When participants were asked to verbalize their reasons, the ease with which poster attributes could be articulated affected the reasons that were given; more positive attributes were articulated for the humorous poster than for the artistic poster. Ultimately, this difference affected participants' ratings; people who had generated reasons preferred the humorous posters; control participants preferred the artistic posters.

Clearly, the act of using language—the telling of a story, giving reasons for a decision, activating a schema with a lexical item—can play an important role in subsequent cognitive processes. This is not linguistic determinism in the Whorfian sense; language is not determining how one thinks about things. But it is a type of linguistic relativity because the use of language is influencing subsequent cognitive operations. In the next section, a particular instance of language use with potential cognitive consequences is discussed in some detail.

IMPLICIT CAUSALITY

One feature of language that might play an important role in person perception and attribution is a phenomenon referred to as implicit causality. The first research reports of implicit causality were published in the late 1960s and early 1970s (Abelson & Kanouse, 1966; Garvey & Caramazza, 1974; Kanouse, 1972; McArthur, 1972). But it was Brown and Fish (1983) who are probably most responsible for bringing the phenomenon to the attention of psychologists. Dozens of papers have now been published, and the effect appears to be reliable, robust, and sizable (see Rudolph & Forsterling, 1997, for a review). Although there is some debate about the mechanisms responsible for implicit causality, it represents a clear demonstration of a relationship between language and thought. Whether it represents linguistic determinism in the Whorfian sense is, as we'll see, an open, empirical question.

Implicit causality can best be described with an example. When people are asked to assign causality for simple sentences such as "Ann helped Barb," they are more likely to believe that Ann is the cause rather than Barb. In contrast, when asked to assign causality for the simple sentence "Ann hated Barb," they tend to believe Barb is the causal locus. Note that Ann and Barb occupy the same grammatical roles in both sentences; Ann is the subject and Barb is the object. So, why is Ann the cause in the first and Barb in the second? The difference is due to the implicit causality believed to be inherent in certain verbs. Brown and Fish used case grammar (Fillmore, 1968) to suggest that Ann and Barb occupy different semantic roles, and judgments of causality are influenced by these semantic roles.

The first sentence involves what is termed an action verb (help) with the corresponding semantic roles of agent (someone or something that brings about an action) and patient (someone or something that undergoes a changed state). In general, people tend to assign greater causal weight to the agent (e.g., Ann) than to the patient (e.g., Barb). It is important to note that this is not a grammatical effect; the agent is assigned greater causal weight regardless of whether it is the grammatical subject or object. So, regardless of whether people judge "Ann, helped Barb" or "Barb was helped by Ann," they tend to assign greater causal weight to Ann than to Barb.[2]

The second sentence—Ann hated Barb—involves a state verb—with the corresponding semantic roles of experiencer (someone having a particular experience) and stimulus (someone or something giving rise to a particular experience). In general, people tend to assign greater causal weight to the stimulus (Barb) than to the experiencer (Ann). Again, this is not a grammatical effect. In fact, Brown

---

[2]As noted by Rudolph and Forsterling (1997), it is possible for grammatical role to influence causal assignments.

and Fish (1983) proposed two classes of state verbs—those with the experiencer in the subject role (termed experiencer-stimulus verbs) and those with the stimulus in the subject role (stimulus-experiencer verbs). For both experiencer-stimulus verbs (e.g., like, hate) and stimulus-experiencer verbs (e.g., impress, bore) the tendency is to assign greater causal weight to the stimulus, even though grammatical role varies over verb type.

The most common method for investigating implicit causality has been to present participants with minimal sentences (e.g., Ted helped Joe) and ask them to indicate whether this occurred because of something about the subject (Ted) or something about the object (Joe). Sometimes an open-ended format is used; participants are asked to complete minimal sentences such as "Ted helped Joe because. . . ." With these and related paradigms, the research strongly supports the implicit causality predictions for state verbs (stimulus attributions are far more likely than experiencer attributions) (e.g., Au, 1986; Brown & Fish, 1983; Corrigan, 1988; Hoffman & Tchir, 1990). The results for action verbs have generally been in line with predictions. However, contradictory findings have been reported by Au (1986), Van Kleek, Hillger, and Brown (1988), and others. But these contradictory results appear to be explained if action verbs are subdivided based on whether the action was initiated by the agent or was a response to something in the environment (primarily the other person). A distinction along these lines was made by Heider (1958) and has been adopted by many researchers working in this area (e.g., Au, 1986; Corrigan, 1993; Rudolph & Forsterling, 1997). For action verbs that are essentially reactions or are evoked, the tendency is to assign greater causal weight to the patient (Rudolph & Forsterling, 1997). For example, Ann is usually assigned greater causal weight than Barb in "Barb congratulated Ann." For action verbs that are not reactions, it is usually the agent that is the perceived causal locus.

The Linguistic Category Model

A slightly different verb classification system has been proposed by Semin and Fiedler (1988, 1991). Termed the linguistic category model, this approach overlaps implicit causality by elucidating the causal properties of classes of verbs. It differs, however, in that it is concerned with additional psychological dimensions of verb types. I describe the causal dimension first, and then discuss the other psychological dimensions.

As with other implicit causality schemes, the linguistic category model distinguishes between state verbs and action verbs. However, two types of action verbs are proposed: interpretive action verbs and descriptive action verbs. Descriptive action verbs are concrete and objective descriptions of observable events (e.g., call, meet, visit); interpretive action verbs are less objective (and more "interpretive") than descriptive action verbs (e.g., help, cheat, imitate). The two other categories in the scheme correspond to state verbs in the Brown and Fish taxonomy.

The first, termed state action verbs, is identical to stimulus-experiencer verbs (e.g., amaze, anger, excite); the second, termed state verbs, is identical to experiencer-stimulus verbs (e.g., admire, like, hate). Both refer to internal, emotional (and hence not directly observable) states. State action verbs are specific reactions to some external action and are contextually grounded. State verbs, on the other hand, are more enduring and do not require the emotional response to be a reaction to a specific action.

As with the Brown and Fish taxonomy, attributions of causality vary over these verb classes in systematic ways. Thus, state verbs are roughly equivalent to the experiencer-stimulus category and result in object attributions, and state action verbs are roughly equivalent to stimulus-experiencer verbs and result in subject attributions. Similarly, descriptive action verbs and interpretive action verbs are action verbs (of the agent-patient variety) and, hence, generally result in subject attributions.

However, the model extends verb classification to include dimensions other than perceived causality, and in doing so demonstrates additional ways in which language and thought may be related. The primary dimension here is one of abstractness-concreteness, although there are additional properties associated with this general dimension including verifiability (low for adjectives; high for descriptive action verbs), revealingness (high for adjectives; low for descriptive action verbs), and so on (see Table 6.1). Descriptive action verbs (e.g., talk) are the least abstract and revealing of the actor, but the easiest to verify. To describe someone as talking says very little about that person; talk is a concrete, easily verifiable and agreed-upon description of an observable act.

The next category on the continuum is interpretive action verbs. These are more abstract than descriptive action verbs and hence more revealing about the person being described; to say one person helped another says more about that person than saying that the person talked to another. Relatedly, interpretive action verbs are less easy to verify and subject to greater observer disagreement; it is less easy to identify a behavior as constituting help than a behavior constituting talk.

TABLE 6.1
Linguistic Category Model (after Semin and Fiedler, 1988)

	Most Concrete	Least Revealing	Most Verifiable
Descriptive Action Verbs			
Interpretive Action Verbs	↕	↕	↕
State Action Verbs			
State Verbs			
Adjectives			
	Least Concrete	Most Revealing	Least Verifiable

The continuum then continues with state action verbs (e.g., surprise), followed by state verbs (e.g., like), and lastly adjectives (e.g., honest). As internal states, both state verb classes are less observable—and hence less verifiable and agreed on—than action verbs. State verbs are also more enduring than state action verbs, and hence more abstract and revealing about the person (an internal reaction that persists reveals more of an actor than one that is a momentary reaction to an event). Relative to verbs, adjectives (e.g., honest) are more abstract (they are not tied to a specific behavior) and reveal more about the person being described. Relatedly, they are less objective and verifiable than verbs.

Almost any particular action can be encoded at different levels, and the verb (or adjective) chosen to describe that action will have important cognitive consequences. So, for example, Andy could be described as "hitting" Bob (a descriptive action verb), or more abstractly as "hurting" Bob (an interpretive action verb), or more abstractly yet as "hating" Bob (a state verb). Or, rather than describing the action, Andy might simply be referred to an aggressive person.

These linguistic choices have important interpersonal consequences. For example, they can play a role in the perpetuation of intergroup stereotypes, a phenomenon referred to as the linguistic intergroup bias, or tendency to use differing levels of abstraction when describing the positive and negative actions of in-group and in-group members (Fiedler, Semin, & Finkenauer, 1993; Maass & Arcuri, 1996; Maass, Milesi, Zabbini, & Stahlberg, 1995; Maass, Salvi, Arcuri, & Semin, 1989). For example, in a study conducted by Maass and associates (1989), members of different riding groups in Italy were shown pictures of cartoons (one half socially desirable and one half socially undesirable) involving members of these different riding groups, including each participant's own club (and hence one's in-group). Participants were asked to choose an alternative that described the scene (Experiment 1) or to provide a free description of the scene (Experiment 2). When the cartoon depicted in-group members engaged in positive behaviors, participants were more likely to use adjectives, words that reflect relatively enduring and stable qualities. When in-group members were depicted as engaging in negative behaviors, participants described the behavior more concretely (with descriptive action verbs), thereby implicating that the behaviors were unique and unstable and not revealing of the personal qualities of the actor. Of course, this tendency was reversed for cartoons depicting out-group members; their positive behaviors were described concretely (descriptive action verbs) and their negative behaviors more abstractly (although the results were stronger for the positive than for the negative behaviors).

Recently, Webster, Kruglanski, and Pattison (1997) have demonstrated the existence of individual differences in the intergroup bias. People who score high on the need for closure (a desire to possess a definite answer on some topic) are more likely than those scoring low on this dimension to use a high level of abstraction when describing positive in-group behavior and negative out-group behavior. Finally, note how this feature of language may play a role in the communication and perpetuation of stereotypes. The use of more-abstract language when describing the negative behaviors of an out-group may result in the recipient of such communications forming more stereotypical views of the out-group; the abstract language serves to induce dispositional attributions regarding the out-group (e.g., Wigboldus, Semin, & Spears, 2000).

Explanations of Implicit Causality

Several explanations have been proposed for implicit causality (see Rudolph & Forsterling, 1997, for a review) and some of them are consistent with Whorf's hypothesis. These explanations suggest that language imposes a structure on causal thinking that overrides basic, nonlinguistic, attributional mechanisms. Non-Whorfian approaches, on the other hand, assume that the structure of language reflects (rather than determines) basic human tendencies regarding causal thinking. Thus, basic attributional principles guide assessments of causality and simultaneously have influenced the structure of language. But note that even these explanations invoke linguistic relativity (though not determinism).

One Whorfian explanation—first proposed but then rejected by Brown and Fish (1983)—is termed the priming or lexical hypothesis. The basic idea is that interpersonal verbs have associated with them dispositional terms referencing the sentence subject, object, or both. The derived dispositional terms associated with the verbs *help, like,* and *amaze* are *helpful, likeable,* and *amazing,* respectively. Now, the interesting thing about this is that the derived dispositional terms are not symmetrical, but rather parallel quite closely the causal reasoning tendencies for these verbs. Specifically, for action verbs (of the agent-patient variety) most of the dispositional terms reference the agent rather than the patient (e.g., *help → helpful),* thereby mirroring the tendency to perceive the agent rather than patient as the causal locus. And both stimulus-experiencer verbs (e.g., *impress → impressive)* and experiencer-stimulus verbs (e.g., *like → likeable)* have dispositional terms referencing the stimulus rather than the experiencer. Again, the preponderance of dispositional terms favors the role most likely to be perceived as causally responsible. In an extensive analysis of approximately 900 English interpersonal verbs, Hoffman and Tchir (1990) found that over 90% of the action verbs had dispositional terms referencing the agent, and only 25% of the terms referenced the patient. For state verbs, over 75% had terms referencing the stimulus and fewer than 50% referencing the experiencer.

The lexical hypothesis suggests that the implicit causality effect is mediated by these derived dispositional terms. In a specific test of this hypothesis, Hoffman and Tchir (1990) orthogonally varied semantic role and whether the verb had a dispositional term referencing the expected causal focus (agents for action verbs and stimuli for state verbs). They reported a significant Semantic Role X Dispositional term interaction; there was a larger implicit causality effect for verbs with terms referencing the expected causal locus than for those that did not have a dispositional term (but see Rudolph & Forsterling, 1997 for an alternative interpretation).

Hoffman and Tchir (1990) also conducted an experimental test of the hypothesis. Participants were given nonsense verbs (e.g., gelf) that were described in terms of either the sentence subject (a person who gelfs) or sentence object (a person who is gelfable). When participants were asked to indicate causality, they were more likely to rate agents and stimuli as more important when the verb had been described in terms of dispositions referencing agents and patients respectively.

Additional support for the lexical hypothesis was provided by Holtgraves and Raymond (1995). In these studies, participants were provided minimal sentences with action and state verbs and were asked to form impressions of the people described by the sentences. A short time later they were given a list of the verbs and asked to recall the names that had been presented with the verbs. Participants were more likely to recall the names of agents (rather than patients) and stimuli (rather than experiencers). The authors argued that the explanation most consistent with these results is the lexical (priming) hypothesis. Specifically, the dispositional terms associated with the verbs serve as retrieval routes for recalling the names. Thus, Ann is more likely to be recalled than Barb in "Ann helped Barb" because the dispositional term (helpful) references Ann rather than Barb.

The lexical hypothesis can be regarded as a Whorfian effect; perceptions of interpersonal causality are constrained by the lexicon. Note that it is a kind of Whorfian effect, however, because how we think about interpersonal events is constrained by the lexicon and not by any inherent limitations of the language. That is, dispositional terms referencing any semantic role are possible in English (and other languages as well). Still, the existing lexicon can guide or constrain our thoughts about causality.

There are several non-Whorfian explanations for the implicit causality effect. The major alternative was termed the causal schema hypothesis by Brown and Fish (1983); Rudolph and Forsterling (1997) refer to it as the covariation hypothesis. In this view, the lexicon is a result of primitive schemas people have for thinking about interpersonal causality. Thus, because of an agent-patient schema, we tend to assign causality to agents rather than patients, and because of a stimulus-experiencer schema, we tend to assign causality to stimuli rather than to experiencers. Note that these schemas operate independent of language; in fact, their existence is assumed to influence language. That these basic patterns of thinking exist and affect language can be seen in the fact that for interpersonal verbs there are relatively few experiencer and patient derived dispositional terms (although such terms are possible).

These causal schemas are part of the meaning of verbs, and as such convey covariation information that then shows up in terms of perceived causality. Thus, action verbs (agent-patient) convey low consensus and low distinctiveness, and hence the agent is perceived as causally responsible. Experiencer-stimuli verbs convey high consensus and high distinctiveness, and hence the stimulus is perceived as causally responsible. Note that this patterning is presumed to reflect reality. Everyone likes others, but fewer are regarded as likeable; hence, it is the stimulus that is usually perceived as responsible.

There is support for this view. Brown and Fish (1983) presented participants minimal sentences (e.g., Tom helps Bob) and assessed estimates of consensus (Tom helps most others) and distinctiveness (Most others help Bob) information. Consensus and distinctiveness ratings were highly related to verb type along the lines suggested above. Other researchers (e.g., Hoffman & Tchir, 1990) presented minimal sentences to participants and assessed ratings of distinctiveness and consensus in addition to attributions of causality. Distinctiveness and consensus ratings paralleled those reported by Brown and Fish (1983). But more important, when these ratings were statistically controlled, the implicit causality effect for attributions disappeared, a result that is consistent with the idea that covariation information mediates the implicit causality effect. An experimental test of this hypothesis (McArthur, 1972) provides additional support for this view.

There are other non-Whorfian explanations that are similar in some respects to the covariation hypothesis. Kasof and Lee (1993), for example, argue that perceived salience mediates implicit causality. For action verbs (in the active voice), the agent is presumably more salient than the patient and, hence, more likely to be perceived as the causal locus. The salience hypothesis is quite similar to the covariation hypothesis; salience and covariation are related concepts. The important point for the present discussion is the idea that covariation (and salience) information is part of the meaning of verbs, and this meaning is derived from basic cognitive operations in terms of how people think about causality.

With few exceptions, most implicit causality research has not been concerned with testing Whorf's hypothesis. And really, none of this research can be taken as supporting linguistic determinism. In terms of causality, languages seem to be sufficiently flexible so as to allow the development of lexical items with any causal locus. Still, this does not mean that the lexicon, as it currently exists, cannot influence thinking about the people referenced with certain verbs. Someone who is told that Fred helped Mark (everything else being equal) may be more likely to have her impression of Fred altered than her impression of Mark. Note that in this case it is the *use* of language—the choice of one word rather than another—that influences perceptions.

Of course, the speaker may have chosen the verb *help* for exactly this reason—in order to convey information about what a helpful person Fred is (rather than what a needy person Mark is). But to describe another is to make choices among linguistic items, and the set of such items is not infinite. The items that are available may play a role in how we think about the person being described. Of course, the items that exist may reflect social reality; everyone needs help at some time, but not everyone is a helpful person. This illustrates how difficult it is to disentangle the reciprocal nature of the relationship between language and thought.

CONVERSATIONAL PRAGMATICS
AND COGNITION

Most of the research discussed so far in this chapter has been concerned with lex-ical effects. But linguistic relativity is not limited to word meanings. For example, Whorf argued that grammar has a particularly powerful effect on thought, although grammatical effects have rarely been tested. Likewise, the impact of pragmatics on cognition has received relatively little attention within a Whorfian framework. But intuitively, certain pragmatic features would seem to play an important role in how we think. Consider, for example, how languages differ in the extent to which interlocutors must mark relative status. Some languages (e.g., Korean) grammaticalize status; others (e.g., English) do not.[3] It is not unreason-able to suspect that speakers of the former will be more attuned to status than are speakers of the latter (e.g., Holtgraves & Yang, 1992).

    Although not concerned explicitly with Whorf's ideas, there is an area of research that has developed over the past 15 years regarding the role of pragmatics, primarily conversational implicature, in reasoning. Prior to this development, most research on judgment and reasoning centered on internal, intrapersonal processes (inference, attention, memory, etc.). A common theme running through this literature was that human judgment and reasoning are often nonoptimal. For example, people fail to use base rate information (Kahneman & Tversky, 1973), they ignore the effects of situa-tions on people's behavior (Nisbett & Ross, 1980), they use nondiagnostic informa-tion in their decisions (the dilution effect; Nisbett, Zukier, & Lemley, 1981), they are susceptible to leading questions (Loftus & Palmer, 1974), and so on.

    But some researchers, in particular Norbert Schwarz and Denis Hilton, have argued that these judgmental biases are not biases at all, but rather reflect the operation of basic pragmatic principles. In this view these "biases" are a result of basic principles regarding how people converse; they represent interpersonal effects rather than (or in addition to) intrapersonal effects. This explanation rests largely on Grice's (1975) theory of conversational implicature (see chap. 1). According to Grice, conversations are guided by the cooperative principle and corresponding maxims of quality (be truthful), quantity (be appropriately inform-ative), relation (be relevant), and manner (be clear). Because people communicate with the *expectation* that another's contributions will be in accord with these max-ims, when these maxims are violated people construct interpretations that are consistent with the cooperative principle.

    These conversational principles are assumed to operate in all communicative situations, including situations in which the reasoning skills of experimental par-ticipants are being examined.[4] That is, participants in such studies will generally

---

[3]English marks status in terms of address, but not in terms of verbs.

[4]Clearly there are exceptions to this such as courtroom trials, when the conversational maxims are suspended (e.g., Levinson, 1979).

interpret the communications of an experimenter (including the stimulus materials used in the experiment) as if they were in accord with Grice's (1975) maxims. This can result in an interpretation of the materials that is at odds with what the experimenter intends.

Several examples can illustrate this point. Consider first the classic Kahneman and Tversky (1973) demonstration that people fail to adequately utilize base-rate information. In their study, participants were provided with person descriptions such as the following:

Jack is a 45-year-old man. He is married and has four children. He is generally conservative, careful, and ambitious. He shows no interest in political and social issues and spends most of his free time on his many hobbies, which include home carpentry, sailing, and mathematical puzzles.

The following are the instructions that were given to participants:

A panel of psychologists have interviewed and administered personality tests to 30 (70) engineers and 70 (30) lawyers, all successful in their respective fields. On the basis of this information, thumbnail descriptions of the 30 (70) engineers and 70 (30) lawyers have been written. You will find on your forms five descriptions, chosen at random from the 100 available descriptions. For each description, please indicate your probability that the person described is an engineer, on a scale from 0 to 100.

In this study, participants were far more likely to predict that Jack was an engineer rather than a lawyer, even when the base-rate for lawyers was far greater than that for engineers. The usual interpretation of this finding is that participant judgments were based on the degree of similarity between a sample and a population (the description above matches most closely the stereotype of an engineer), and that participants failed to appropriately use the base-rate information that had been provided.

What seems to be crucial here is the instructions. Participants were told the description was based on personality tests administered by a panel of psychologists. Now, personality tests administered by psychologists clearly represent individuating information rather than base-rate information, and because the experimenter gives this information to participants as part of the experimental procedure, it seems reasonable that participants will assume this information should be used in making their judgments. They assume the information is relevant (in Grice's sense). And so they use it; their responses reflect this information and hence the putative operation of the representativeness heuristic.

Several studies have demonstrated that if this task is changed in various ways, then the likelihood that participants will "inappropriately" use individuating information is decreased. For example, if the presumed relevance of the individuating information is undermined, people are far less likely to use it. Schwarz,

Strack, Hilton, and Naderer (1991) tested this by telling some participants that the personality description, rather than being written by a psychologist based on a personality test, was compiled by a computer that randomly drew descriptive sentences bearing on the target person. Under these circumstances, participants were far less likely to use the individuating information, and instead placed greater weight on the base-rate information.

Other research has demonstrated how various features of the Kahneman and Tversky task contributes to the assumed relevance and hence use of the personality descriptions. Participants are usually given five different descriptions of the target (hence the individuating information changes) but always the same base-rate information. Because of this, participants may assume that it is the descriptions rather than the base-rate information that is most relevant for the task. If this is the case, then varying the base-rate information but leaving the description constant should result in greater use of base-rate information. And it does (Schwarz et al., 1991; Experiment 2).

Consider, now, the order with which the information in the Kahneman and Tversky study was presented. Participants first received the base-rate information followed by the individuating information. In general, the information a speaker considers the most important is presented last (e.g., the given new contract; Clark, 1985). If individuating information is provided after the base-rate information, then base-rate information must not be sufficient for performing the task; otherwise it would not have been presented. Consistent with this reasoning, Krosnick, Li, and Lehman (1990) found that base-rate information was more likely to be used if presented after, rather than before, individuating information. This effect appears to be mediated by the assumed relevance of information that is presented last. The finding that information presented last is weighed most heavily disappears when participants are told the order with which the information was presented was randomly determined.

There are other judgmental "biases" that can be interpreted as reflecting principles of conversational reasoning. For example, the well-known fundamental attribution error, or tendency to "erroneously" infer internal states based on non-diagnostic information, can be interpreted in this way. Participants in the classic Jones and Harris (1967) study read an essay presumably written by another student and were then asked to judge the essay writer's true opinion regarding the issue. Some participants were told the essay writer had been instructed by the experimenter to adopt the position conveyed (forced-choice condition); other participants were told the writer's position had been freely chosen (free-choice condition). The major finding was that participants inferred the author's position to be in line with the position advocated in the essay, even when that position had been assigned and hence was not diagnostic of the writer's true opinion.

Note the similarity here to the Kahneman and Tversky study. Participants are given information to use in performing a specific task (judging the essay writer's opinion), and it is reasonable for them to assume that such information should be used (why else was it provided?). That is, the experimenter's contribution is assumed to be relevant. When the relevance of the information is lessened, people are much less likely to use it. Wright and Wells (1988) replicated the Jones and Harris (1967) study, but some participants were told that the information given to them had been randomly selected and hence might not be relevant for the judgment task they were to perform. In this condition, the fundamental attribution error was dramatically reduced.

It is not only probability judgments and attitudinal attributions that are affected by conversational principles. Indeed, conversation principles may be operative any time research questions are asked; the presumption of relevance almost always holds. For example, the Loftus and Palmer (1974) study regarding the effects of leading questions (e.g., How fast was the car going when it smashed/hit the truck?) can be interpreted as reflecting participants' beliefs in the relevance of the verb (*smashed* vs. *hit*) in the question.

Conversational principles appear to play a role in the manner in which people interpret survey questions. For example, Strack, Schwartz, and Wanke (1991) asked respondents to rate their happiness and their satisfaction with life, two questions that are obviously highly related. For some participants the two items were presented together at the end of a questionnaire; for others the life satisfaction item was presented as the first item in an ostensibly unrelated questionnaire. In the first situation, the second question would appear to be redundant; it violates Grice's maxim of quantity. Because of this, participants might reason that the second question must mean something different from the first. Why else would it be asked? Responses to the two questions differed significantly when they were part of the same questionnaire. Such a concern does not arise when the two items are part of two separate questionnaires, and responses to the two items were almost identical in this situation.

Linguistic relativity is not limited to lexical effects. Equally important are the cognitive consequences of conversational pragmatics. Like language use in general, these effects are not strictly determined by one's language, but rather are best viewed as a by-product of the use of that language. The clearest demonstration of such effects is the role of Grice's (1975) conversational principle in reasoning tasks. As this research has shown, many cognitive biases may actually reflect the principles that guide conversations. These effects may extend far beyond these research settings because many times the products of our cognitive processes are elicited in a conversational context. We are *asked* our opinion about this, whether that is likely to occur, and so on. The manner in which the question is asked and our beliefs about the state of the questioner's knowledge can influence the answer we give. Our answer, then, is not simply the result of intrapersonal cognitive processes; it is the result of an interaction between those processes and certain relevant, pragmatic principles regarding communication.

Moreover, Grice's conversational maxims are very basic principles that apply to actions in general, and not just conversational interaction. Even when our thoughts are not elicited in a conversational context, the manner in which they are formulated and the direction that they take may be influenced by the principles of relevance, quality, quantity, and so on. For example, the intrapersonal process of repression may be viewed as changing the topic of one's internal thought process-es; in effect, a relevance violation (cf. Billig, 1999). Now, such an occurrence may reflect the influence of language use on thought, or it may reflect the reverse. But at the very least it demonstrates the manner in which thought and language can be closely intertwined.

CONCLUSION

This chapter has focused on the role of language in how we think about our world. The chapter began with a discussion of linguistic determinism, the idea that lan-guage determines much of the way in which we think. But Whorf's hypothesis, as this proposed effect is frequently called, has had a checkered past, and it is quite doubtful that language fully determines thought. Early research designed to test Whorf's hypothesis demonstrated that certain basic cognitive processes such as color perception are not influenced by one's language (e.g., Berlin & Kay, 1969). There appears to be an underlying physiological basis for color perception that makes this process somewhat immune from language.

However, language clearly plays a role in thought, and that role is especially large in the social domain. There is probably no underlying physiological basis for person perception in the way that there may be for color perception. Perceiv-ing others and thinking about them is fraught with ambiguity; people are more likely to disagree regarding their perceptions of another person than they are about their perceptions of a color. It is within this ambiguity that language plays a role. And it does so in several ways.

First, the very dimensions that are used in perceiving others—and communi-cating those perceptions—are constrained by one's language. The available lexi-con provides channels for viewing people. Because languages differ in the terms they provide, person perception may vary over cultures (Hoffman, et al., 1986). In much the same way, basic attributional processes may be constrained by the per-ceiver's language. A language that provides a multitude of dispositional terms may increase the likelihood that those dispositional terms will be used, and hence that internal rather than external attributions for behavior will be made. The most obvious attributional effect related to language is implicit causality; the verbs used for describing actions can convey information regarding the presumed caus-es of those actions. Although this may not reflect linguistic determinism in an absolute sense, there is an asymmetry in the causal locus of many verbs, and this may bias the attributions that people make.

Second, many times social perception is as much an interpersonal process as it is an intrapersonal process. We *talk* about our perceptions with others, getting feedback on those thoughts and sometimes altering them as a function of this process. In this case it is the *use* of language, rather than anything inherent in language itself, that influences social perception. This can happen in a variety of ways. Chunks of knowledge identified with a lexical item may be activated and influence the manner in which information about others is processed (i.e., schema effects). The act of talking about someone creates a verbal representation that can influence what is remembered later (e.g., Schooler & Engstler-Schooler, 1990). Telling a story, the act of putting one's thoughts into words, may create a representation that determines how the story object is thought about (McGregor & Holmes, 1999). The words people choose may subtly convey their attitudes toward the objects of their talk. They may describe their successes (or those of their in-group) with interpretive action verbs, or even adjectives, as a means of suggesting that such actions are the usual state of affairs. One's negative actions might then be described much more concretely (e.g., with descriptive action verbs) so as to convey the sense that such actions are an aberration

Finally, the manner in which people talk about others can be constrained by pragmatic principles, and this can have a corresponding effect on the manner in which we think and reason about others. When attitudes, judgments, perceptions, and so on are elicited by others in a casual conversation or an experimental session, the attitudes, judgments, and perceptions that are provided may be influenced by general principles regarding conversational interaction (Grice, 1975).

Probably more than any other chapter in this volume, the material covered in this chapter has clear and direct relevance for traditional areas of social psychological research such as attribution, stereotypes, prejudice, attitudes, and even research methods. Language, and especially language use, is implicated in all of these phenomena. Consider, for example, the role of language in the creation and maintenance of stereotypes and its corresponding effects on prejudice. Stereotypes exist within individuals, of course; they are an intrapersonal phenomenon. But stereotypes are acquired via social communication—sometimes through the media and sometimes through conversations (van Dijk, 1987). As the linguistic intergroup bias suggests, people tend to use more abstract words when describing positive in-group behaviors and negative out-group behaviors. In this way a speaker can convey the view that the positive behaviors are more representative of the in-group and negative behaviors more representative of out-groups. This has clear implications for the recipient of a communication; dispositional inferences are more likely when a speaker uses relatively more abstract language (e.g., Wigboldus et al., 2000). In other words, language may be a crucial mediator for the transmission of stereotypes. The abstractness of one's language has other important implications. Given that it reflects stereotypic thinking on the part of the speaker, the abstractness of one's talk about in-group and out-group members may be taken as an indicator of prejudice, as von Hippel, Sekaquaptewa, and Vargas (1997) have recently demonstrated.

Differential abstractness of language use is not motivated only by in-group favoritism; this aspect of language use appears related to basic cognitive processes. For example, expectancy consistent information in general tends to be described at a relatively higher level of abstraction (Wigboldus et al., 2000). The temporal aspects of memory retrieval are influenced by abstractness; abstract predicates used as memory prompts elicit earlier memories (memories more removed in time) than concrete predicates (Semin & Smith, 1999).

The phenomenon with the greatest relevance for the field of social psychology as a whole is the role of conversational pragmatics in experimental research (a phenomenon that is relevant for any human research involving self-report measures). A very large portion of social psychological research involves participants making judgments; indicating their perceptions; and reporting their feelings, opinions, behaviors, and so on. This is generally a response to questions put to them by the experimenter (either verbally or in the context of a written questionnaire). It is thus a communicative situation, or a dialogue, and the principles guiding conversations will play a role in participants' responses.

In many respects, researchers have only begun to scratch the surface of these issues, and there are many important questions here deserving of future research. Consider, for example, how researchers frequently use multiple items to assess a single construct. The use of multiple items is recommended as a means of increasing the reliability of the measurement of a construct. But there may be additional considerations here. If participants are asked to respond to multiple items, and the items are very similar to one another (as is usually the case, given that they are presumably tapping the same construct), participants may assume that the questioner really intends to assess slightly different things; they will perceive different meanings in the items based on the assumption of conversational informativeness (Grice, 1975). One solution would be to distribute the items over proportedly different questionnaires (e.g., see Strack et al., 1991).

Social life is largely verbal; even when not talking with others, people may use language internally as they think about themselves and others. Language is thus a major medium for social thought at both the intra- and interpersonal levels. Understanding its role can contribute greatly to our understanding of these processes.

7

Summary:
Language as Social Action

Human language is many things. For certain linguists and philosophers, it is an abstract, symbolic system that humans seem uniquely capable of acquiring. Viewed in this way, studying language apart from its use is a legitimate enterprise. But viewing language in this way does not tell us very much about what people are doing as they produce and comprehend utterances. Language, when it is used, is an action. More important, it is also a social action—an action embedded within a web of many interpersonal determinants and consequences. It is these interpersonal considerations of language as social action that have been the core focus of much of this book. In this chapter I provide a review and integrative summary of these factors, and then elaborate on the specific implications of language use for social psychology and the social bases of language use.

LANGUAGE AS ACTION

First, and most fundamentally, to use language is to perform an action. It is an attempt to alter the world in some way (as with declaratives and directives) or to commit oneself to a particular depiction of the world (as with assertives) or to describe one's inner state (as with expressives). Obviously one alters the world with declaratives (e.g., "I declare war on Ohio."). But all utterances are actions in the same sort of way, albeit on a much smaller scale. They are social actions—actions that are directed toward other people.

If language is viewed as action, then the criteria for evaluating it is no longer grammaticality (although this is a component of the locutionary act). Instead, to perform these acts successfully (or felicitously) requires the meeting of relevant situational requirements, including having the requisite beliefs and attitudes. It is as if language use were a game (Wittgenstein, 1953), with the moves in this game being constrained by regulative rules and constituted by constitutive rules (e.g., Searle, 1969). Language use involves a grammar of its own, a grammar of actions. Competent language users must possess some type of action grammar. They must know how to translate their intentions into linguistic actions in a particular conversational and social context. They need to do so in such a way that they will have a fair chance of accomplishing their goals, that their intentions will be recognized, that others will not be offended, and so on. Of course they must be equally skilled at recognizing the intentions of others.

Now, the game being played is not solitaire; it involves two or more people who alternate the speaker and hearer roles. Just as you cannot play poker or baseball or checkers alone, because others are required to recognize and ratify and react to what you have done, so too you cannot use language in a conversation alone. An interlocutor is required to recognize and ratify and react to what you have done via your utterances.

But what exactly does a recipient recognize? What does conversational understanding entail? No doubt there must be some comprehension of the sense and reference of a conversational turn. But conversational turns are often not well-formed, grammatical sentences; they are fragmented, elliptical, and ungrammatical. When abstracted from the conversational context, there may be little sense and reference to discern. But recipients must recognize *something* if they are to make reasonable contributions to an exchange. It is likely that what is recognized is the speaker's intention in producing a particular turn; in speech act terms, it is the turn's illocutionary force.

Note that recognition of illocutionary force is different than the question of comprehension in the usual sense. It is possible to understand the sense and reference of a remark (recognize the locutionary act) without recognizing the action that the speaker is performing (the illocutionary act). It is possible to comprehend, in the usual sense, a remark like "I had the highest GPA on my floor last year" without recognizing that the speaker is bragging. Similarly, it is possible to understand a remark like "It's warm in here" without recognizing that the speaker is performing a request.

Recognition of illocutionary force or speaker intention has received scant empirical attention, so we really don't know the extent to which language use involves understanding at this level. It seems unlikely that a specific intention will be recognized for each and every turn that a conversationalist produces. Because conversations are elliptical and fragmented, intentions are probably conveyed and recognized over a series of turns. Of course, language use is not just about conveying intentions. In fact, one of the major themes of this book is that language users communicate much information unintentionally, or unwittingly. Moreover, a speaker's intention in producing an utterance may be ambiguous; he may have only a very vague sense of what he intends with a remark. Or he might have mixed or conflicting thoughts about what it is that he intends with a remark. Many communicative settings have an approach-avoidance quality; we may want to request something from a person but simultaneously desire to avoid imposing on that person. In these instances a speaker may simply leave it up to the hearer to decide how an utterance should be interpreted (Blum-Kulka & Weizman, 1988).

Still, it seems likely that a speaker's intention and the recipient's attempt to recognize that intention will play an important and fundamental role in language use. But how is this accomplished? This is a particularly difficult issue; often there is no one-to-one correspondence between sentence meaning and what a speaker means (or intends to accomplish) with a remark. Many speech acts are performed indirectly, and the speaker's intention cannot be simply and directly derived from a consideration of the remark in isolation.

Now, the whole notion of indirect speech acts is somewhat controversial, based as it is on a distinction between literal and nonliteral (or direct and indirect) meaning, a distinction that in some instances may be difficult to make (Gibbs, 1984; Dascal, 1987). Still, for many (though not all) utterances it is possible to specify a context-free literal meaning and a context-dependent nonliteral or indirect meaning. This raises the difficult task of explaining how people recognize a speaker's indirect meaning (when they do so).

The standard view of this process, derived primarily from Grice's (1975) theory of conversational implicature, has served as a baseline for much of the research in this area. Empirical evidence in support of this process is actually quite sparse (see chap. 1). The preponderance of evidence suggests that this type of inferential processing is not required for the comprehension of many types of indirect utterances. Instead, many indirect meanings are recognized directly, reflecting perhaps the metaphorical nature of our thinking (Gibbs, 1994a).

It is important to recognize, however, that only a relatively few types of indirect utterances (requests and figures of speech) have been examined empirically. Indirect meanings are pervasive in conversations, and research has only begun to scratch the surface regarding how these remarks are produced and understood. Indirect utterances can vary in many ways, and it seems reasonable that different processes will be involved in their comprehension. For example, conversational indirectness may be distinguished from literary or metaphorical indirectness. Literary indirectness reflects our tendency to occasionally think metaphorically and to speak nonliterally. Most figures of speech would fall in this group and represent what Grice (1975) called generalized implicatures, or inferences that transcend the specific occasion of their use and thereby reflect the metaphorical nature of thought.

But not all indirectness is metaphorical. Some instances—what I term conversational indirectness—represent what Grice (1975) called particularized implicatures, or inferences that are specific to a particular occasion of use. Because talk is embedded within a matrix of social activities—a web that provides a context for the talk—understanding conversational indirectness requires a consideration of the discourse context, the operation of interpersonal processes, and interactant coordination, factors that I discuss next.

Language as Contextualized Action

Conversational utterances are not solitary things; they occur in the context of other conversational utterances. As a part of a conversation, their meaning is partially derived from their placement in a conversational context. Hence, recognizing a speaker's action cannot be accomplished without a consideration of the context within which it occurs. This idea lies at the heart of Grice's (1975) ideas regarding conversational implicature; an implicature is an interpretation of an utterance that makes sense in terms of the overall conversation—one that conforms to the accepted purpose and direction of the exchange. But the accepted purpose and direction of an exchange is not always easy to discern. Indeed, interactants may have conflicting views regarding the underlying purpose of their exchange. But conversations are structured—they have a beginning and an ending, people take turns talking, questions usually follow answers, and so on—and this structure provides a framework for the interpretation of conversation turns.

Conversation analysts (e.g., Sacks, 1992) have provided most of the evidence regarding the structural regularities existing in conversational interaction. The most basic structural unit is an adjacency pair (e.g., question-answer), a two-turn format that probably developed very early on in the evolution of language use. The significance of adjacency pairs lies in the manner in which they structure sequences of talk, and not just the two turns that comprise them. The occurrence of insertion sequences, the use of adjacency pairs or presequences as a means of initiating subsequent stretches of talk, and their use in opening and closing conversations all illustrate how their role extends far beyond the two turns of talk of which they are comprised. For example, a summons ("Heh Jack")—answer ("What?") adjacency pair is frequently used to begin a conversation. But its significance extends beyond the initial two turns. The onus is on the first speaker to make the next move—to justify his use of a summons. Jack has the ball, at least initially, and his interlocutor will be attuned to and directed toward an understanding of his intentions; the recipient's orientation is affected by being the recipient of a summons. Even the termination of the conversation may be affected by the initial summons-answer sequence. It is generally the person issuing the summons who has the responsibility of beginning the terminal phase of a conversation (Schegloff & Sacks, 1973).

In a similar way, adjacency pairs can serve to launch a story, make a request, issue an invitation, and so on. In all instances, adjacency pairs provide a mechanism allowing people to cooperatively deal with issues and preconditions underlying the actions they wish to perform. In this way they provide an alternative analysis of speech act performance, especially the performance of indirect speech acts (Levinson, 1983). So, a person wishing to make a request can use the first-pair part of an adjacency pair to check the hearer-based felicity conditions (e.g., the hearer's ability to perform the act). Depending on the recipient's response (the second-pair part), the person can then make the request, check on additional preconditions should they exist, or accept the other's offer to perform the act (in which case the request has been avoided altogether).

Adjacency pairs have important implications for conversational interpretation; they represent a template for both the production and the comprehension of language. Given the occurrence of a specific first-pair part (e.g., a question), a specific second-pair part (e.g., an answer) is expected. This expectation puts pressure on the next speaker to produce the expected second-pair part. But this expectation also serves as a frame for interpreting the manner in which that pressure is handled; it frames the interpretation of what follows. Failing to provide the expected second-pair part is likely to instigate an inference process. In this way this structural regularity helps to specify the conditions under which a conversational inference will be made (a weakness in Grice's model). So, failing to comply with a request, accept an offer, answer a question, return a greeting, and so on all violate the adjacency pair format and instigate a search for meaning, an attempt to understand why the expected second-pair part did not occur, and what the speaker meant (if anything) in failing to provide it.

Conversational structure extends beyond adjacency pairs and the stretches of talk associated with them. In fact, a striking feature of (most) conversations is their coherency, a coherency that is not predictable at the beginning but is clearly apparent when viewed in retrospect. People generally address the same topic, yet they are able to cover a series of topics within a conversation, with the topic changes often (though not always) occurring seamlessly. How this happens is really something of a mystery. In fact, it is exceedingly difficult, if not impossible, to formally define conversational coherence. Yet, it happens. Interlocutors are clearly mutually attuned to the notion of topic, they use various moves to mark topic changes, and more subtly they may maneuver a conversation around to a topic on which they wish to contribute. But the on-line processes involved in this behavior are really unknown at this point. We do it, but we don't know how we do it. Conversation analytic research has illuminated many of the regularities and discourse mechanisms underlying conversational structure. What remains is to relate those regularities to on-line mental processes, including interactants' interpersonal goals.

Language as Interpersonal Action— Interpersonal Determinants

Why has our system of language use evolved in the way that it has? Why is it structured the way that it is, with topical coherence, turn-taking regularity, and the frequent occurrence of adjacency pairs? Why does indirectness occur? It is easy to imagine things being different. We could, for example, possess a much more direct and efficient language-based communicative system. We could always say what we mean and mean what we say. Topic shifts could be abrupt, turn taking could be random and haphazard, and so on.

Obviously many forces have influenced the manner in which people communicate verbally. Efficiency and comprehensibility certainly top the list. But they cannot be alone. Indeed, one of the major hallmarks of language use it its inefficiency and occasional incomprehensibility. Some of this is due to temporary factors such as distraction, fatigue, and so on. But not all of it. Much of the inefficiency can be traced to the operation of interpersonal concerns that exist in most communicative settings. One of the major theses of this book has been that these concerns have played an influential role in shaping the manner in which we use language.

Interpersonal concerns can be seen quite clearly at the utterance level, and the concept that seems to capture these concerns best is Goffman's (1967) notions of face and face-work. Face, or one's public identity, is a "sacred thing" that is always at stake when interacting with others. People generally try to support one another's face during conversations, and to do so helps ensure that one's own face will be similarly supported. So, people frequently engage in face-work; they mutually affirm their recognition of and respect for one another (e.g., with greetings and good-byes), they tread lightly on threatening topics, they avoid pointing out another's faults, and so on.

Now, the most interesting aspect of this process is the manner in which it is manifested in the linguistic minutiae of our conversations. There are an almost infinite number of ways in which any verbal action (or speech act) can be performed, and face management is probably a major reason for why these options exist. Face management is likely the major motivation for why speakers choose one form rather than another in any particular context. Politeness theory (Brown & Levinson, 1987) provides a parsimonious account of these phenomena; linguistic patterning is assumed to reflect face management, and face management is linked to two basic and universal dimensions of interaction: power and solidarity. Variability in power and solidarity influence an individual's concern with face management, and this determines one's degree of politeness.

Research on politeness and indirectness has provided some support for these ideas, especially for directives and the interpersonal variable of relative power. Greater indirectness is associated with greater politeness (up to a point), politeness increases as a function of face threat, and face threat increases as a function of the power of the recipient (Holtgraves, 1992). For other speech acts and other interpersonal variables the results are much less clear. Moreover, there are many unresolved issues regarding what politeness is, how it can be categorized and measured, the extent to which people try to manage (rather than threaten) each others' face, and so on. But the basic idea, the idea that people are engaged in face management during their conversations, working to maintain their face and those of their interlocutors, and that this concern is manifested in the particulars of their utterances, particularly in terms of the indirectness dimension, seems correct. It is this concern with managing face that may have motivated or brought about the politeness system in the first place. It is for this reason that we don't always say what we mean.

Face-management processes also play a role in conversational structure beyond the level of single utterances. Consider, for example, the strong preference for agreement that is associated with adjacency pairs (Pomerantz, 1984). Dispreferred seconds (e.g., a disagreement) are produced in a manner that is very different from their preferred counterparts (e.g., an agreement). Dispreferred turns are delayed, prefaced, and indirect; their preferred counterparts are quick, simple, and direct. Why? Why did this feature of conversations develop as it did? It could have developed differently. By indicating that a turn is dispreferred, the speaker is displaying some attention to the recipient's face, at least in some cultures. To disagree quickly and directly and without any hesitation or preface will often threaten the recipient's face. Delaying one's disagreement (even just slightly, for less than one second) and prefacing it with an apology can serve to indicate that although the speaker does disagree with the prior speaker's opinion or assessment or whatever, the sacred being of one's self remains worthy of respect.

Or consider the strong preference for self- over other repair. Conversation analytic researchers have demonstrated a strong tendency for interactants to allow speakers to correct or repair their own conversational errors rather than repairing the errors for them (Schegloff, Jefferson, & Sacks, 1977). Why? Well, there is the matter of economy; few conversational resources are used for self-repair. But again there is the matter of face management. To repair another's mistakes (conversational or otherwise) is a clear threat to that person's face. Thus people generally avoid this. Instead, they allow the speaker to correct any problems and enter in only after it is clear that the speaker is not going to do so.

In terms of identification, there appears to be a strong preference for interactants to avoid self-identification at the start of a telephone conversation. The ideal is to be identified by the other, with little attention being paid to the identification process (Schegloff, 1979). And again, face management seems to be playing a role here. Rather than avoiding a face threat, the preference for other recognition over self-identification represents an approach-based (rather than avoidance) affiliative move. To recognize another without an explicit recognition process indicates a relatively high degree of familiarity, a marker of positive politeness.

Finally, consider the manner in which conversation topics are managed. To unilaterally change a conversational topic implies the speaker has the right to do so; thereby putting the other person in a one-down position and having his face threatened. Hence, abrupt, unilateral topic changes are relatively rare. Instead, interactants negotiate the introduction of new topics, enacting a series of moves so as to make clear the relevance of their contribution for the current interaction.

In addition to affecting how people phrase their utterances, face management can also play a role in how people interpret conversation turns. When an utterance occurs that is somewhat less than absolutely clear (i.e., not in accord with Grice's [1975] maxims), recipients will often reinterpret the remark (i.e., generate a conversational implicature). But what specific interpretation will a recipient make? Because face management is a major motivation for the production of indirectness and because people are mutually aware of this fact, face management should help disambiguate potential indirect interpretations of an utterance. Specifically, recipients should recognize that the speaker is engaging in face management, and therefore that the most likely interpretation of the remark is one that would be face threatening in this situation (Holtgraves, 1998). Moreover, this process can be facilitated with the use of dispreferred markers. Because dispreferred markers (e.g., pauses and prefaces) can reflect the operation of face management, their occurrence signals the recipient that face management is being undertaken, and hence that a face management interpretation of the remark is very likely correct. It is in these ways that face management can play a simultaneous role in both language production and language comprehension.

Language as Interpersonal Action— Interpersonal Consequences

Just as interpersonal concerns influence the way we use language, so too does language use affect our interpersonal worlds in many ways. When we talk with people we are concerned not only with conveying intentions and determining the intentions of our interlocutors. We are also simultaneously attempting to manage others' impressions of us, as well as trying to form clear and coherent impressions of them. The sense we develop of our conversation partners is part of the meaning that is conveyed through their use of language; it is one of the perlocutionary effects of language use. Of course the sense they develop of us is part of the meaning conveyed through our use of language.

Language use is one of the major channels through which we gain information about other people; it should play a substantial role in our perceptions of others. Much research suggests that it does. Impression formation and management flows from language use in many ways, but two are primary. First, how we talk— our accent, speech rate, politeness level, and so on—are pieces of information that others can use in forming impressions of us. Some of these linguistic-based impressions are mediated by group identification. To speak with a particular accent or style can identify one as belonging to a particular group or social class (Labov, 1972a). Similar to other group or class membership indicators, this can result in group-based stereotypic inferences.

Other language variables—particularly extralinguistic and content variables—can affect impressions more directly, without any activation of group member-ship. Many times this is unintended—impressions "given off" in Goffman's (1959) terms. People cannot help but disclose aspects of their identity when they talk. Although such effects have been widely documented, detailed examination of the processes by which they occur are relatively rare. To what extent, for exam-ple, do these effects represent the automatic activation of stereotypes? Or might more conscious mediation be involved? Do language-based impressions require cognitive resources on the part of the perceiver? And so on.

At the same time, many of these language variables are modifiable and hence give people some control over the impressions others form of them. People can alter their speech style or accent or dialect. In this way they can influence the impressions others form of them, impressions "given" in Goffman's (1959) terms. This type of stylistic variation is an important tool in the impression manager's repertoire. One can speak quickly to convey competence, impolitely to display power, slang to convey closeness. Again, relatively little is known about how such processes work. What, for example, is the nature of the impression manager's intention? Often, it would seem to be a covert intention, one that is not intended to be recognized (we don't want our interlocutors to recognize our attempts at impression management).

That people can manage their impressions linguistically implies some consen-sus (within a particular group) regarding the implications of a language variable; language use, in this sense, is socially meaningful. But (with some exceptions) its meaning is not universal. The identity implications may be quite variable—noti-cable by some and not others, influencing impressions in one direction for some, and in another direction for others. Linguistic-based impression management is fraught with ambiguity. Because language variation is multiply determined, per-ceptions of a speaker may be affected on any of several different dimensions. Does lack of politeness indicate power or a close relationship? Such ambiguity can contribute greatly to interpersonal misunderstandings, and those misunder-standings may be particularly common in interethnic communication.

Language-based impression management also illustrates the reciprocal nature of the relationship between language and the social context. Language use reflects the social context in the sense that how one talks is affected by who one is (class, ethnicity, personality, etc.) as well as the context that one is in (e.g., for-mal vs. informal). Reciprocally, how one talks can define the interpersonal nature of the situation. Politeness phenomena illustrate this quite nicely. Interpersonal variables such as power influence levels of politeness in a particular context, and levels of politeness can be a source of information regarding the speaker's view of her power. And because of this, people can attempt to negotiate their power in a relationship by varying their level of politeness (e.g., Holtgraves & Yang, 1992). Politeness is both socially meaningful and a means of managing one's impressions.

The language-social context relationship becomes quite complicated because language and context are constantly changing—they exist in a dynamic relationship with one another. Changes in socially meaningful language variables can alter the context, and changes in the context (e.g., new people entering the conversation) can alter participants' use of language. People can use their partners' language use as a guide or standard for their own language use, attempting to converge or diverge with their partner's manner of speaking (e.g., Giles et al., 1991). These dynamic changes can play a role in the impressions that interactants form of each other.

The second way in which language use plays a role in impression formation and management is in terms of what one says, or the content of one's remarks (e.g., Berry et al., 1997). Often it is not the content alone that is important, but rather the content as it is conveyed in a particular conversational context. This is not to say the content of one's utterances is unimportant. If you admit to being a serial murderer others' impressions of you will be affected, regardless of the context of your disclosure. But with less-extreme instances the contextual placement of one's contributions can interact with the context to affect impressions. In one sense, this is simply an instance of rule violators being negatively evaluated. Conversational and interactional rules constrain what one can say at various points in a conversation, and those violating such rules will tend to be viewed negatively.

There is a more interesting dimension to this phenomenon, however, a dimension that is intimately linked with conversational comprehension processes. Rule violations are unexpected, and like unexpected behaviors in general, people try to make sense of them; they attempt to construct an explanation for why they occurred. This phenomenon lies at the heart of Grice's (1975) proposal regarding how we interpret indirect speech acts. A person notices that a speaker has violated a conversational maxim and generates an indirect meaning as a means of making sense of the utterance. However, such sense making need not be restricted to the meaning of the utterance alone. This sense-making process may include inferences about the speaker (e.g., personality and motives) and the situation. Sometimes understanding a person's utterance entails an understanding of the person who made the remark; conversational comprehension and social perception merge and may be part of the same process (Holtgraves & Grayer, 1994).

Language as Thoughtful Action

Now, there is an entirely different way in which language and social perception may be related; language can also influence our intrapersonal world in terms of how we think and reason about people. Language is a tool that may be used for perceiving and thinking about others, and the nature of this tool may play an important role in these processes. Consider the myriad number of ways in which we might perceive the behavior of another person. Obviously the lexical items available to us will constrain this process; it is difficult to categorize someone without a word to denote the category. Thus, the very building blocks of the person-perception process—the categories that are applied to incoming social information—may be influenced by the language that one is using. In this way person perception can vary cross-culturally, as a function of the differing trait terms that languages provide their users (Hoffman et al., 1986). Or consider how languages differ in the manner in which they force their users to orient to interpersonal variables. Because speakers of Korean must mark verbs in terms of relative status, it is not unreasonable to assume that they will attend to the status dimension more so than speakers of, say, English. In this way one's perceptual processes might be influenced by language use, as one thinks in order to speak (Slobin, 1996).

Of course the idea that language determines, or at least influences, thought is controversial. And for good reason. Explicit tests of various versions of Benjamin Whorf's hypothesis have yielded mixed results. It is important to keep in mind, however, that the language-thought relationship may vary over domains. Is color perception affected by the lexicon? Probably not. But people—and social stimuli in general—are a different matter. There are an infinite number of dimensions that can be used for perceiving others, and so language might easily constrain the dimensions that are used. Color perception, on the other hand, represents a single dimension with a physiological basis; language should be less influential in this domain.

It is also clear that the use of language can have an effect on cognitive operations, even if the structure of one's language does not. The distinction is an important one. It is one thing to argue that a linguistic system constrains the perceptions and thought processes of its users. It is another thing to suggest that a specific act of using a language will have cognitive consequences. For example, there may be nothing about language per se that influences decision making. But if one is asked to verbalize the reasons for a decision, to use language to justify a decision, then that activity can influence the quality of the decision that is made. Some factors affecting decisions are easier to verbalize than others, and it is the easily verbalized factors that tend to be articulated and influence one's decisions (Wilson & Schooler, 1991).

Or consider stories. Many times the information we convey to others is packaged as a story or narrative, a natural device for conveying information in a conversational context (Schank & Abelson, 1995). In telling a story, however, certain details will need to be glossed over (everything can't be included in a story) and a sequential structure imposed on the material. The act of telling a story, then, creates a new representation that is partly a result of the storytelling act. This new representation can have an impact on later impressions of, and memory for, the incident described (McGregor & Holmes, 1999).

Or consider how the use of certain verbs may influence the recipient's beliefs about the situation the speaker describes. To say that Mark helped Fred is to point to Mark as the initiator of the action (Mark is a helpful person) rather than Fred (Fred is a needy person). Similarly, to say that Andy hurt Bob is more descriptive of Andy than to say that Andy hit Bob. The hearer of the former is more likely to form a clear and negative impression of Andy than is the recipient of the latter.

To use language in this way, to justify a decision, tell a story, describe a person to another, is to create a linguistic representation of a particular phenomenon, a linguistic representation that to a certain extent has a life of its own—a representation that now serves as the source for information about that decision, event, or person. Thus, the act of using language can alter the way we think about the object of our thought. This is not an unusual occurrence; many times social perception and thought are as much interpersonal processes as they are intrapersonal processes. People talk about others, exchanging information, comparing notes, asking for opinions, and so on. All of this may take place during a conversation. Not only does the act of talking influence subsequent thoughts, certain conversational principles (e.g., Grice, 1975) can influence what and how things get talked about. Thus, the opinions and judgments that people articulate (the putative products of their thought processes) are partly a result of conversational principles (Gruenfeld & Wyer, 1992; Schwarz, 1996).

Language as Coordinated Action

Language use is clearly a social enterprise. When we perform speech acts, we expect others to recognize the acts we perform, we expect our words to have some effect on the recipient. Even if we don't want our intention to be recognized—an attempt at impression management, for example—we still need to have some idea that the recipient will draw the inferences we want them to draw. Abiding by Grice's (1975) conversational maxims requires some estimate of what the recipient knows; giving an appropriately informative answer (the quantity maxim) would not be possible otherwise. Of course, we need to have some idea that whatever it is that we are talking about—the sense and reference of our utterance—will be correctly identified by the recipient. In short, people must engage in some sort of perspective taking when they talk.

In general, people are aware of this requirement and structure their utterances accordingly. Speakers frequently alter their descriptions of referents based on some sense of the perspective of their interlocutor (Fussell & Krauss, 1989a, b; Kingsbury, 1968). The explanations given to another person vary as a function of what that person knows, and the terms used for describing a person vary as a function of beliefs regarding the recipient's attitude toward the person being described. Clearly, people are sensitive to the perspective's of their interlocutors.

But taking the perspective of another is not an easy thing to do. Complete and perfect perspective taking is impossible, as each person's perspective is unique.

During the course of a conversation it is difficult to continually monitor another's perspective; it is simply too demanding and time consuming. As a result, there is a tendency for people to (at least initially) rely too much on their own perspective when they assess another person's perspective. As Keysar (1998) has demonstrated, people tend to use privileged information when describing and attempting to identify described objects. At the level of speaker meaning, there is a tendency to assume that the meanings one takes to be obvious will be obvious to others as well. People adjust their perspective, however, especially when they are given evidence that the other person does not understand them, and if they have enough time to do so. The conversational system provides for the possibility of feedback, and it is this feedback that allows people to coordinate their perspectives, to adjust their perspective so that it is in line with that of another (Clark, 1996a).

Perspective taking may be necessary for communication, but it is not sufficient. To a certain extent, perspective taking must be mutual; it requires that people have mutual awareness that their perspectives coincide. Thus, not only must a recipient take the perspective of the speaker, he must also believe that the speaker has taken his perspective into account when formulating his utterance. Capturing this process is exceedingly difficult because complete mutual perspective taking (each interactant is aware of the other interactant's awareness and is aware that the other is aware of that awareness, and so on) is not possible. Many aspects of language use are conventionalized, however, and for these aspects mutual perspective taking is not a serious problem. Word meanings, syntax, and phonology are all conventional. Even many indirect meanings are conventionalized. Thus, people can make conventional indirect requests with syntactic constructions such as "Can you x?" There may also be politeness values conventionally associated with syntactic forms. Even many language-based impression effects are conventional, such as the conventional association between perceptions of status and the use of prestigious language varieties.

Still, conventionality only goes so far. People can use language in so many ways and with such a variety of meanings that conventionality only provides a foundation. Even conventionality itself requires perspective taking of some sort; interlocutors must occasionally check to see that they are adhering to the same conventions.

To a large extent, mutual perspective taking is achieved through the process of the verbal interaction itself, as interactants collectively coordinate their use of language (Clark, 1996a). People must continuously provide positive evidence that another's contribution has been understood; they must ground their contributions. This can be indicated in a variety of ways. Verbal continuers, head nods, a gaze, or a relevant subsequent contribution can all be taken as indicating acceptance of a prior turn (that it has been grounded). In this way, the conversation itself is a resource for the coordination of interactants' perspectives. Thus, many of the structural regularities of conversations play a role in this process. Providing the second-pair part to the other speaker's first-pair part grounds the first speaker's contribution. Perspective taking is a process that is tentative, a series of hypotheses about others' perspectives that is supported, or not, on a turn-by-turn basis.

The discourse as it unfolds, the building up of common ground through the grounding process, and interactants' mutual copresence all serve as heuristics for the recognition of mutual perspective taking. This must occur for all levels of language use—referent identification, speech act performance, level of politeness, and so on. The system is not perfect, of course. Misunderstandings do occur, and they occur because of the difficulty in perspective taking and because of the ambiguities inherent in the grounding process. Initially egocentric perspectives may not be corrected entirely, evidence for grounding may be ambiguous, estimated knowledge based on community membership may be faulty, and so on. But the attempt to adopt another's perspective, coupled with the assumption that one's interlocutor is doing the same, seems to be fundamental for successful language use.

LINGUISTIC UNDERPINNINGS
OF SOCIAL BEHAVIOR

The study of language can contribute greatly to our understanding of social behavior. This is for a very simple reason: Language is the medium through which many social psychological processes operate. This fact, of course, borders on the obvious. Numerous scholars have indeed undertaken linguistic analyses of social behavior. But sustained, experimental work on this topic remains rare. One of the obstacles has been the lack of conceptual machinary required to parse language into socially meaningful units that can be manipulated and analyzed. Many of the linguistic phenomena discussed in this book—illocutionary force and perlocutionary effects, politeness, conversational implicature, adjacency pairs, and so on—provide entry points into language use and can facilitate the analysis of its role in social life. In the following sections I revisit some core areas of social psychology for which research has demonstrated, and future research could demonstrate, the important role played by lanuage.

Person Perception and
Impression Management

Person perception has been one of the core areas of social psychology for decades. Although research in this area has waxed and waned over this period, it has clearly drawn intense interest during the past 25 years. During this time, researchers have undertaken detailed analyses of the cognitive processes involved in person perception, and they have developed complex, comprehensive models in this domain (e.g., Wyer & Srull, 1986). In general, the emphasis in this research has been on the manner in which people combine and represent pieces of information; much less is known about how raw social stimuli are transformed so as to be used in this process. Beginning with Asch (1946), participants in social cognition experiments are often provided lists of traits describing a person and are asked to form an impression of that person. But this sidesteps the issue of how people obtain such information in the first place (e.g., Hastie, Park, Weber, 1984; Wyer & Gruenfeld, 1995). This first step may be crucial. The acquisition of information is an active process that may change the very nature of the information that is acquired.

Language use is one of the major sources of raw social information; it is the very stuff out of which impressions are formed. Although nonlinguistic variables—physical appearance for example (Zebrowitz, 1997)—are clearly important, it is our interactions with others that are the major sites for forming impressions of others. Those interactions are largely verbal interactions. Even when we receive second-hand information about people—someone tells us something about another person—that process is communicative and can influence our perceptions, in this case the communicator more than the person described (e.g., Skowronski et al., 1998).

What specific role, then, does language play in the person-perception process? Well, at the most basic level, language is a socially meaningful behavior, meaningful in the sense that there are identity implications for many aspects of language use. To a certain extent, how we speak can define who we are. Accent, dialect, linguistic style, and one's language all serve to indicate membership in social groups, an identification that can greatly influence the person-perception process. Not all language variables are mediated by group identification, however. Lexical content, for example, appears to have direct effects on perceptions of a speaker's personality (Berry et al., 1997). Many extralinguistic variables—speech rate, for example—operate in the same way.

Other linguistic variables are largely relationship based; they reveal the speaker's view of the relationship with the interlocutor. Politeness is a good example. Politeness variability reveals the speaker's view of her relative status and the psychological distance between herself and her partner, a view that can influence how she is perceived by her partner. Other identity-relevant aspects of language use are derived from the operation of conversational rules, guidelines for constructing (both the form and content) of one's conversational contributions. Deviations from conversational rules—bragging in certain contexts, for example, or abruptly changing the conversational topic—can influence overall evaluations of the speaker. But conversational rules are complex things and can influence perceptions in other ways as well; reasoning about why a violation occurred can affect perceptions of speakers on different dimensions as perceivers attempt to determine why the violation occurred.

These effects are neither simple nor straighforward. Interlocutors are not only perceiving others, they are also being perceived, and people can alter their language use so as to achieve various effects. Slight variations in one's linguistic behavior can be used to alter the social context of the talk, to defuse a tense situation with a joke, or to turn a formal situation into an informal one. More importantly, language use is a major means for managing the impressions we convey to others. We cannot change our physical appearance (except cosmetically, of course), but we can and do vary our talk. Thus, a person can attempt to portray himself as having relatively high status by lowering his level of politeness and issuing direct commands. Or he may attempt to convey competence by speaking quickly with a powerful linguistic style and prestigious language variety, or closeness by speaking fankly and adopting an in-group dialect, and so on. One can manipulate some conversational rules so as to mitigate the effects of violating other conversational rules. For example, a person can gently negotiate the conversational topic so as to be able to provide a context for a positive self-disclosure, thereby lessening the negative implications of bragging. Or one can subtly alter one's linguistic style so as to converge with the style of one's interlocutor, a move often resulting in more favorable impressions of the speaker. As a socially meaningful activity, language is a resource that people can use to pursue various impression-management strategies. So, if we want to know how people manage their impressions, and we really do not understand this very well, than language use is a good place to look.

Impression management is not a solitary activity, interlocutors are not only acting, they are also reacting to the behavior, linguistic and otherwise, of others. In this way language use might be a major source for many interpersonal expectancy effects. It has been demonstrated, for example, that beliefs about one's interaction partner can influence how one behaves toward that person, and these behavioral effects can alter that person's behavior (e.g., Snyder, Tanke, & Berscheid, 1977). But how does this happen? Exactly how does one elicit behaviors that confirm an expectancy? No doubt subtle aspects of language use are important here—speaking warmly to elicit warmth, rudely to elicit rudeness. Or gently bringing up topics for which the other is likely to have a positive (or negative) contribution. And so on.

Language is both a source and a resource for person perception and impression management. But it can play a role in these processes in other ways as well. Specifically, person perception can be affected by interpersonal processes because we often talk about our perceptions of others, and the act of talking, as we have seen, can influence our representation of, and memory for, the topic of that talk. As an interpresonal process, our talking about others can be affected by a host of linguistic variables such as the nature of our relationship with the other (Semin, 1998), our beliefs about the recipient's opinion of the other person (Higgins & Rholes, 1978), what we presume the other knows about the target (Slugoski, 1983). And so on.

And last, but not least, person perception might be influenced by the dimensions that are available to be used in this process. Granted, the evidence is less clear on this point. But still, there are a myriad of ways in which we might perceive others, and such choices would seem to be constrained by the words that are available for doing this (Hoffman et al., 1986). It is very difficult to perceive others on a dimension without the existence of a lexical item that captures that difference. To perceive others as finicky, flirtatious, or frugal requries the existence of these words. Benjamin Whorf may have overstated his case—language does not fully determine thought—but he did foster an awareness of the subtle influences that language has on certain aspects of cognition, with person perception being primary in this regard. The available lexicon, then, is a framework within which the person-perception process operates. Similarly, thoughtful impression management may also require some type of linguistic basis for the planning of an identity that one may wish to convey.

Social Reasoning

Reasoning is typically regarded as an intrapersonal process. What else could it be? It is something we do by ourselves; we recall and combine information and make comparisons and form a judgment and so on. But a key insight of recent research in this area is that this process is often socially situated, and because of this, certain aspects of language use can play an influential role in the process of social reasoning. The products of reasoning are often elicited in a conversational context. We ask others why they thought this way or that, why this happened rather than that, and so on. Most crucially, thousands of participants in reasoning exeriments are asked such things, and they are done so in a communicative context, a context in which communicative principles can play an important role.

When people are asked to make attributions, or judge the likelihood of some event, or the probability that a person belongs to a particular group, and so on, the answers that they provide can be constrained by conversational principles. This can be manifested in many ways. First, when people are asked a question, they generally try to provide an informative answer; they strive to abide by the quantity maxim and provide just the right amount of information, information that is believed to be unknown to the questioner, but not more information than what the questioner might want. The answer that is given, then, is not simply the endproduct of an internal judgment process. Instead, the answer is shaped by interpersonal processes—estimates of what one's interlocutor knows, and how an answer would mesh with that knowledge (Slugoski, 1983). Perspective taking is crucial in this regard.

Second, the manner in which people interpret questions about their judgments can be influenced by these same principles (Hilton, 1995). Not only do people generally abide by conversational maxims, they expect others to do so as well. Thus, they expect questions from another to be informative, to not be requesting information that is already possessed by the questionner. So, if asked "How's your family?" right after being asked "How's your wife?" survey respondents will reason that the second question includes family members other than one's wife. The answer they provide will likely be different than if the first question had not been asked (Strack et al., 1991).

Third, when people are asked to make a judgment and are given pieces of information with which to do so, they are likely to use the provided information in making that judgment (Hilton, 1995). And why not? Why would someone give me information for making a decision unless that information was to be used in doing so? The tendency for respondants to use individuating information in a typical judgmental heuristics study may be as much a result of the researcher giving them this information as it is a result of a failure to appropriately use, for example, base-rate information.

These effects all serve to illustrate the interpersonal side of social reasoning, how conversational principles and assumptions regarding the questioner's knowledge influence the output of one's reasoning. But social reasoning is also an internal, intrapersonal process, and here too language may play an important role. Consider, for example, how the properties of certain verbs influence the manner in which the objects of those verbs are thought about. When told that Bill helped Al, our thoughts about these two will be directed by the causality implicit in the verb *help*. We are more likely to believe that Bill is a helpful guy than that Al is a needy one. Or consider how the existence (or lack thereof) of certain linguistic structures may faciliate (or hinder) particular types of thought. Languages that provide devices for thinking counterfactually may facilitate this type of reasoning and make it easier and possibly more likely to occur (Bloom, 1981). Or consider how attributions might be influenced by the available lexicon. A surfeit of dispositional terms may increase the likelihood of making internal attributions for another person's behavior, the dispositional terms prompting the perceiver to look for internal causes, possibly at the expense of equally legitimate external causes.

In the end, social reasoning is both an internal, intraindividual process, as well as often being a socially situated communicative phenomenon. Language, it appears, can play an important role in both aspects of this process.

Attitudes and Prejudice

Attitudes and prejudice are two of the most central topics in social psychology, and they are also two of the most elusive constructs. They are illusive because people do not always report their true attitude. Of course prejudice is notoriously difficult to detect. Accordingly, researchers have recently focused on the detection and measurement of implicit attitudes and stereotypes (e.g., Greenwald & Banaji, 1995). Language is important in this regard because how one talks about a topic may reflect certain aspects of the speaker's attitude toward that topic (Van Dijk, 1987; Von Hippel et al., 1997). Simply put, how we talk about, describe, and refer to others may be indicative of our underlying attitudes toward those others.

The language variable receiving the most experimental attention in this regard is the linguistic ingroup bias (Maas et al., 1989)—a tendency to speak abstractly about the positive behaviors of one's in-group and negative behaviors of one's outgroup. There is now a fair amount of research documening the existence of this effect and demonstrating that it is largely automatic and out-of-awareness (e.g., Semin & de Poot, 1997), and hence an appropriate indicator of a speaker's implicit attitudes. Unlike other indicators of implicit attitudes (e.g., reaction time measures), however, linguistic abstractness can also play an important role in the transmission and maintenance of stereotypes (Ruscher, 1998). How we talk about others may not only reflect our implicit attitudes, it may also impact the recipient's attitudes. As Wigboldus and colleagues (2000) have demonstrated, when speakers are asked to describe the positive and negative behaviors of in-group and out-group members, recipients of those messages tend to make dispositional attributions for the negative behaviors of out-group, but not in-group, members, an effect that is reversed for positive behaviors. Place this tendency in a real-life context—parent-child conversations, family discussions, workplace encounters—and it is easy to imagine how the linguistic expression of attitudes can play an important role in the creation, maintenance, and transmission of prejudicial attitudes.

Aggression, Altruism, and Beyond

Research has clearly demonstrated the role played by language in person perception and impression management, social reasoning, and attitudes. But investigations of its role in other social psychological processes is somewhat rarer. Simple reflection, however, suggests many other possibilities in this regard. Interpersonal processes, especially, would seem to be a gold mine. Consider, in alphabetical order, just a few of the standard topics in social psychology.

What facilitates interpersonal aggression? The priming of hostile thoughts, anger, alchohol, and the presence of weapons have all been examined and clearly play a role. But agressive acts often arise during the course of a verbal interaction, and clearly aspects of that interaction—its course, content, and structure—can play a role in the eventual likelihood of an aggressive act. People who are skilled communicators may be less likely to use physical force than are less-skilled communicators (Bandura, 1973). But why? One possibility is that those who commit violent acts may be more likely to interpret others' communications in a negative way, or to take offense at another's remarks (Dodge, 1980). In this case, the manner in which people tend to interpret others' communications can influence the likelihood of aggression.

Regardless of interpretation differences, another's utterances may elicit or provoke aggressive actions. Fighting words may be just that. Language cannot only precipitate aggression, it is also a form of aggression. Psychological abuse, fighting words, and racial epitats are all instances of language being used to harm others. Some of this may be quite subtle. For example, in the trial of Bernie Goetz— the subway vigalante who was charged with shooting unarmed juveniles on a subway—the politeness of requests made to him by his victims was an issue. Goetz argued that his victims had threatened him with direct requests "Give me five dollars"; a request that he perceived as threatening and menacing, and hence justifying his actions. Not so, said the victims. They claimed their request had been phrased politely—"Mister, can I have five dollars?" a polite phrase that did not justify an aggressive action.

There is some evidence suggesting that there are systematic linguistic differences between couples who are abusive and those who are not (Cordova, Jacobs, Gottman, Rushe, & Cox, 1993; Sabourin & Stamp, 1995). Abusive couples appear to use vague rather than precise language, to emphasize relational rather than content talk, and to be oppositional rather than collaborative (Sabourin & Stamp, 1995). The precise nature of these communication patterns and *how* they increase the likelihood of aggression is an important avenue for future research.

The flip-side of aggression—altruism—may also have linguistic underpinnings, especially in terms of how one makes an appeal for help. For example, overly vague requests for help in an emergency situation may go unheeded (Cialdini, 1984)—the ambiguity of the communication allowing the recipient an out and preventing him from recognizing its emergency status. Of course, greater directness may not always be best. In nonemergency situations direct—and hence impolite—requests can backfire, inducing reactance and the likelihood of securing help.

Finally persuasion—a topic with a very long history in social psychology—is largely a verbal activity. Yet, systematic research on the role of language variables in persuasion has not been extensive. The strength of one's arguments is usually important (Petty & Cacioppo, 1986), but what exactly makes an argument strong? It appears that adapting the content of one's arguments to the beliefs of the recipients is helpful. Messages that are based on a premise with which the audiance agrees are more successful than the same message based on a less-acceptable premise (Holtgraves & Bailey, 1991).

It is not just the content of one's arguments that are important, *how* one conveys an appeal is important as well. The use of powerful language—for some communicators in some situations—can facilitate persuasion (Holtgraves & Lasky, 1999). More recently, the role of metaphors in persuasion has been examined (Ottati, Rhoads, & Graesser, 1999). But really only the surface has been scratched here. The role played by language variables in persuasion is clearly an important avenue for future research.

SOCIAL BASES OF LANGUAGE USE

Just as the study of language can illuminate many social psychological processes, so too can the study of social psychological processes shed light on many aspects of language use. Talk usually occurs in a social context—in the context of a relationship (however temporary) existing between two or more interactants. Most talk is not idle chatter. Even when it is idle chatter, it is really anything but idle from a psychologist's perspective. People are pursuing agendas and reacting to the agendas pursued by others, they are trying to maintain a relationship or alter it in various ways, they are trying to manage the impressions others are forming of them as well as gleaning information about the people with whom they are inter-acting. These social activities are pursued through language use, and so it is diffi-cult to separate language from the complex web of social activities within which it is embedded.

What does this entail for the study of language? At one level it requires a con-sideration of language use as a collaborative activity. It requires, for example, a consideration of how interactants coordinate—and mutually verify their coordi-nation—as they use language and how they collectively understand what is being accomplished through their talk. This fundamental feature of language use has been staked out and pursued most vigorously by Herb Clark and his collegues (Clark, 1996a). This is an area that underpins all apsects of language use.

But it also involves a consideration of production and comprehension as inter-personal acts, acts that are intimately bound up with the interactants' goals and motives and the relationship between them. Consider comprehension. What exactly does it mean to comprehend a conversational utterance? Well, it involves the identification of referents, an integration of that utterance into an overall dis-course model, and so on. Is that all? Probably not. But we really do not know because little research has been conducted on conversational comprehension. Instead, the emphasis in psycholinguistic research has been on text processing; witness the number of text processing chapters in the *Handbook of Psycholin-guistics* (Gernsbacher, 1994). Accordingly, much is known about levels of repre-sentation, the types of inferences that readers tend to generate and when they gen-erate them, the extent to which antecedents are reactivated, and so on.

However, texts and conversations are different things; conversation turns are social acts in a way that sentences in a text are not. Now, clearly, texts are the products of social processes. There is a writer and an audience. The writer has particular goals in producing a text, and readers have particular goals in reading that text. But the writer and the audience are not in face-to-face contact, their use of language is not interactive, and they are not alternating the speaker and hearer role. The audiance is often implicit for the text writer, but explicit for the conver-sationalist. There is, of course, a middle ground here. Mediated communication such as e-mail, discussion boards, and chat rooms have qualities that are similar to face-to-face conversation and qualities that are similar to written texts. But still, there are differences, and these differences suggest that the comprehension of conversational utterances may differ from the comprehension of sentences in a written text. For example, conversational turns have to be grounded (Clark, 1996a), a requirement that does not exist for texts. Interactants must ground the referents of their utterances—they strive to be sure they are talking about the same thing.

But there may be additional levels of discourse representation for conversa-tions. People are performing actions with their words, and so interlocutors must ground their actions as well as their referents. The details of conversational inter-action suggest that they do (see chap. 5). Now, every conversational turn need not perform a specific action; actions may often be realizied over a stretch of turns, and this may often be collaborative. But, clearly, speakers who produce conversational turns are performing actions in a way that writers of a text are not. How and in what way are speech acts recognized? What, exactly, is the nature of this process? Action recognition has to be derived or inferred from stretches of talk; in a sense, it is an inference. But it is unlike inferences typically generated by readers of a text. Because conversations are part of a larger social activity, it seems likely that social considerations will play a role in the nature of the comprehension process.

There are numerous possibilites in this regard. First, various features of the social context might predispose interactants to comprehend conversation turns in particular ways, with these interpretations flowing directly from the context, in effect, short-circuiting an inference process. Consider, for example, two people involved in a conversation in which one has more power than the other—a boss talking with an employee, for example. In the context of a workplace discussion, the employee might be predisposed to directly comprehend the boss' utterances as directives, and this might occur without any inferential processing (Holtgraves, 1994; Katz, & Pexman, 1997). Or consider the role of dispreferred markers. A brief delay and/or preface at the beginning of a speaker's turn can prompt the recipient to recognize that the turn is dispreferred and probably face threatening (Holtgraves, 2000). In this way, the recipient might recognize the speaker's intention before a word is uttered.

Second, when an inference process is required to uncover a speaker's meaning, the social context can guide the recipient to a particular interpretation of the turn. Consider, for example, the mutual requirement of face management, or tendency to structure one's talk so as to be sensitive to the identities of the involved parties. Mutual awareness of this sensitivity can influence the manner in which hearers interpret maxim violations. A mutually recognized concern with face management may guide the reader to interpret maxim violations as attempts to convey face-threatening information (Holtgraves, 1998). The face-management motive guides the hearer to a particular implicature, an important consideration because the number of implicatures is infinite.

But conversational comprehension may be more complex than this. Face management is not the only motive operating in conversations, and other motives may play a role in conversation interpretation as well. Face-to-face interaction raises a host of concerns, chief among them being the development of a sense of the nature of one's interlocutors—who they are, what they think, what they are likely to do next, and so on. In short, it is a striving to reduce uncertainty (Berger & Bradac, 1982). Comprehenders may attempt to not only recognize the illocutionary force of a speaker's utterance, they may also strive to understand why the speaker is producing this utternace in this situation. This search may play a role in the recognition of intended, indirect meanings, as noted above. But other inferences are also possible—inferences regarding the speaker's motives, personality, and so on. These inferences may occur as part of the recipient's attempt to make sense of a speaker's turn, particularly if that turn in some way violates a conversational maxim. Although it is likely that a recipient will first attempt to determine a speaker's intended meaning, that failing, other inferences may then be generated in an attempt to make sense of the utterance (Holtgraves & Grayer, 1994).

Just as understanding conversational comprehension requires a consideration of the social context, so too does language production. Much more has been established in this arena, at least insofar as it has been demonstrated—by many researchers in varying disciplines across a range of domains—that people alter various aspects of their talk as a function of various characteristics of their interlocutors, the setting, and so on. What remains to be investigated is how and when these concerns come into play. Although researchers have investigated the sequence of steps involved in producing an utterance (e.g., Levelt, 1989), the point at which various pragmatic factors enter into this process is not clear. It is possible, for example, that a speaker's high status allows him to spend less time and effort in formulating polite utterances. But does the formulation of polite versions of one's intentions come after the construction of a default version of the utterance? Or does it occur earlier?

Language use is a social behavior that is part of a larger complex set of social behaviors. This embedding raises many issues regarding how people actually use language. It is clear that social concerns affect how people interpret utterances, recognize speech acts, keep track of topics, plan what to say and how to say it, and so on. But all of this happens very quickly, and how this occurs remains something of a mystery.

CONCLUSION

To use language is to engage in a "meaningful" activity, with "meaning" existing at multiple levels. There is the sense and reference of an utterance, of course. But there is also the speaker's intention(s) in uttering a particular string of words. And then there are the perlocutionary effects, the number of which can be quite large and include, among other things, judgments of the speaker's personality and motives. Perlocutionary effects also include the manner in which the recipient's behavior is altered, including a subsequent utterance, a remark that now has its own layers of meaning.

There are a multitude of meanings, in large part because language is a social action. Language users are doing things with their words—they are requesting, promising, apologizing, and so on. In doing this they will have varying degrees of awareness of the interpersonal concerns that may be simmering on the back burner. Moreover, they must monitor the reactions of their interlocutors so as to coordinate the management of these multiple layers of meaning. These layers of meaning are not always separate and distinct; they mutually influence one another. For example, speech act recognition may sometimes involve attention to the interpersonal dimension (e.g., recognition of an order may require a consideration of the speaker's power and hence the right to issue an order). Sometimes understanding what a person means with an utterance will entail an understanding of who the speaker is, a sense of motives and personality. Of course, understanding who a person is may require an understanding of what she is doing with her remarks.

All of these meanings are only partly in the words themselves; words influence these meanings but do not fully determine them. Referents can be ambiguous, the number of potential interpretations of an utterance can be quite large, and the perlocutionary effects can be infinite in number. So, sense and reference must be interpreted, speech acts inferred, perlocutionary effects estimated, and so on. Language use can involve a multitude of inferences. But talk happens very quickly. Thus some aspects of meaning are only potential. They may sometimes play an on-line role in language use; other times they may operate off-line, as when we rehash the meaning of a previous conversation. But the meaning potentials are always there and must be considered in explaining how people use language.

What does it take to be a user of language? Clearly, syntactic and semantic competence is required. But so too is pragmatic competence. Users need to know how to translate their intentions into a linguistic form so that they will be recognized by others; they must also be able to recognize the intentions that others are trying to convey. Moreover, they must have some sense of how their utterances will be taken by others, or what impressions their words will convey; they must also recognize the impressions that others are intending to convey. Whether or not communicative competence is completely distinct from linguistic competence is not entirely clear and is subject to considerable debate (e.g., Pinker, 1994). What is clear is that an understanding of how people use language and an understanding of how speakers produce and hearers understand conversation turns will require a consideration of the factors discussed in this book. It is quite possible that this may alter our view of the nature of linguistic competence.

References

Abelson, R. P., & Kanouse, D. E. (1966). Subjective acceptance of verbal generalizations. In S. Feldman (Ed.), *Cognitive consistency: Motivation antecedents and behavioral consequents* (pp. 171–197). New York: Academic Press.

Alford, D. M. (1981, February). Is Whorf's relativity Einstein's relativity? *Proceedings of the seventh annual meeting of the Berkeley Linguistics Society,* 13–26.

Allport, G. W. (1954). *The nature of prejudice.* New York: Addison-Wesley.

Ambady N., Koo, J., Lee, F., & Rosenthal, R. (1996). More than words: Linguistic and nonlinguistic politeness in two cultures. *Journal of Personality and Social Psychology, 70,* 996–1011.

Amrhein, P. C. (1992). The comprehension of quasi-performative verbs in verbal commitments: New evidence for componential theories of lexical meaning. *Journal of Memory and Language, 31,* 756–784.

Argyle, M. (1973). *Social interaction.* London: Tavistock.

Aronsson, K., & Satterlund-Larsson, U. (1987). Politeness strategies and doctor-patient communication: On the social choreography of collaborative thinking. *Journal of Language and Social Psychology, 6,* 1–27.

Asch, S. E. (1946). Forming impressions of personality. *Journal of Abnormal and Social Psychology, 41,* 1230–1240.

Atkinson, J. M., & Drew, P. (1979). *Order in the court: The organization of verbal interaction in judicial settings*. London: Macmillan.

Au, T. (1983). Chinese and English counterfactuals: The Sapir-Whorf hypothesis revisited. *Cognition, 15,* 155–187.

Au, T. (1984). Counterfactuals: In reply to Alfred Bloom. *Cognition, 17,* 289–302.

Au, T. (1986). A verb is worth a thousand words: The causes and consequences of interpersonal events implicit in language. *Journal of Memory and Language, 25,* 104–122.

Austin, J. L. (1962). *How to do things with words*. Oxford: Clarendon Press.

Bach, K., & Harnish, R. M. (1979). *Linguistic communication and speech acts*. Cambridge, MA: MIT Press.

Bahrick, H. P., & Boucher, B. (1968). Retention of visual and verbal codes of the same stimuli. *Journal of Experimental Psychology, 78,* 417–422.

Bakan, D. (1966). *The duality of human existence*. Chicago: Rand McNally.

Bandura, A. (1973). *Aggression: A social learning analysis*. Upper Saddle River, NJ: Prentice Hall.

Bauman, I. (1988, May). *The representational validity of a theory of politeness*. Paper presented at the annual meeting of the International Communication Association Convention, New Orleans, LA.

Bavelas, J. B., Black, A., Chovil, N., & Mullet, J. (1990). *Equivocal Communication*. Newbury Park, CA: Sage.

Baxter, J. C. (1970). Interpersonal spacing in natural settings. *Sociometry, 33,* 444–456.

Baxter, L. A. (1984). An investigation of compliance gaining as politeness. *Human Communication Research, 10,* 427–456.

Beattie, G. W. (1983). *Talk: An analysis of speech and nonverbal behavior in conversation*. Milton Keynes, UK: Open University Press.

Bell, A. (1984). Language style as audience design. *Language in Society, 13,* 145–204.

Berger, C. R., & Bradac, J. J. (1982). *Language and social knowledge*. London: Edward Arnold.

Berlin, B., & Kay, P. (1969). *Basic color terms: Their universality and evolution*. Berkeley: University of California.

Berry, D. S., Pennebaker, J. W., Mueller, J. S., & Hiller, W. S. (1997). Linguistic bases of social perception. *Personality and Social Psychology Bulletin, 23,* 526–537.

Billig, M. (1999). *Freudian repression: Conversation creating the unconscious*. Cambridge, UK: Cambridge University Press.

Bilous, F. R., & Krauss, R. M. (1988). Dominance and accommodation in the conversational behaviors of same and mixed gender dyads. *Language and Communication, 8,* 183–194.

Blom, J. P., & Gumperz, J. J. (1972). Social meaning in linguistic structure: Code-switching in Norway. In J. J. Gumperz & D. Hymes (Eds.), *Directions in sociolinguistics* (pp. 407–434). New York: Holt, Rinehart & Winston.

Bloom, A. H. (1981). *The linguistic shaping of thought: A study in the impact of language on thinking in China and the West*. Hillsdale, NJ: Erlbaum.

Blum-Kulka, S. (1987). Indirectness and politeness in requests: Same or different? *Journal of Pragmatics, 11,* 131–146.

Blum-Kulka, S., Danet, B., & Gherson, R. (1985). The language of requesting in Israeli society. In J. Forgas (Ed.), *Language in social situations* (pp. 113–139). New York: Springer-Verlag.

Blum-Kulka, S., & Weizman, E. (1988). The inevitability of misunderstandings: Discourse ambiguities. *Text, 8,* 219–241.

Bourhis, R. Y., & Giles, H. (1976). The language of co-operation in Wales: A field study. *Language Sciences, 42,* 13–16.

Bradac, J. J. (1990). Language attitudes and impression formation. In H. Giles & W. P. Robinson (Eds.), *Handbook of language and social psychology* (pp. 287–421). Chichester, UK: Wiley.

Bradac, J. J., Bowers, J. W., & Courtright, J. A. (1979). Three language variables in communication research: Intensity, immediacy, and diversity. *Human Communication Research, 5,* 257–269.

Bradac, J. J., & Wisegarver, R. (1984). Ascribed status, lexical diversity, and accent: Determinants of perceived status, solidarity, and control of speech style. *Journal of Language and Social Psychology, 3*, 239–256.

Bransford, J. J., & Johnson, M. K. (1972). Contextual prerequisites for understanding: Some investigations of comprehension and recall. *Journal of Verbal Learning and Verbal Behavior, 11*, 717–726.

Brennan, S. E. (1998). The grounding problem in conversations with and through computers. In S. Fussell & R. Kreuz (Eds.), *Social and cognitive approaches to interpersonal communication* (pp. 201–225). Mahwah, NJ: Erlbaum.

Brennan, S. E., & Clark, H. H. (1996). Conceptual pacts and lexical choice in conversation. *Journal of Experimental Psychology: Learning, Memory, and Cognition, 22*, 1482–1493.

Brown, B. L. (1980). Effects of speech rate on personality attributions and competency evaluations. In H. Giles, W. P. Robinson, & P. Smith (Eds.), *Language: Social psychological perspectives* (pp. 294–300). Oxford: Pergamon.

Brown, B. L., Giles, H., & Thakerar, J. N. (1985). Speaker evaluations as a function of speech rate, accent and context. *Language and Communication, 5*, 107–220.

Brown, P., & Fraser, C. (1979). Speech as a marker of situation. In K. R. Scherer & H. Giles (Eds.), *Social markers in speech* (pp. 33–108). Cambridge, UK: Cambridge University Press.

Brown, P., & Levinson, S. (1978). Universals in language usage: Politeness phenomena. In E. Goody (Ed.), *Questions and politeness* (pp. 56–289). Cambridge, UK: Cambridge University Press.

Brown, P., & Levinson, S. (1987). *Politeness: Some universals in language usage.* Cambridge, UK: Cambridge University Press.

Brown, R. (1958). *Words and things.* New York: The Free Press.

Brown, R. (1965). *Social psychology.* New York: The Free Press.

Brown, R., & Fish, D. (1983). The psychological causality implicit in language. *Cognition, 14*, 237–273.

Brown, R., & Ford, M. (1961). Address in American English. *Journal of Abnormal and Social Psychology, 62*, 375–385.

Brown, R., & Gilman, A. (1989). Politeness theory and Shakespeare's four major tragedies. *Language in Society, 18*, 159–212.

Brown, R., & Lenneberg, E. (1954). A study in language and cognition. *Journal of Abnormal and Social Psychology, 49*, 454–462.

Bucci, W. (1997). *Psychoanalysis and cognitive science: A multiple code theory.* New York: Guilford.

Bull, P. & Elliot, J. (1998). Level of threat: A means of assessing interviewer toughness and neutrality. *Journal of Language and Social Psychology, 17*, 220–244.

Byrne, D. (1971). *The attraction paradigm.* New York: Academic Press.

Cacciari, C., & Glucksberg, S. (1991). Understanding idiomatic expressions: The contribution of word meanings. In G. Simpson (Ed.), *Understanding word and sentence meaning* (pp. 217–240). Amsterdam: North-Holland.

Cacciari, C., & Glucksberg, S. (1994). Understanding figurative language. In M. A. Gernsbacher (Ed.), *Handbook of psycholinguistic research* (pp. 447–478). San Diego, CA: Academic Press.

Cansler, D. C., & Stiles, W. B. (1981). Relative status and interpersonal presumptuousness. *Journal of Experimental Social Psychology, 17*, 459–471.

Cargile, A. C., Giles, H., Ryan, E. B., & Bradac, J. J. (1994). Language attitudes as a social process: A conceptual model and new directions. *Language and Communication, 14*, 211–236.

Carli, L. (1990). Gender, language and influence. *Journal of Personality and Social Psychology, 59*, 941–951.

Carmichael, L., Hogan, H. P., & Walter, A. A. (1932). An experimental study of the effect of language on the reproduction of visually perceived form. *Journal of Experimental Psychology, 15*, 73–86.

Carroll, J. B., & Casagrande, J. B. (1958). The function of language classifications in behavior. In E. E. Maccoby, T. M. Newcomb, & E. L. Hartley (Eds.), *Readings in social psychology* (pp. 18–31). New York: Holt, Rinehart & Winston.

Chen, Y. (1990). *The functionality of back channel responses in face-to-face interaction.* Unpublished master's thesis, Columbia University, New York.

Cheng, P. W. (1985). Pictures of ghosts: A critique of Alfred Bloom's *The Linguistic Shaping of Thought. American Anthropologist, 87,* 917–922.

Chiu, C., Krauss, R. M., & Lau, I. Y-M. (1998). Some cognitive consequences of communication. In S. R. Fussell & R. J. Kreuz (Eds.), *Social and cognitive approaches to interpersonal communication* (pp. 259–278). Mahwah, NJ: Erlbaum.

Chomsky, N. (1965). *Language and mind.* New York: Harcourt, Brace, & Jovanovich.

Choy, S., & Dodd, D. (1976). Standard-English speaking and nonstandard Hawaiian-English speaking children: Comprehension of both dialects and teachers' evaluations. *Journal of Educational Psychology, 68,* 184–193.

Cialdini, R. B. (1984). *Influence.* New York: William Morrow & Co.

Clark, H. H. (1979). Responding to indirect speech acts. *Cognitive Psychology, 11,* 430–477.

Clark, H. H. (1985). Language use and language users. In G. Lindzey & E. Aronson (Eds.), *The handbook of social psychology* (3rd ed., Vol. 2, pp. 179–232). Reading, MA: Addison-Wesley.

Clark, H. H. (1992). *Arenas of language use.* Chicago: University of Chicago Press.

Clark, H. H. (1996a). *Using language.* Cambridge, UK: Cambridge University Press.

Clark, H. H. (1996b). Communities, commonalities, and communication. In J. J. Gumperz & S. C. Levinson (Eds.), *Rethinking linguistic relativity* (pp. 324–358). Cambridge, UK: Cambridge University Press.

Clark, H. H., & Brennan, S. E. (1991). Grounding in communication. In L. B. Resnick, J. M. Levine, & S. D. Teasley (Eds.), *Perspectives on socially shared cognition* (pp. 127–149). Washington, DC: American Psychological Association.

Clark, H. H., & Carlson, T. B. (1981). Context for comprehension. In J. Long & A. Addeley (Eds.), *Attention and performance IX* (pp. 313–329). Hillsdale, NJ: Erlbaum.

Clark, H. H., & Carlson, T. B. (1982). Hearers and speech acts. *Language, 58,* 332–373.

Clark, H. H., & Clark, E. V. (1977). *Psychology and language: An introduction to psycholinguistics.* San Diego, CA: Harcourt Brace Jovanovich.

Clark, H. H., & Gerrig, R. J. (1983). Understanding old words with new meanings. *Journal of Verbal Learning and Verbal Behavior, 22,* 591–608.

Clark, H. H., & Marshall, C. R. (1981). Definite reference and mutual knowledge. In A. K. Joshi, B. L. Webber, & I. A. Sag (Eds.), *Elements of discourse understanding* (pp. 10–63). Cambridge, UK: Cambridge University Press.

Clark, H. H., & Murphy, G. L. (1982). Audience design in meaning and reference. In J. F. Le Ny & W. Kintsch (Eds.), *Language and comprehension* (pp. 287–299). New York: North Holland.

Clark, H. H., & Schaefer, E. F. (1987). Concealing one's meaning from overhearers. *Journal of Memory and Language, 26,* 209–225.

Clark, H. H., & Schaefer, E. F. (1989). Contributing to discourse. *Cognitive Science, 13,* 259–204.

Clark, H. H., & Schunk, D. (1980). Polite responses to polite requests. *Cognition, 8,* 111–143.

Clark, H. H., & Wilkes-Gibbs, D. (1986). Referring as a collaborative process. *Cognition, 22,* 1–39.

Cohen, C. E. (1981). Person categories and social perception: Testing some boundaries of the processing effects of prior knowledge. *Journal of Personality and Social Psychology, 40,* 441–452.

Cohen, P. R., & Levesque. H. J. (1990). Rational interaction as the basis for communication. In P. R. Cohen, J. Morgan, & M. E. Pollack (Eds.), *Intentions in communication* (pp. 221–256). Cambridge, MA: MIT Press.

Cordova, J. V., Jacobs, N. S., Gottman, J. M., Rushe, R., & Cox, G. (1993). Negative reciprocity and communication in couples with a violent husband. *Journal of Abnormal Psychology, 102,* 559–564.

Corrigan, R. (1988). Who dun it? The influence of actor-patient animacy and type of verb in the making of causal attributions. *Journal of Memory and Language, 27,* 447–465.

Corrigan, R. (1993). Causal attributions to states and events described by different classes of verbs. *British Journal of Social Psychology, 32,* 335–348.

Coupland, N. (1984). Accommodation at work: Some phonological data and their implications. *International Journal of the Sociology of Language, 46,* 49–70.

Coupland, J., Coupland, N., Giles, H., & Wiemann, J. (1988). My life is in your hand: Processes of self-disclosure in intergenerational talk. In N. Coupland (Ed.), *Styles of Discourse* (pp. 201–253). London: Croom Helm.

Coupland, N., Giles, H., & Wiemann, J. M. (Eds.). (1991). *"Miscommunication" and problematic talk.* Newbury Park, CA: Sage.

Craig, R. T., Tracy, K., & Spivak, F. (1986). The discourse of requests: Assessment of a politeness approach. *Human Communication Research, 12,* 437–468.

Crosby, F., & Nyquist, L. (1977). The female register: An empirical study of Lakoff's hypothesis. *Language in Society, 6,* 313–322.

Dascal, M. (1987). Defending literal meaning. *Cognitive Science, 11,* 259–281.

Davidson, J. (1984). Subsequent versions of invitations, offers, requests and proposals dealing with potential or actual rejection. In J. M. Atkinson & J. C. Heritage (Eds.), *Structures of social action: Studies in conversation analysis* (pp. 102–128). Cambridge, UK: Cambridge University Press.

Davis, D. (1982). Determinants of responsiveness in dyadic interaction. In W. Ickes & E. Knowles (Eds.), *Personality, roles, and social behavior* (pp. 85–139). New York: Springer-Verlag.

Davis, D., & Holtgraves, T. (1984). Perceptions of unresponsive others: Attributions, attraction, understandability, and memory for their utterances. *Journal of Experimental Social Psychology, 20,* 383–408.

DePaulo, B. M., & Coleman, L. (1986). Talking to children, foreigners, and retarded adults. *Journal of Personality and Social Psychology, 51,* 945–959.

Dillard, J. P., Wilson, S. R., Tusing, K. J., & Kinney, T. A. (1997). Politeness judgments in personal relationships. *Journal of Language and Social Psychology, 16,* 297–325.

Dodge, K. A. (1980). Social cognition and children's aggressive behavior. *Child Development, 51,* 162–170.

Dubois, B. L., & Crouch, I. (1975). The question of tag questions in women's speech: They don't really use more of them, do they? *Language in Society, 4,* 289–294.

Duncan, S., & Fiske, D. W. (1977). *Face to face interaction: Research, methods and theory.* Hillsdale, NJ: Erlbaum.

Durkheim, E. (1915). *The elementary forms of religious life.* London: Allen & Unwin.

Edwards, D. & Potter, J. (1992). *Discursive psychology.* London. Sage.

Erickson, B., Lind, A. E., Johnson, B. C., & O'Barr, W. M. (1978). Speech style and impression formation in a court setting: The effects of "powerful" and "powerless" speech. *Journal of Experimental Social Psychology, 14,* 266–279.

Ervin-Tripp, S. (1976). Is Sybil there? The structure of American English directives. *Language in Society, 5,* 25–66.

Ferguson, C. (1964). Diglossia. In D. Hymes (Ed.), *Language in culture and society* (pp. 429–439). New York: Harper & Row.

Fiedler, K., Semin, G. R., & Finkenauer, C. (1993). The battle of words between gender groups: A language-based approach to intergroup processes. *Human Communication Research, 19,* 409–441.

Fielding, G., & Evered, C. (1980). The influence of patients' speech upon doctors. In R. N. St. Clair & H. Giles (Eds.), *The social and psychological contexts of language* (pp. 51–72). Hillsdale, NJ: Erlbaum.

Fillmore, C. (1968). The case for case. In E. Bach & R. G. Harms (Eds.), *Universals in linguistic theory* (pp. 1–87). New York: Holt, Rinehart & Winston.

Fishman, P. M. (1980). Conversational insecurity. In H. Giles, W. P. Robinson, & P. M. Smith (Eds.), *Language: Social psychological perspectives* (pp. 127–132). New York: Pergamon Press.

Fitch, K. L., & Sanders, R. E. (1994). Culture, communication, and preferences for directness in expression of directives. *Communication Theory, 4,* 219–245.

Forgas, J. P. (1999a). Feeling and speaking: Mood effects on verbal communication strategies. *Personality and Social Psychology Bulletin, 25,* 850–863.

Forgas, J. P. (1999b). On feeling good and being rude: Affective influences on language use and request formulations. *Journal of Personality and Social Psychology, 76,* 928–939.

Foss, D. J., & Hakes, D. R. (1978). *Psycholinguistics: An introduction to the psychology of language.* Upper Saddle River, NJ: Prentice Hall.

Francik, E. P., & Clark, H. H. (1985). How to make requests that overcome obstacles to compliance. *Journal of Memory and Language, 24,* 560–568.

Fraser, B. (1990). Perspectives on politeness. *Journal of Pragmatics, 14,* 219–236.

Fraser, B., & Nolan, W. (1981). The association of deference with linguistic form. *International Journal of the Sociology of Language, 26,* 93–109.

Furnham, A. (1990). The language of personality. In H. Giles & W. P. Robinson (Eds.), *Handbook of language and social psychology* (pp. 73–95). Chicester, UK: Wiley.

Fussell, S. R., & Krauss, R. (1989a). The effects of intended audience on message production and comprehension: Reference in a common ground framework. *Journal of Experimental Social Psychology, 25,* 203–219.

Fussell, S. R., & Krauss, R. (1989b). Understanding friends and strangers: The effects of audience design on message comprehension. *European Journal of Social Psychology, 19,* 509–526.

Fussell, S. R., & Krauss, R. (1991). Accuracy and bias in estimates of others' knowledge. *European Journal of Social Psychology, 21,* 445–454.

Fussell, S. R., & Krauss, R. (1992). Coordination of knowledge in communication: Effects of speakers' assumptions about what others know. *Journal of Personality and Social Psychology, 62,* 378–391.

Gaertner, S., & Bickman, L. (1971). Effects of race on the elicitation of helping behavior. *Journal of Personality and Social Psychology, 20,* 218–222.

Garfinkel, H. (1967). *Studies in ethnomethodology.* Upper Saddle River, NJ: Prentice Hall.

Garvey, C., & Caramazza, A. (1974). Implicit causality in verbs. *Linguistic Inquiry, 5,* 459–464.

Gazdar, G. (1979). *Pragmatics: implicature, presupposition, and logical form.* New York: Academic Press.

Gergen, K. J. (1989). Warranting voice and the elaboration of the self. In J. Shotter & K. J. Gergen (Eds.), *Texts of identity* (pp. 70–81), Greenwich, Conn: JAI Press.

Gernsbacher, M. A. (1990). *Language comprehension as structure building.* Hillsdale, NJ: Erlbaum.

Gernsbacher, M. A. (Ed.) (1994). *Handbook of psycholinguistic research.* San Diego, CA: Academic Press.

Gerrig, R. J., Ohaeri, J. O., & Brennan, S. E. (2000). Illusory transparency revisited. *Discourse Processes, 29,* 137–159.

Gibbs, R. W., Jr. (1980). Spilling the beans on understanding and memory for idioms. *Memory & Cognition, 8,* 449–456.

Gibbs, R. W., Jr. (1983). Do people always process the literal meaning of indirect requests? *Journal of Experimental Psychology: Learning, Memory, and Cognition, 9,* 524–533.

Gibbs, R. W., Jr. (1984). Literal meaning and psychological theory. *Cognitive Science, 8,* 225–304.

Gibbs, R. W., Jr. (1986). What makes some indirect speech acts conventional? *Journal of Memory and Language, 25,* 181–196.

Gibbs, R. W., Jr. (1994a). *The poetics of mind.* Cambridge, UK: Cambridge University Press.

Gibbs, R. W., Jr. (1994b). Figurative thought and figurative language. In M. A. Gernsbacher (Ed.), *Handbook of psycholinguistic research* (pp. 411–446). San Diego, CA: Academic Press.

Gibbs, R. W., Jr. (1998). The varieties of intentions in interpersonal communication. In S. Fussell & R. Kreuz (Eds.), *Social and cognitive psychological models of interpersonal communication* (pp. 19–37). Hillsdale, NJ: Erlbaum.

Gibbs, R. W., Jr. (1999). *Intentions in the experience of meaning*. Cambridge, UK: Cambridge University Press.

Gildea, P., & Glucksberg, S. (1983). On understanding metaphor: The role of context. *Journal of Verbal Learning and Verbal Behavior, 22,* 577–590.

Giles, H. (1970). Evaluative reactions to accents. *Educational Review, 22,* 211–227.

Giles, H. (1973). Accent mobility: A model and some data. *Anthropological Linguistics, 15,* 87–105.

Giles, H. (1979). Ethnicity markers in speech. In K. Scherer & H. Giles (Eds.), *Social markers in speech* (pp. 251–289). Cambridge, UK: Cambridge University Press.

Giles, H., & Coupland, N. (1991). *Language: Contexts and consequences.* Pacific Grove, CA: Brooks/Cole.

Giles, H., Coupland, J., & Coupland, N. (1991). *Contexts of accommodation: Developments in applied sociolinguistics.* Cambridge, UK: Cambridge University Press.

Giles, H., & Sassoon, C. (1983). The effects of speakers' accent, social class, background and message style on British listeners' social judgments. *Language and Communication, 3,* 305–313.

Giles, H., & Smith, P. M. (1979). Accommodation theory: Optimal levels of convergence. In H. Giles and R. N. St. Clair (Eds.), *Language and social psychology* (pp. 45–65). Oxford: Basil Blackwell.

Giles, H., Taylor, D. M., & Bourhis, R. Y. (1973). Towards a theory of interpersonal accommodation through speech: Some Canadian data. *Language in Society, 2,* 117–192.

Givon, T. (1989) *Mind, code, and context: Essays in pragmatics.* Hillsdale, NJ: Erlbaum.

Glucksberg, S. (1991). Beyond literal meanings: The psychology of allusion. *Psychological Science, 2,* 146–152.

Glucksberg, S., Gildea, P., & Bookin, H. (1982). On understanding nonliteral speech: Can people ignore metaphors? *Journal of Verbal Learning and Verbal Behavior, 21,* 85–98.

Glucksberg, S., & Keysar, B. (1990). Understanding metaphorical comparisons: Beyond similarity. *Psychological Review, 97,* 3–18.

Godfrey, D. H., Jones, E. E., & Lord, C. G. (1986). Self-promotion is not ingratiating. *Journal of Personality and Social Psychology, 50,* 106–115.

Goffman, E. (1959). *The presentation of self in everyday life.* Garden City, NY: Doubleday Anchor.

Goffman, E. (1967). *Interaction ritual: Essays on face to face behavior.* Garden City, NY: Anchor Books.

Goffman, E. (1971). *Relations in public.* New York: Harper & Row.

Goffman, E. (1976). Replies and responses. *Language in Society, 5,* 257–131.

Goguen, J. A., & Linde, C. (1983). *Linguistic methodology for the analysis of aviation accidents.* (Contract No. NA52–11052). Palo Alto, CA: Structural Semantics.

Gonzales, M. H., Manning, D. J., & Haugen, J. A. (1992). Explaining our sins: Factors influencing offender accounts and anticipated victim responses. *Journal of Personality and Social Psychology, 62,* 958–971.

Gonzales, M. H., Pederson, J., Manning, D., & Wetter, D. W. (1990). Pardon my gaffe: Effects of sex, status and consequence severity on accounts. *Journal of Personality and Social Psychology, 58,* 610–621.

Goodwin, C. (1986). *Conversational organization: Interaction between speakers and hearers.* New York: Academic Press.

Gordon, D., & Lakoff, R. (1975). Conversational postulates. In P. Cole & J. Morgan (Eds.), *Syntax and semantics 3: Speech acts* (pp. 83–106). New York: Academic Press.

Gottman, J. M. (1979). *Marital interaction: Experimental investigations.* New York: Academic Press.

Gottschalk, L. A., & Gleser, G. C. (1969). *The measurement of psychological states through the content analysis of verbal behavior.* Berkeley: University of California Press.

Graesser, A. C., Singer, M., & Trabasso, T. (1994). Constructing inferences during narrative text comprehension. *Psychological Review, 101,* 371–395.

Greenwald, A. G., & Banaji, M. R. (1995). Implicit social cognition: Attitudes, self-esteem, and stereotypes. *Psychological Review, 102,* 1–27.

Grice, H. P. (1957). Meaning. *Philosophical Review, 67,* 377–388.

Grice, H. P. (1975). Logic and conversation. In P. Cole & J. Morgan (Eds.), *Syntax and semantics 3: Speech acts* (pp. 41–58). New York: Academic Press.

Grice, H. P. (1989). *Studies in the way of words.* Cambridge, MA: Harvard University Press.

Grimes, J. (1975). *The thread of discourse.* The Hague: Mouton.

Gruenfeld, D. H., & Wyer, R. S., Jr. (1992). Semantics and pragmatics of social influence: How affirmations and denials affect beliefs in referent propositions. *Journal of Personality and Social Psychology, 62,* 38–49.

Gudykunst, W., Yoon, Y. C., & Nishida, T. (1987). The influence of individualism-collectivism on perceptions of communication in in-group and out-group relations. *Communication Monographs, 54,* 295–306.

Gumperz, J. J. (1982). *Discourse strategies.* Cambridge, UK: Cambridge University Press.

Gumperz, J. J., & Levinson, S. C. (Eds.) (1996). *Rethinking linguistic relativity* Cambridge, UK: Cambridge University Press.

Guy, G. R., & Vonwiller, J. (1984). The meaning of intonation in Australian English. *Australian Journal of Linguistics, 4.1,* 1–17.

Halliday, M. A. K., & Hassan, R. (1976). *Cohesion in English.* London: Longman.

Hardin, C., & Banaji, M. R. (1993). The influence of language on thought. *Social Cognition, 11,* 277–308.

Harré, R. (1986). Selves in talk. *British Journal of Social Psychology, 25,* 271–273.

Harré, R., & Secord, P. (1972). *The explanation of social behavior.* Oxford: Blackwell.

Hastie, R. (1984). Causes and consequences of causal attributions. *Journal of Personality and Social Psychology, 46,* 44–56.

Hastie, R., Park, B., & Weber, R. (1984). Social memory. In R. S. Wyer & T. K. Srull (Eds.), *Handbook of social cognition* (Vol. 2, pp. 151–212). Hillsdale, NJ: Erlbaum.

Heider, E. R. (1972). Universals in color naming and memory. *Journal of Experimental Psychology, 93,* 10–20.

Heider, E. R., & Olivier, D. C. (1972). The structure of the color space in naming and memory for two languages. *Cognitive Psychology, 3,* 337–354.

Heider, F. (1958). *The psychology of interpersonal relations.* New York: Wiley.

Heritage, J. C. (1984). *Garfinkel and ethnomethodology.* Cambridge, UK: Polity Press.

Higgins, E. T., & McCann, C. D. (1984). Social encoding and subsequent attitudes, impressions and memory: "Context-driven" and motivational aspects of processing. *Journal of Personality and Social Psychology, 47,* 27–39.

Higgins, E. T., & Rholes, W. S. (1978). "Saying is believing": Effects of message modification on memory and liking for the person described. *Journal of Experimental Social Psychology, 14,* 363–378.

Hill, B., Sachiko, I., Shoko, I., Kawasaki, A., & Ogino, T. (1986). Universals of linguistic politeness. *Journal of Pragmatics, 10,* 347–371.

Hilton, D. J. (1995). The social context of reasoning: Conversational inference and rational judgment. *Psychological Bulletin, 118,* 248–271.

Hilton, D. J., & Slugoski, B. R. (1986). Knowledge-based causal attributions: The abnormal conditions focus model. *Psychological Review, 93,* 75–88.

Hobbs, J. R., Stickel, M. E., Appelt, D. E., & Martin, P. (1993). Interpretation as abduction. *Artificial Intelligence, 63,* 69–142.

Hoffman, C., Lau, I., & Johnson, D. R. (1986). The linguistic relativity of person cognition: An English-Chinese comparison. *Journal of Personality and Social Psychology, 51,* 1097–1105.

Hoffman, C., & Tchir, M. A. (1990). Interpersonal verbs and dispositional adjectives: The psychology of causality embodied in language. *Journal of Personality and Social Psychology, 58,* 767–778.

Holtgraves, T. M. (1986). Language structure in social interaction: Perceptions of direct and indirect speech act and interactants who use them. *Journal of Personality and Social Psychology, 51,* 305–314.

Holtgraves, T. M. (1989). The form and function of remedial moves: Reported use, psychological reality, and perceived effectiveness. *Journal of Language and Social Psychology, 8,* 1–16.

Holtgraves, T. M. (1992). The linguistic realization of face management: Implications for language production and comprehension, person perception, and cross-cultural communication. *Social Psychology Quarterly, 55,* 141–159.

Holtgraves, T. M. (1994). Communication in context: Effects of speaker status on the comprehension of indirect requests. *Journal of Experimental Psychology: Learning, Memory, and Cognition, 20,* 1205–1218.

Holtgraves, T. M. (1997a). Politeness and memory for the wording of remarks. *Memory & Cognition, 25,* 106–116.

Holtgraves, T. M. (1997b). Yes, but . . . : Positive politeness in conversation arguments. *Journal of Language and Social Psychology, 16,* 222–239.

Holtgraves, T. M. (1997c). Styles of language use: Individual and cultural variability in conversational indirectness. *Journal of Personality and Social Psychology, 73,* 624–637.

Holtgraves T. M. (1998). Interpreting indirect replies. *Cognitive Psychology, 37,* 1–27.

Holtgraves, T. M. (1999). Comprehending indirect replies: When and how are their conveyed meanings activated? *Journal of Memory and Language, 41,* 519–540.

Holtgraves, T. M. (2000). Preference organization and reply comprehension. *Discourse Processes, 30,* 87–106.

Holtgraves, T. M. (2001). Unpublished data, Ball State University, Muncie, Indiana.

Holtgraves, T. M., & Ashley, A. (2001). Comprehending illocutionary force. *Memory & Cognition, 29,* 83–90.

Holtgraves, T., & Bailey, C. (1991). Premise acceptability and message effectiveness. *Basic and Applied Social Psychology, 12,* 157–176.

Holtgraves, T. M., & Drozd, B. (1998). *Cross-cultural differences in conversational interpretation.* Paper presented at the annual meeting of the Midwestern Psychological Association, Chicago.

Holtgraves, T. M., & Dulin, J. (1994). The Muhammad Ali effect: Differences between African-Americans and European-Americans in their perceptions of a truthful bragger. *Language and Communication, 14,* 275–285.

Holtgraves, T. M., Eck, J., & Lasky, B. (1997). Face management, question wording, and social desirability. *Journal of Applied Social Psychology, 27,* 1650–1672,

Holtgraves, T. M., & Grayer, A. R. (1994). I am not a crook: Effects of denials on perceptions of a defendant's guilt, personality, and motives. *Journal of Applied Social Psychology, 24,* 2132–2150.

Holtgraves, T. M., & Lasky, B. (1999). Linguistic power and persuasion. *Journal of Language and Social Psychology, 18,* 196–205.

Holtgraves, T. M., & Raymond, S. (1995). Implicit causality and memory: Evidence for a priming model. *Personality and Social Psychology Bulletin, 21,* 5–12.

Holtgraves, T. M., & Srull, T. K. (1989). The effects of positive self-descriptions on impressions: General principles and individual differences. *Personality and Social Psychology Bulletin, 15,* 452–462.

Holtgraves, T. M. & Yang, J. N. (1990). Politeness as an universal: Cross-cultural perceptions of request strategies and inferences based on their use. *Journal of Personality and Social Psychology, 59,* 719–729.

Holtgraves, T. M., & Yang, J. N. (1992). The interpersonal underpinnings of request strategies: General principles and differences due to culture and gender. *Journal of Personality and Social Psychology, 62,* 246–256.

Horton, W. S., & Keysar, B. (1996). When do speakers take into account common ground? *Cognition, 59,* 91–117.

Hovarth, B. (1986). *Variation in Australian English: A sociolinguistic study of English in Sydney.* Cambridge, UK: Cambridge University Press.

Howeler, M. (1972). Diversity of word usage as a stress indicator in an interview situation. *Journal of Psycholinguistic Research, 1,* 243–248.

Hudson, R. A. (1980). *Sociolinguistics.* Cambridge, UK: Cambridge University Press.

Hunt, E., & Agnoli, F. (1991). The Whorfian hypothesis: A cognitive psychology perspective. *Psychological Review, 98,* 377–389.

Ickes, W. (1993). Empathic accuracy. *Journal of Personality, 61,* 587–610.

Jacobs, S., & Jackson, S. (1982). Conversational argument: A discourse analytic approach. In J. R. Cox & C. A. Willard (Eds.), *Advances in argumentation theory and research* (pp. 205–237). Carbondale: Southern Illinois University Press.

Jefferson, G. (1972). Side sequences. In D. Sudnow (Ed.), *Studies in social interaction* (pp. 294–338). New York: The Free Press.

Jefferson, G. (1978). Sequential aspects of storytelling in conversation. In J. Schenkein (Ed.), *Studies in the organization of conversational interaction* (pp. 219–248). New York: Academic Press.

Jefferson, G. (1986). Notes on latency in overlap onset. *Human Studies, 9,* 153–183.

John, O. (1990). The "Big Five" factor taxonomy: Dimensions of personality in the natural language and in questionnaires. In L. Pervin (Ed.), *Handbook of personality: Theory and research* (pp. 66–100). New York: Guilford.

Johnson-Laird, P. N. (1982). Mutual ignorance: Comments on Clark and Carlson's paper. In N. V. Smith (Ed.), *Mutual knowledge* (pp. 40–45). London: Academic Press.

Jones, E. E. (1964). *Ingratiation.* New York: Appleton-Century-Crofts.

Jones, E. E. (1990). *Interpersonal perception.* New York: W. H. Freeman.

Jones, E. E., & Harris, V. A. (1967). The attribution of attitudes. *Journal of Experimental Social Psychology, 3,* 1–24.

Jones, E. E., & Pittman, T. (1982). Toward a general theory of strategic self-presentation. In J. Suls (Ed.), *Psychological perspectives on the self* (Vol. 1, pp. 231–262). Hillsdale, NJ: Erlbaum.

Jucker, J. (1986). *News interviews: A pragmalinguistic analysis.* Amsterdam: Gieben.

Kahneman, D., & Tversky, A. (1973). On the psychology of prediction. *Psychological Review, 80,* 237–251.

Kalin, R., & Rayko, D. (1980). The social significance of speech in the job interview. In R. N. St. Clair & H. Giles (Eds.), *The social and psychological contexts of language* (pp. 39–50). Hillsdale, NJ: Erlbaum.

Kanouse, D. E. (1972). Language, labeling, and attribution. In E. E. Jones, D. E. Kanouse, H.H. Kelley, R. E. Nisbett, S. Valins, & B. Weiner (Eds.), *Attribution: Perceiving the causes of behavior* (pp. 121–135). Morristown, NJ: General Learning Press.

Kaplan, D. (1979). On the logic of demonstratives. *Journal of Philosophical Logic, 8,* 81–98.

Kasof, J., & Lee, J. Y. (1993). Implicit causality as implicit salience. *Journal of Personality and Social Psychology, 65,* 877–891.

Katriel, T. (1986). *Talking straight: Durgri speech in Israeli Sabra culture.* Cambridge, UK: Cambridge University Press.

Katz, A., & Pexman, P. M. (1997) Interpreting figurutive statements: Speaker occupation can change metaphor to irony. *Metaphor and Symbol, 12,* 19–41.

Katz, J. J. (1977). *Propositional structure and illocutionary force.* New York: Crowell.

Kay, P. (1996). Intra-speaker relativity. In J. J Gumperz & S. C. Levinson (Eds.), *Rethinking linguistic relativity* (pp. 97–114). Cambridge, UK: Cambridge University Press.

Kay, P., & Kempton, W. (1984). What is the Sapir-Whorf hypothesis? *American Anthropologist, 86,* 65–79.

Keenan, E. O. (1976). The universality of conversational implicature. *Language in Society, 5,* 67–80.

Keenan, E. O., & Schieffelin, B. (1976). Topic as a discourse notion. In C. N. Li (Ed.), *Subject and topic* (pp. 337–384). New York: Academic Press.

Kelly, G. A. (1955). *The psychology of personal constructs.* New York: Norton.

Keltner, D., Young, R. C., Heerey, E. A., Oemig, C., & Monarch, N. D. (1998). Teasing in hierarchical and intimate relations. *Journal of Personality and Social Psychology, 75,* 1231–1247.

Kemper, S., & Thissen, D. (1981). How polite? A reply to Clark and Schunk. *Cognition, 9,* 305–309.

Kendon, A. (1967). Some functions of gaze-direction in social interaction. *Acta Psychologia, 26,* 22–63.

Kent, G. G., Davis, J. D., & Shapiro, D. A. (1978). Resources required in the construction and reconstruction of conversation. *Journal of Personality and Social Psychology, 36,* 13–22.

Keysar, B. (1989). On the functional equivalence of literal and metaphorical interpretation in discourse. *Journal of Memory and Language, 28,* 375–385.

Keysar, B. (1994). The illusory transparency of intention: Linguistic perspective taking in text. *Cognitive Psychology, 26,* 165–208.

Keysar, B. (1997). Unconfounding common ground. *Discourse Processes,* 161–172.

Keysar, B. (1998). Language users as problem solvers: Just what ambiguity problem do they solve? In S. Fussell & R. Kreuz (Eds.), *Social and cognitive approaches to interpersonal communication* (pp. 175–200). Mahwah, NJ: Erlbaum.

Keysar, B. (2000). The illusory transparency of intention: Does June understand what Mark means because he means it? *Discourse Processes, 29,* 161–172.

Keysar, B., Barr, D. J., Balin, J. A., & Brauner, J. S. (2000). Taking perspective in conversation: The role of mutual knowledge in comprehension. *Psychological Science, 11,* 32–38.

Keysar, B., Barr, D. J., Balin, J. A., & Paek, T. (1998). Definite reference and mutual knowledge: A processing model of common ground in comprehension. *Journal of Memory and Language, 39,* 1–20.

Keysar, B., & Bly, B. (1995). Intuitions of the transparency of idioms: Can one keep a secret by spilling the beans? *Journal of Memory and Language, 34,* 89–109.

Kingsbury, D. (1968). *Manipulating the amount of information obtained from a person giving directions.* Unpublished honors thesis, Harvard University, Department of Social Relations, Cambridge, Massachusetts.

Kintsch, W., & van Dijk, T. A. (1978). Toward a model of text comprehension and production. *Psychological Review, 95,* 163–182.

Klatsky, R. L., Martin, G. L., & Kane, R. A. (1982). Semantic interpretation effects on memory for faces. *Memory & Cognition, 10,* 195–206.

Kochman, T. (1981). *Black and white styles in conflict.* Chicago: University of Chicago Press.

Kollock, P., Blumstein, P., & Schwartz, P. (1985). Sex and power in interaction: Conversational privileges and duties. *American Sociological Review, 50,* 34–46.

Kosinski, J. (1971). *Being there.* New York: Bantam Books.

Krauss, R. M., & Fussell, S. R. (1991a). Perspective taking in communication: Representations of others' knowledge in reference. *Social Cognition, 9,* 2–24.

Krauss, R. M., & Fussell, S. R. (1991b). Constructing shared communicative environments. In L. B. Resnick, J. M. Levine, & S. D. Teasley (Eds.), *Perspectives on socially shared cognition* (pp. 172–202). Washington, DC: American Psychological Association.

Krauss, R. M., & Fussell, S. R. (1996). Social psychological models of interpersonal communication. In E. T. Higgins & A. W. Kruglanski (Eds.), *Social psychology: Handbook of basic principles* (pp. 655–701). New York: Guilford.

Krauss, R. M., & Weinheimer, S. (1964). Changes in length of reference phrases as a function of social interaction: A preliminary study. *Psychonomic Science, 1,* 113–114.

Krauss, R. M., & Weinheimer, S. (1966). Concurrent feedback, confirmation and the encoding of referents in verbal communication. *Journal of Personality and Social Psychology, 4,* 343–346.

Kreuz, R. J., Kassler, M. A., & Coppenrath, L. (1998). The use of exaggeration in discourse: Cognitive and social facets. In S. R. Fussell & R. J. Kreuz (Eds.), *Social and cognitive approaches to communication* (pp. 91–112). Mahwah, NJ: Erlbaum.

Kreuz, R. J., & Roberts, R. M. (1993). When collaboration fails: Consequences of pragmatic errors in conversation. *Journal of Pragmatics, 19,* 239–252.

Krosnick, J., Li, F., & Lehman, D. R. (1990). Conversational conventions, order of information acquisition, and the effect of base rates and individuating information on social judgment. *Journal of Personality and Social Psychology, 59,* 1140–1152.

Labov, W. (1966). *The social stratification of English in New York City.* Washington, DC: Center for Applied Linguistics.

Labov, W. (1972a). *Sociolinguistic patterns.* Philadelphia: University of Pennsylvania Press.

Labov, W. (1972b). *Language in the inner city*. Philadelphia: University of Pennsylvania Press.

Labov, W., & Fanschel, D. (1977). *Therapeutic discourse*. New York: Academic Press.

LaFrance, M., & Mayo, C. (1976). Racial differences in gaze behavior during conversation: Two systematic observational studies. *Journal of Personality and Social Psychology, 33*, 547–552.

LaFrance M., & Mayo, C. (1978). *Moving bodies: Nonverbal communication in social relationships*. Monterey, CA: Brooks/Cole.

Lakoff, R. (1973). The logic of politeness: Or, minding your p's and q's. *Papers from the Ninth Regional Meeting of the Chicago Linguistic Society* (pp. 292–305).

Lakoff, R. (1975). *Language and woman's place*. New York: Harper & Row.

Lakoff, R. (1977). Women's Language. *Language and Style, 10*, 222–248.

Lakoff, R. (1979). Stylistic strategies within a grammar of style. In J. Orasanu, M. K. Slater, & L. L. Adler (Eds.), *The annals of the New York Academy of Sciences* (pp. 53–80).

Lambert, B. L. (1996). Face and politeness in pharmacist-physician interaction. *Social Science and Medicine, 43*, 1189–1199.

Lambert, W. E., Hodgson, R., Gardner, R. C., & Fillenbaum S. (1960). Evaluative reactions to spoken languages. *Journal of Abnormal and Social Psychology, 60*, 44–51.

Lantz, D., & Stefflre, V. (1964). Language and cognition revisited. *Journal of Abnormal and Social Psychology, 69*, 472–481.

Lavandera, B. (1978). Where does the sociolinguistic variable stop? *Language in Society, 7*, 171–182.

Leech, G. (1983). *Principles of pragmatics*. London: Longman.

Leichty, G., & Applegate, J. L. (1991). Social-cognitive and situational influences on the use of face-saving persuasive strategies. *Human Communication Research, 7*, 451–484.

Lerner, G. (1996). Finding "face" in the preference structure of talk-in-interaction. *Social Psychology Quarterly, 59*, 303–321.

Leung, K. (1988). Some determinants of collective avoidance. *Journal of Cross-Cultural Psychology, 19*, 125–136.

Levelt, W. J. M. (1989) *Speaking: From intention to articulation*. Cambridge, MA: MIT Press.

Levin, H., & Lim, T. (1988). An accommodating witness. *Language and Communication, 8*, 195–198.

Levinson, S. (1983). *Pragmatics*. Cambridge, UK: Cambridge University Press.

Levinson, S. (1979). Activity types and language. *Linguistics, 17*, 365–399.

Lewis, D. K. (1969). *Convention: A philosophical study*. Cambridge, MA: Harvard University Press.

Lim, T., & Bowers, J. W. (1991). Face-work, solidarity, approbation, and tact. *Human Communication Research, 17*, 415–450.

Liu, L. G. (1985). Reasoning counterfactually in Chinese: Are there any obstacles? *Cognition, 21*, 239–270.

Loftus, E. F. (1977). Shifting human color memory. *Memory & Cognition, 5*, 696–699.

Loftus, E. F., & Palmer, J. C. (1974). Reconstruction of automobile destruction: An example of the interaction between language and memory. *Journal of Verbal Learning and Verbal Behavior, 13*, 585–589.

Lucy, J. A., & Schweder, R. A. (1979). Whorf and his critics: Linguistic and nonlinguistic influences on color memory. *American Anthropologist, 81*, 581–615.

Maass, A., & Arcuri, S. (1996). Language and stereotyping. In C. N. Macrae, C. Stangor, & M. Hewstone (Eds.), *Stereotypes and stereotyping* (pp. 193–226). New York: Guilford.

Maass, A., Milesi, A., Zabbini, S., & Stahlberg, D. (1995). The linguistic intergroup bias: Differential expectancies or in-group protection? *Journal of Personality and Social Psychology, 68*, 116–126.

Maass, A., Salvi, D., Arcuri, L., & Semin, G. (1989). Language use in intergroup contexts: The linguistic intergroup bias. *Journal of Personality and Social Psychology, 57*, 981–993.

Mahl, G. F. (1972). People talking when they can't hear their voices. In A. W. Siegman & B. Pope (Eds.), *Studies in dyadic communication* (pp. 211–264). New York: Pergamon.

Markus, H. R., & Kitayama, S. (1991). Culture and the self: Implications for cognition, emotion, and motivation. *Psychological Review, 98*, 224–253.

Matsumoto, Y. (1988). Reexamination of the universality of face: Politeness phenomena in Japanese. *Journal of Pragmatics, 12,* 403–426.

McAdams, D. P. (1985). *Power, intimacy, and the life story.* Homewood, IL: Dempsey.

McAdams, D. P. (1993). *The stories we live by: Personal myths and the making of the self.* New York: William Morrow.

McArthur, L. Z. (1972). The how and what of why: Some determinants and consequences of causal attributions. *Journal of Personality and Social Psychology, 22,* 171–188.

McCann, C. D., & Hancock, R. D. (1983). Self-monitoring in communicative interactions: Social-cognitive consequences of goal-directed message modification. *Journal of Experimental Social Psychology, 19,* 109–121.

McGregor, I., & Holmes, J. G. (1999). How storytelling shapes memory and impressions of relation-ship events over time. *Journal of Personality and Social Psychology, 76,* 403–419.

McLaughlin, M. L., Cody, M., & O'Hair, H. D. (1983). The management of failure events: Some con-textual determinants of accounting behavior. *Human Communication Research, 9,* 208–224.

Mead, G. H. (1934). *Mind, self, and society.* Chicago: University of Chicago Press.

Merritt, M. (1976). On questions following questions (in-service encounters). *Language in Society, 5,* 315–357.

Miller, A. G., Schmidt, D., Meyer, C., & Colella, A. (1984). The perceived value of constrained behav-ior: Pressures toward biased inference in the attitude attribution paradigm. *Social Psychology Quarterly, 47,* 160–171.

Miller, D. T., & Prentice, D. A. (1996). The construction of social norms and standards. In E. T. Hig-gins & A. W. Kruglanski (Eds.), *Social psychology: Handbook of basic principles* (pp. 799–829). New York: Guilford.

Miller, J. (1984). Culture and the development of everyday social explanation. *Journal of Personality and Social Psychology, 46,* 961–978.

Miller, K. F., & Stigler, J. (1987). Counting in Chinese: Cultural variation in a basic cognitive skill. *Cognitive Development, 2,* 279–305.

Milroy, L., & Milroy, J. (1978). Speech and context in an urban setting. *Belfast Working Papers in Language and Linguistics, 2,* 1–85.

Miyawaki, K., Strange, W., Verbrugge, R., Liberman, A. M., Jenkins, J. J., & Fujimura, O. (1975). An effect of linguistic experience: The discrimination of /r/ and /l/ by native speakers of Japanese and English. *Perception and Psychophysics, 18,* 331–340.

Morisaki, S., & Gudykunst, W. B. (1994). Face in Japan and the United States. In S. Ting-Toomey (Ed.), *The challenge of face-work* (pp. 47–94). Albany: State University of New York Press.

Mullen, B., Dovidio, J. F., Johnson, C., & Copper, C. (1992). Ingroup-outgroup differences in social projection. *Journal of Experimental Social Psychology, 28,* 422–440.

Najjar, O. (1998, July). Presentation at symposium: Politeness and Face—State of the Art. Annual meeting of the International Communication Association, Jerusalem, Israel.

Natale, M. (1975). Convergence of mean vocal intensity in dyadic communications as a function of social desirability. *Journal of Personality and Social Psychology, 32,* 790–804.

Natale, M., Entin, E., & Jaffe, J. (1979). Vocal interruptions in dyadic communication as a function of speech and social anxiety. *Journal of Personality and Social Psychology, 37,* 865–878.

Newcombe, N., & Arnkoff, D. B. (1979). Effects of speech style and sex of speaker on person percep-tion. *Journal of Personality and Social Psychology, 37,* 1293–1303.

Newtson, D., & Czerlinski, T. (1974). Adjustment of attitude communications for contrasts by extreme audiences. *Journal of Personality and Social Psychology, 30,* 829–837.

Ng, S. H., Bell, D., & Brooke, M. (1993). Gaining turns and achieving high influence ranking in small conversational groups. *British Journal of Social Psychology, 32,* 265–275.

Nickerson, R. S. (1999). How we know—and sometimes misjudge—what others know: Imputing one's own knowledge to others. *Psychological Bulletin, 125,* 737–759.

Nisbett, R. E., & Ross, L. (1980). *Human inference: Strategies and shortcomings of social judgment.* Upper Saddle River, NJ: Prentice Hall.

Nisbett, R. E., Zukier, H., & Lemley, R. E. (1981). The dilution effect: Nondiagnostic information weakens the implications of diagnostic information. *Cognitive Psychology, 13*, 248–277.

Noller, P., & Venardos, C. (1986). Communication awareness in married couples. *Journal of Social and Personality Relationships, 3*, 31–42.

O'Barr, W. (1982). *Linguistic evidence: Language, power, and strategy in the courtroom*. New York: Academic Press.

O'Barr, W., & Atktins, B. K. (1980). "Women's language" or "powerless" language? In S. McConnell-Ginet, R. Borker, & N. Furman (Eds.), *Women and language in literature and society* (pp. 3–110). New York: Praeger.

Ohlschlegel, S., & Piontkowski, V. (1997). Topic progression and social categorization. *Journal of Language and Social Psychology, 16*, 444–455.

Okamoto, S., & Robinson, W. P. (1997). Determinants of gratitude expression in England. *Journal of Language and Social Psychology, 16*, 411–433.

Olson, D. R. (1970). Language and thought: Aspects of a cognitive theory of semantics. *Psychological Review, 77*, 257–273.

Ortony, A., Schallert, D., Reynolds, D., & Antos, S. (1978). Interpreting metaphors and idioms: Some effects of context on comprehension. *Journal of Verbal Learning and Verbal Behavior, 16*, 465–477.

Ottati, V., Rhoads, S., & Graesser, A. C. (1999). The effect of metaphor on processing style in a persuasion task: A motivational resonance model. *Journal of Personality and Social Psychology, 77*, 688–697.

Parsons, T. (1937). *The structure of social action*. New York: McGraw-Hill.

Penman, R. (1990). Face-work and politeness: Multiple goals in courtroom discourse. *Journal of Language and Social Psychology, 9*, 15–38.

Pennebaker, J. W., & King, L. (1999). Linguistic styles: Language use as an individual difference. *Journal of Personality and Social Psychology, 77*, 1296–1312.

Pennington, D. L. (1979). Black-white communication: An assessment of research. In M. K. Asante, E. Newmark, & C. Blake (Eds.), *Handbook of intercultural communication* (pp. 383–401). Beverly Hills, CA: Sage.

Pennington, N., & Hastie, R. (1988). Explanation-based decision making: Effects of memory structure on judgment. *Journal of Experimental Psychology, Learning, Memory, and Cognition, 14*, 521–533.

Person, N. K., Kreuz, R. J., Zwaan, R. A., & Graesser, A. C. (1995). Pragmatics and pedagogy: Conversational rules and politeness strategies may inhibit effective tutoring. *Cognition and Instruction, 13*, 161–188.

Petty, R. E., & Cacioppo, J. T. (1986). *Communication and persuasion: Central and peripheral routes to attitude change*. New York: Springer-Verlag.

Piaget, J. (1926). *The language and thought of the child*. New York: Harcourt Brace.

Pinker, S. (1994). *The language instinct*. New York: William Morrow & Co.

Planalp, S., & Tracy, K. (1980). Not to change the subject but . . . : A cognitive approach to the management of conversation. In D. Nimmo (Ed.), *Communication yearbook 4* (pp. 237–260). New Brunswick, NJ: Transaction.

Pomerantz, A. (1978). Compliant responses: Notes on the co-operation of multiple constraints. In J. Schenkein (Ed.), *Studies in the organization of conversational interaction* (pp. 79–112). New York: Academic Press.

Pomerantz, A. (1984). Agreeing and disagreeing with assessments: Some features of preferred/ dispreferred turn-shapes. In J. Atkinson & J. Heritage (Eds.), *Structures of social action: Studies in conversation analysis* (pp. 79–112). Cambridge, UK: Cambridge University Press.

Potter, J. (1996). *Representing reality: Discourse, rhetoric and social construction*. London: Sage.

Potter, J. (1998) Cognition as context (whose cognition?). *Research on Language and Social Interaction, 31*, 29–44.

Potter, J., & Wetherall, M. (1987). *Discourse and social psychology: Beyond attitudes and behavior.* London: Sage.

Purnell, T., Idsardi, W., & Baugh, J. (1999). Perceptual and phonetic experiments on American English dialect identification. *Journal of Language and Social Psychology, 18,* 10–30.

Ramsey, R. (1966). Personality and speech. *Journal of Personality and Social Psychology, 4,* 116–118.

Reichman, R. (1978). Conversational coherency. *Cognitive Science, 2,* 283–327.

Reichman, R. (1985). *Getting computers to talk like you and me.* Cambridge, MA: MIT Press.

Reisman, K. (1974). Contrapuntal conversations in an Antigual village. In R. Bauman & I. Sherzer (Eds.), *Explorations in the ethnography of speaking* (pp. 110–124). Cambridge UK: Cambridge University Press.

Richter, L., & Kruglanski, A. W. (1999). Motivated search for common ground: Need for closure effects on audience design in interpersonal communication. *Personality and Social Psychology Bulletin, 25,* 1101–1114.

Rips, L. J., Brem, S. K., & Bailenson, J. N. (1999). Reasoning dialogues. *Current Directions in Psychological Science, 6,* 172–177.

Robinson, W. P. (1998). Language and social psychology: An intersection of opportunities and significance. *Journal of Language and Social Psychology, 17,* 276–301.

Roger, D., & Bull, P. (1989). *Conversation: An interdisciplinary perspective.* Clevedon, UK: Multilingual Matters.

Roger, D., & Nesserhaver, W. (1987). Individual differences in dyadic conversational strategies: A further study. *British Journal of Social Psychology, 26,* 247–255.

Rommetveit, R. (1974). *On message structure: A framework for the study of language and communication.* New York: Wiley.

Rosaldo, M. Z. (1982). The things we do with words: Ilongot speech acts and speech act theory in philosophy. *Language in Society, 11,* 203–237.

Rosch, E. (1973). Natural categories. *Cognitive Psychology, 4,* 328–350.

Ross, L., Greene, D., & House, P. (1977). The "false consensus effect": An egocentric bias in the social perception and attribution process. *Journal of Experimental Social Psychology, 13,* 279–301.

Ross, L., & Nisbett, R. E. (1991). *The person and the situation.* New York: McGraw-Hill.

Rubin, D. L., & Nelson, M. W. (1983). Multiple determinants of stigmatized speech style: Women's language, powerless language, or everyone's language? *Journal of Language and Social Psychology, 26,* 273–290.

Rudolph, U., & Forsterling, F. (1997). The psychological causality implicit in verbs: A review. *Psychological Bulletin, 121,* 192–218.

Rundquist, S. (1992). Indirectness: A gender study of flouting Grice's maxims. *Journal of Pragmatics, 18,* 431–449.

Ruscher, J. B. (1998). Prejudice and stereotyping in everyday conversation. In M. Zanna (Ed.), *Advances in Experimental Social Psychology* (Vol. 30, pp. 241–307). San Diego, CA: Academic Press.

Russell, A. W., & Schober, M. F. (1999). How beliefs about a partner's goals affect referring in goal-discrepant conversations. *Discourse Processes, 27,* 1–33.

Ryan, E. B., Carranza, M. A., & Moffie, R. W. (1977). Reactions towards varying degrees of accentedness in the speech of Spanish-English. *Language and Speech, 20,* 267–273.

Ryan, E. B., Giles, H., & Sebastian, R. (1982). An integrative perspective for the study of attitudes toward language variation. In E. B. Ryan & H. Giles (Eds.), *Attitudes toward language variation* (pp. 1–19). London: Edward Arnold.

Ryan, E. B., & Sebastian, R. (1980). The effects of speech style and social class background on social judgments of speakers. *British Journal of Social and Clinical Psychology, 19,* 229–233.

Ryave, A. L. (1978). On the achievement of a series of stories. In J. Schenkein (Ed.), *Studies in the organization of conversational interaction* (pp. 113–132). New York: Academic Press.

Sabourin, T. C., & Stamp, G. H. (1995). Communication and the experience of dialectical tensions in family life: An examination of abusive and nonabusive families. *Communication Monographs, 62,* 213–242.

Sacks, H. (1974). An analysis of the course of a joke's telling in conversation. In R. Baumann & J. Sherzer (Eds.), *Explorations in the ethnography of speaking* (pp. 337–353). Cambridge, UK: Cambridge University Press.

Sacks, H. (1992). *Lectures on conversations.* G. Jefferson (Ed.) (2 Vols.) Oxford: Basil Blackwell.

Sacks, H., & Schegloff, E. A. (1979). Two preferences in the organization of reference to persons in conversation and their interaction. In G. Psathas (Ed.), *Everyday language: Studies in ethnomethodology* (pp. 15–21). Hillsdale, NJ: Erlbaum.

Sacks, H., Schegloff, E. A., & Jefferson, G. (1974). A simplist systematics for the organization of turn-taking in conversation. *Language, 4,* 696–735.

Sampson, E. E. (1983). Deconstructing psychology's subject. *Journal of Mind and Behavior, 4,* 135–164.

Sankoff, D., Thibault, P., & Berube, H. (1978). Semantic field variability. In D. Sankoff (Ed.), *Linguistic variation: Models and methods* (pp. 23–44). New York: Academic Press.

Santa, J. L., & Baker, L. (1975). Linguistic influence on visual memory. *Memory and Cognition, 3,* 445–450.

Santa, J. L., & Ranken, H. B. (1972). Effects of verbal coding on recognition memory. *Journal of Experimental Psychology, 93,* 268–278.

Sapir, E. (1921). *Language: An introduction to the study of speech.* New York: Harcourt, Brace.

Saussure, F. de (1916/1968). *Cours de linguistique generale.* Paris: Payot.

Schank, R. C. (1977). Rules and topics in conversation. *Cognitive Science, 1,* 421–441.

Schank, R. C., & Abelson, R. P. (1977). *Scripts, plans, goals and understanding.* Hillsdale, NJ: Erlbaum.

Schank, R. C., & Abelson, R. P. (1995). Knowledge and memory: The real story. In R. J. Wyer, Jr. (Ed.), *Advances in social cognition* (Vol. 8, pp. 1–86). Hillsdale, NJ: Erlbaum Press.

Schegloff, E. A. (1968). Sequencing in conversational openings. *American Anthropologist, 70,* 1075–1095.

Schegloff, E. A. (1972). Notes on a conversational practice: Formulating place. In D. Sudnow (Ed.), *Studies in social interaction* (pp. 75–119). New York: The Free Press.

Schegloff, E. A. (1979). Identification and recognition in telephone conversation openings. In G. Psathas (Ed.), *Everyday language: Studies in ethnomethodology* (pp. 23–78). New York: Irvington.

Schegloff, E. A. (1982). Discourse and an interactional achievement: Some uses of "uh huh" and other things that come between sentences. In D. Tannen (Ed.), *Analyzing discourse: Text and talk. Georgetown University Roundtable on Languages and Linguistics, 1981* (pp. 71–93). Washington, DC: Georgetown University Press.

Schegloff, E. A. (1992a). To Searle on conversation: A note in return. In H. Parret and J. Verschueren (Eds.), *(On) Searle on conversation* (pp. 113–128). Philadelphia: John Benjamins.

Schegloff, E. A. (1992b). Repair after next turn: The last structurally provided defense of intersubjectivity in conversation. *American Journal of Sociology, 97,* 1295–1345.

Schegloff, E. A., Jefferson, G., & Sacks, H. (1977). The preference for self-correction in the organization of repair in conversation. *Language, 53,* 361–382.

Schegloff, E., & Sacks, H. (1973). Opening up closings. *Semiotica, 8,* 289–327.

Schenkein, J. (1978). Identity negotiation in conversation. In J. Schenkein (Ed.), *Studies in the organization of conversational interaction* (pp. 57–78). New York: Academic Press.

Scherer, K. (1979). Personality markers in speech. In K. Scherer & H. Giles (Eds.), *Social markers in speech* (pp. 147–209). Cambridge, UK: Cambridge University Press.

Schiffer, S. R. (1972). *Meaning.* Oxford: Oxford University Press.

Schlenker, B. R. (1980). *Impression management.* Monterey, CA: Brooks/Cole.

Schlenker, B. R., & Darby, B. W. (1981). The use of apologies in social predicaments. *Social Psychology Quarterly, 44,* 271–278.

Schober, M. F. (1993). Spatial perspective taking in conversation. *Cognition, 47,* 1–24.

Schober, M. F. (1998). Different kinds of conversational perspective taking. In S. Fussell & R. Kreuz (Eds.), *Social and cognitive approaches to interpersonal communication* (pp. 145–174). Mahwah, NJ: Erlbaum.

Schober, M. R., & Clark, H. H. (1989). Understanding by addressees and overhearers. *Cognitive Psychology, 21,* 211–232.

Schooler, J. W., & Engstler-Schooler, T. Y. (1990). Verbal overshadowing of visual memories: Some things are better left unsaid. *Cognitive Psychology, 22,* 36–71.

Schuman, H., & Presser, S. (1981). *Questions and answers in attitude surveys.* New York: Academic Press.

Schutz, A. (1970). *On phenomonology and social relations.* Chicago: University of Chicago Press.

Schwarz, N. (1996). *Cognition and communication: Judgmental biases, research methods, and the logic of conversation.* Mahwah, NJ: Erlbaum.

Schwarz, N., Strack, F., Hilton, D., & Naderer, G. (1991). Base rates, representativeness, and the logic of conversation: The contextual relevance of "irrelevant" information. *Social Cognition, 9,* 67–84.

Scollon, R., & Scollon, S. (1981). *Narrative, literacy, and face in interethnic communication.* Norwood, NJ: Ablex.

Searle, J. R. (1969). *Speech acts.* Cambridge, UK: Cambridge University Press.

Searle, J. R. (1975). Indirect speech acts. In P. Cole & J. Morgan (Eds.), *Syntax and semantics 3: Speech acts* (pp. 59–82). New York: Academic Press.

Searle, J. R. (1979). *Expression and meaning.* Cambridge, UK: Cambridge University Press.

Searle, J. (1990). Collective intentions and actions. In P. Cohen, J. Morgan, & M. Pollack (Eds.), *Intentions in communication* (pp. 401–416). Cambridge, MA: MIT Press.

Searle, J. (1992). Conversation. In H. Parret & J. Verschueren (Eds.), *(On) Searle on conversation* (pp. 7–30). Philadelphia: John Benjamins.

Searle, J. R., & Vanderveken, D. (1985). *Foundations of illocutionary logic.* Cambridge, UK: Cambridge University Press.

Sedikides, C. (1990). Effects of fortuitously activated constructs versus activated communication goals on person impressions. *Journal of Personality and Social Psychology, 58,* 397–408.

Seggre, I. (1983). Attribution of guilt as a function of ethnic accent and type of crime. *Journal of Multilingual and Multicultural Development, 4,* 197–206.

Seligman, C., Tucker, G. R., & Lambert, W. E. (1972). The effects of speech style and other attributes on teachers' attitudes toward pupils. *Language in Society, 1,* 131–142.

Selman, R. L. (1981). The child as a friendship philosopher. In S. R. Asher & J. M. Gottman (Eds.), *The development of children's friendships* (pp. 242–272). Cambridge, UK: Cambridge University Press.

Semin, G. R. (1998). Cognition, language, and communication. In S. R. Fussell & R. J. Kreuz (Eds.), *Social and cognitive approaches to interpersonal communication* (pp. 229–258). Mahwah, NJ: Erlbaum.

Semin, G. R., & de Poot, D. J. (1997). The question-answer paradigm: You might regret not noticing how a question is worded. *Journal of Personality and Social Psychology, 73,* 472–480.

Semin, G. R., & Fiedler, K. (1988). The cognitive functions of linguistic categories in describing persons: Social cognition and language. *Journal of Personality and Social Psychology, 54,* 558–568.

Semin, G. R., & Fiedler, K. (1991). The linguistic category model, its bases, applications and range. In W. Stroebe & M. Hewstone (Eds.), *European review of social psychology* (Vol. 2, pp. 1–30). Chichester, UK: Wiley.

Semin, G. R., & Smith, E. R. (1999). Revisiting the past and back to the future: Memory systems and the linguistic representation of social events. *Journal of Personality and Social Psychology, 76,* 877–892.

Shatz, M., & Gelman, R. (1973). The development of communication skills: Modification of the speech of young children as a function of the listener. *Monographs of the Society for Research in Child Development, 38,* 1–38.

Siegman, A. W., & Pope, B. (1972). *Studies in dyadic communication.* New York: Pergamon.

Simard, L., Taylor, D. M., & Giles, H. (1976). Attribution processes and interpersonal accommodation in a bilingual setting. *Language and Speech, 19,* 374–387.

Sinclair, J. M., & Coulthard, R. M. (1975). *Towards an analysis of discourse.* Oxford: Oxford University Press.

Singer, M., Halldorson, M., Lear, J. C., & Andrusiak, P. (1992). Validation of causal bridging inferences in discourse understanding. *Journal of Memory and Language, 31,* 507–524.

Skowronski, J. J., Carlston, D. E., Mae, L., & Crawford, M. T. (1998). Spontaneous trait transference: Communicators take on the qualities they describe in others. *Journal of Personality and Social Psychology, 74,* 837–848.

Slobin, D. (1996). From "thought and language" to "thinking for speaking." In J. J. Gumperz & S. C. Levinson (Eds.), *Rethinking linguistic relativity* (pp. 70–96). Cambridge, UK: Cambridge University Press.

Slugoski, B. R. (1983). *Attributions in conversational context.* Paper presented at the Annual Social Psychology Section Conference of the British Psychological Society, Sheffield.

Slugoski, B. R., & Hilton, D. J. (in press). Conversation. In H. Giles & W. P. Robinson (Eds.), *Handbook of language and social psychology* (2nd edition). London: Wiley.

Slugoski, B., Lalljee, M., Lamb, R., & Ginsburg, G. P. (1993). Attributions in conversational context: Effects of mutual knowledge on explanation giving. *European Journal of Social Psychology, 23,* 219–238.

Slugoski, B., & Turnbull, W. (1988). Cruel to be kind and kind to be cruel: Sarcasm, banter and social relations. *Journal of Language and Social Psychology, 7,* 101–121.

Smith, S. M., & Schaffer, D. R. (1995). Speed of speech and persuasion: Evidence for multiple effects. *Personality and Social Psychology Bulletin, 21,* 1051–1060.

Smitherman, G. (1977). *Talking and testifying: The language of Black America.* Boston: Houghton Mifflin.

Snyder, M. (1979). Self-monitoring processes. In L. Berkowitz (Ed.), *Advances in experimental social psychology* (Vol 12, pp. 86–131). New York: Academic Press.

Snyder, M., Tanke, E. D., & Berscheid, E. (1977). Social perception and interpersonal behavior: On the self-fulfilling nature of social stereotypes. *Journal of Personality and Social Psychology, 35,* 656–666.

Sperber, D., & Wilson, D. (1986). *Relevance.* Cambridge, MA: Harvard University Press.

Stalnaker, R. C. (1978). Assertion. In P. Cole (Ed.), *Syntax and semantics 9: Pragmatics* (pp. 315–322). New York: Academic Press.

Steedman, J. J., & Johnson-Laird, P. N. (1980). The production of sentences, utterances, and speech acts: Have computers anything to say? In B. Butterworth (Ed.), *Language production: Vol. 1, Speech and talk* (pp. 111–141). London: Academic Press.

Stefflre, V., Castillo Vales, V. S., & Morley, L. (1966). Language and cognition in Yucatan: A cross-cultural replication. *Journal of Personality and Social Psychology, 4,* 112–115.

Stiles, W. (1978). Verbal response modes and dimensions of interpersonal roles: A method of discourse analysis. *Journal of Personality and Social Psychology, 36,* 693–703.

Stiles, W. (1992). *Describing talk.* Newbury Park, CA: Sage.

Stiles, W., Putnam, S. M., & Jacob, M. C. (1982). Verbal exchange structure of initial medical interviews. *Health Psychology, 1,* 315–336.

Strack, F., Schwarz, N., & Wanke, M. (1991). Semantic and pragmatic aspects of context effects in social and psychological research. *Social Cognition, 9,* 111–125.

Street, R. L., Jr., Brady, R. M., & Putman, W. B. (1983). The influence of speech rate stereotypes and rate similarity on listeners' evaluations of speakers. *Journal of Language and Social Psychology, 2,* 337–356.

Tannen, D. (1984). *Conversational style: Analyzing talk among friends.* Norwood, NJ: Ablex.

Tannen, D. (1990). *You just don't understand.* New York: Morrow.

Thakerar, J. N., & Giles, H. (1981). They are—so they speak: Noncontent speech stereotypes. *Language and Communication, 1,* 251–256.

Ting-Toomey, S. (1988). Intercultural conflict styles. In Y. Y. Kim & W. B. Gudykunst (Eds.), *Theories in intercultural communication* (pp. 213–238). Beverly Hills, CA: Sage.

Titone, D. A., & Connine, C. M. (1994). Comprehension of idiomatic expressions: Effects of familiarity and literality. *Journal of Experimental Psychology: Learning, Memory and Cognition, 20,* 1126–1138.

Tracy, K. (1990). The many faces of face-work. In H. Giles & P. Robinson (Eds.), *Handbook of language and social psychology* (pp. 209–226). London: Wiley.

Tracy, K., & Tracy, S. J. (1998). Rudeness at 911: Reconceptualizing face and face attack. *Human Communication Research, 25,* 225–251.

Traxler, M. J., & Gernsbacher, M. A. (1992). Improving written communication through minimal feedback. *Language and Cognitive Processes, 7,* 1–22.

Traxler, M. J., & Gernsbacher, M. A. (1993). Improving written communication through perspective taking. *Language and Cognitive Processes, 8,* 311–334.

Trees, A. R., & Manusov, V. (1998). Managing face concerns in criticism: Integrating nonverbal behaviors as a dimension of politeness in female friendship dyads. *Human Communication Research, 24,* 564–583.

Triandis, H. (1995). *Individualism and collectivism.* Boulder, CO: Westview Press.

Trudgill, P. (1974). *The social differentiation of English in Norwich.* Cambridge, UK: Cambridge University Press.

Van Dijk, T. A. (1987). *Communicating racism: Ethnic prejudice in thought and talk.* Newbury Park, CA: Sage.

Van Dijk, T. A. (Ed.). (1998). *Discourse studies: A multidisciplinary introduction* (2 Vol.). London: Sage.

Van Kleek, M. H., Hillger, L. A., & Brown, R. (1988). Pitting verbal schemas against information variables in attribution. *Social Cognition, 6,* 89–106.

Von Hippel, W., Sekaquaptewa, D., & Vargas, P. (1997). The linguistic intergroup bias as an implicit indicator of prejudice. *Journal of Experimental Social Psychology, 33,* 490–509.

Vuchinich, S. (1977). Elements of cohesion between turns in ordinary conversation. *Semiotica, 20,* 229–257.

Watts, R. J. (1992). Linguistic politeness and politic verbal behavior: Reconsidering claims for universality. In R. J. Watts, S. Ide, & K. Ehlich (Eds.), *Politeness in language: Studies in its history, theory, and practice* (pp. 43–70). Berlin: Morton de Gruyter.

Webster, D. M., & Kruglanski, A. (1994). Individual differences in need for cognitive closure. *Journal of Personality and Social Psychology, 67,* 1049–1062.

Webster, D. M., Kruglanski, A. W., & Pattison, D. A. (1997). Motivated language use in intergroup contexts: Need-for-closure effects on the linguistic intergroup bias. *Journal of Personality and Social Psychology, 72,* 1122–1131.

Weiner, S. L., & Goodenough, D. R. (1977). A move toward a psychology of conversation. In R. O. Freedle (Ed.), *Discourse production and comprehension (Vol. 1): Discourse processes: Advances in theory and research* (pp. 213–224). Norwood, NJ: Ablex.

Weizman, E., & Blum-Kulka, S. (1992). Ordinary misunderstanding. In M. Stamenov (Ed.), *Current advances in semantic theory* (pp. 417–432). Philadelphia: John Benjamins.

Werker, J. F. (1991). The ontogeny of speech perception. In I. G. Mattingly & M. Studder-Kennedy (Eds.), *Modularity and the motor theory of speech perception.* Hillsdale, NJ: Erlbaum.

Wheeler, L., Reis, H. T., & Bond, M. H. (1989). Collectivism-individualism in everyday social life: The middle kingdom and the melting pot. *Journal of Personality and Social Psychology, 54,* 323–333.

Whorf, B. L. (1956). *Language, thought, and reality.* J. B. Carroll (Ed.). Cambridge, MA: MIT Press.

Wigboldus, D. H. J., Semin, G. R., & Spears, R. (2000). How do we communicate stereotypes? Linguistic bases and inferential consequences. *Journal of Personality and Social Psychology, 78,* 5–18.

Wilkes-Gibbs, D., & Clark, H. H. (1992). Coordinating beliefs in conversation. *Journal of Memory and Language, 31,* 183–194.

Williams, F., Whitehead, J. L., & Miller, L. (1972). Relations between attitudes and teacher expectancy. *American Educational Research Journal, 9,* 263–277.

Wilson, S. R., (1992). Face and face-work in negotiation. In L. L. Putnam and M. E. Roloff (Eds.), *Communication perspectives in negotiation* (pp. 176–205). Newbury Park, CA: Sage.

Wilson, S. R., Aleman, C. G., & Leathan, G. B. (1998). A revised analysis of face-threatening acts and application to seeking compliance with same-sex friends. *Human Communication Research, 25,* 64–96.

Wilson, T. D., Lisle, D. J., Schooler, J. W., Hodges, S. D., Klaaren, K. J., & LaFleur, S. J. (1993). Introspecting about reasons can reduce post-choice satisfaction. *Personality and Social Psychology Bulletin, 19,* 331–339.

Wilson, T. D., & Schooler, J. W. (1991). Thinking too much: Introspection can reduce the quality of preferences and decisions. *Journal of Personality and Social Psychology, 60,* 181–192.

Wish, M., D'Andrade, R. G., & Goodenough, J. E. (1980). Dimensions of interpersonal communication: Correspondences between structures for speech acts and bipolar scales. *Journal of Personality and Social Psychology, 39,* 848–860.

Wish, M., Deutsch, M., & Kaplan, S. (1976). Perceived dimensions of interpersonal relations. *Journal of Personality and Social Psychology, 33,* 409–420.

Wittgenstein, L. (1953). *Philosophical investigations.* Oxford: Blackwell.

Wood, L. A., & Kroger, R. O. (1991). Politeness and forms of address. *Journal of Language and Social Psychology, 10,* 145–168.

Wooten, A. (1981). The management of grantings and rejections by parents in request sequences. *Semiotica, 37,* 59–89.

Wright, E. F., & Wells, G. L. (1988). Is the attitude-attribution paradigm suitable for investigating the dispositional bias? *Personality and Social Psychology Bulletin, 14,* 183–190.

Wyer, R. S., Budesheim, T. L., & Lambert, A. J. (1990). Person memory and judgment: The cognitive representation of informal conversations. *Journal of Personality and Social Psychology, 58,* 218–235.

Wyer, R. S., & Gruenfeld, D. H. (1995). Information processing in social contexts: Implications for social memory and judgment. In M. P. Zanna (Ed.), *Advances in experimental social psychology* (Vol. 27, pp. 52–93). New York: Academic Press.

Wyer, R. S., & Srull, T. K. (1986). Human cognition in its social context. *Psychological Review, 93,* 322–359.

Yngve, V. H. (1970). On getting a word in edgewise. In *Papers from the sixth regional meeting of the Chicago Linguistics Society.* Chicago: Chicago Linguistics Society.

Zajonc, R. B. (1960). The process of cognitive tuning and communication. *Journal of Abnormal and Social Psychology, 61,* 159–167.

Zebrowitz, L. A. (1997). *Reading faces: Windows to the soul?* Boulder, CO: Westview.

Zimmerman, D. H., & West, C. (1975). Sex roles, interruptions, and silences in conversation. In B. Thorne & N. Henley (Eds.), *Language and sex: Differences and dominance* (pp. 105–129). Rowley, MA: Newbury House.

Author Index

Two indexes are provided: this author index
and a subject index beginning on page 229.

A

Abelson, R. P., 161, 163, 187
Agnoli, F., 151, 156, 158
Aleman, C. G., 140
Alford, D. M., 152
Allport, G. W., 161
Ambady, N. 52, 53, 58, 62
Amrhein, P. C., 18
Andrusiak, P., 60, 85
Antos, S., 29
Appelt, D. E., 60
Applegate, J. L., 53, 54
Arcuri, S., 3, 166, 194
Argyle, M., 107
Arnkoff, D. B., 71
Asch, S., 190
Ashley, A., 19
Atkins, B. K., 71
Atkinson, J. M., 96, 104
Au, T., 156, 164
Austin, J. L., 10–12, 17, 33

B

Bach, K., 14
Bahrick, H. P., 160
Bailenson, J. N., 113
Bailey, C. 196
Bakan, D., 40
Baker, L., 161
Balin, J. A., 132

Banaji, M.. R., 69, 151, 158, 194
Bandura, A., 195
Barr, D. J., 132
Baugh, J., 68
Bauman, I., 49
Bavelas, J. R., 50
Baxter, L. A., 50, 52, 54
Beattie, G. W., 70
Bell, A., 79
Bell, D., 118
Berger, C. R., 81, 198
Berlin, B., 153, 174
Berry, D., 3, 73–74, 81, 186, 191
Berscheid, D., 192
Berube, H., 66
Bickman, L., 68
Billig, M., 174
Bilous, F. R., 80
Black, A., 50
Blom, J. P., 75
Bloom, A. H., 155–156, 194
Blum-Kulka S., 49, 51, 53, 54, 119, 179
Blumstein, P., 71
Bly, B., 145
Bond, M. H., 58
Bookin, H., 30, 31
Boucher, B., 160
Bourhis, R. Y., 68, 79, 80
Bowers, J. W., 52, 53, 54, 72, 100
Bradac, J. J., 67, 68, 72, 81, 198
Brady, R. M., 72
Bransford, J. J., 161
Brauner, J. S., 132

221

Subject Index

Two indexes are provided: an author index beginning on page 221 and this subject index.